The Eagle and the Dove

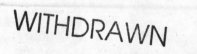

Syracuse Studies on Peace and Conflict Resolution

HARRIET HYMAN ALONSO, CHARLES CHATFIELD, AND LOUIS KRIESBERG
SERIES EDITORS

The U.S. Delegation at the International Congress of Women at The Hague, May 1915. The Women's International League for Peace and Freedom. Courtesy Swarthmore College Peace Collection.

The Eagle and the Dove

THE AMERICAN PEACE MOVEMENT AND UNITED STATES FOREIGN POLICY 1900–1922

Second Edition

Edited and with an Introductory Essay by

JOHN WHITECLAY CHAMBERS II

SYRACUSE UNIVERSITY PRESS

Peace
JX
1961
.U6
E24
1991
X

Second Edition 1991
91 92 93 94 95 96 97 98 99   6 5 4 3 2 1

First Edition, copyright 1976, Garland Publishing, Inc.

About the frontispiece: This photograph was apparently taken in Washington, D.C., before the departure of the delegation. Among the forty-five persons in this picture are a number who are mentioned in this book, including:
Front row: Jane Addams, second from left.
Second row, standing: Alice Hamilton, second from left.
Third row, from left: Emily Green Balch, first; Sophonisba, P. Breckinridge, fourth and slightly behind the row; Julia Grace Wales, sixth.
Back row: Mary Heaton Vorse O'Brien, first and hatless; Juliet Barrett Rublee, third and with hat; Grace Abbott, fourth, next to Rublee and hatless; Leonora O'Reilly, fifth, diagonally in front and to the right of Abbott, with her chin concealed by the hat of the woman in front of her; Rebecca Shelley, second woman to the right of O'Reilly and wearing a light-colored outfit; and Louis Lochner, second from the upper right, a peace activist.

The paper used in this publication meets the minimum requirements of American National Standard for Information Sciences—Permanence of paper for Printed Library Materials, ANSI Z39.48-1984. ∞™

Library of Congress Cataloging-in-Publication Data

The Eagle and the dove: the American peace movement and United States
    foreign policy. 1900–1922/edited and with an introductory essay by
    John Whiteclay Chambers II.—2nd ed.
        p. cm.—(Syracuse studies on peace and conflict resolution)
    Includes bibliographical references and index.
    ISBN 0-8156-2518-9 (cloth).—ISBN 0-8156-2519-7 (paper)
        1. Peace Movements—United States—History—20th century—Sources.
    2. United States—Foreign relations—20th century—Sources
    3. World War, 1914–1918—Protest movements—United States—Sources.
    I. Chambers, John Whiteclay. II. Series.
    JX1961.U6E24, 1991   91-26515
    327.1'72'0973—dc20   CIP

Manufactured in the United States of America

To the Memory of

WARREN F. KUEHL
(1924–1987)

CHARLES DEBENEDETTI
(1943–1987)

JOHN WHITECLAY CHAMBERS II is Associate Professor of History at Rutgers University, New Brunswick, New Jersey. A Fulbright Scholar and a Rockefeller Humanities Fellow, he is the author of *The Tyranny of Change: America in the Progressive Era,* and *To Raise an Army: The Draft Comes to Modern America,* and has edited several anthologies, including (with Charles Moskos) the forthcoming work, *The New Conscientious Objection: The Secularization of Objection to Military Service.* He received his Ph.D. in U.S. History at Columbia University, and he taught there, at Barnard College, for ten years. He is a past president of the Council on Peace Research in History.

Contents

Editor's Note

As this book was in the process of publication, momentous events in the Persian Gulf—from the Iraqi invasion of Kuwait in August 1990 to the U.S. led counterassault in January and February 1991—reinforced the relevance and importance of issues of war and peace in international relations. Once again, Americans debated various diplomatic, economic, and military options as responses to acts of international violence.

Debates over war as an instrument of national policy necessarily involve larger principles as well as specific details. Although the details and time frames differed considerably, the debates of 1990–1991 and those of 1914–1918 examined in this volume did share many common concerns. Both dealt variously with questions of law, morality, and human welfare; economic and political interests; and effective and acceptable means of sustaining national and international goals.

On a broader plane, dramatic changes in the international environment transpired during the two eras—the initial decades and the final years of the twentieth century. In the period from 1900 to 1920 occurred the beginning of the decline of the British Empire; the rise of militantly expansionist Germany and Japan; the challenge of revolutions in Mexico, China, and Russia; and the emergence of the United States as an activist world power. In recent years have occurred the demise of the cold war between the United States and the Soviet Union; the re-emergence of independent nations in Eastern Europe; and challenges to the West from economic, cultural, political, and even military forces in the third world; and apparently the beginning of a relative decline of the global economic influence of the Unites States.

At the close of the twentieth century, as at its beginning, Americans debate the larger question of the proper role of the United States in a newly emerging world order. Thus the questions raised in the earlier era and addressed in this book have a particular relevance today.

Preface to the Second Edition

To a substantial extent this is a new book. The introductory essay has stood the test of time, but I have recast much of the rest of the anthology in light of recent scholarship in a variety of areas—women, peace movements, foreign policy, the Progressive Era, and World War I. Although this is an abridged version of the first edition, more than half of the documents are new to this work.

Women figure much more prominently in this volume than in the first edition because the historical profession, previously dominated by men, now emphasizes the study of women in the American past. The role women played in the peace movement, for example, is today seen by many men and women historians as being important to women, society, and the world.

In the early years of the twentieth century, the peace movement provided significant opportunities for educated women with a limited range of choices in a society that still imposed formidable restrictions outside the home. All-female organizations, whether pacifist groups or other women's organizations with an active interest in the cause of peace, offered opportunities for creating a sense of sisterhood and building networks for mutual support and influence. Pacifist organizations such as the Woman's Peace party (WPP), or the nongender-defined American Union Against Militarism (AUAM), American Neutral Conference Committee, Emergency Peace Federation, or the Committee on the Limitation of Armaments, enabled women to exercise organizational leadership at many levels, whether in their local or state organization or in the national or international arena. The Women's International League for Peace and Freedom (WILPF), which grew out of the Woman's Peace party, quickly became a substantial international pressure group, and two of its early presidents, Jane Addams and Emily Greene Balch, won Nobel Peace prizes for their work.[1]

The cause of peace was seen as a legitimate public role for women in the Progressive Era precisely because it fit the prevailing ideology that linked women to domestic tasks and ideals. Women were viewed as more sensitive, nurturing, and moral than men. As Barbara Steinson and others have shown, many of the middle- and upper-class women in the peace movement accepted these assumptions even while challenging the inequities women confronted in the economic, legal, and political spheres of society.[2] Thus many of them argued that women were particularly qualified to work for peace in the world (just as they did in the family), thereby limiting the aggressive and destructive impulses of males and protecting women and children who traditionally suffered from the ravages of war.

Given the basic assumption that women do have a particular connection to peace, the question of causation has been one of the issues of concern in women's studies and in peace studies in recent years. Although not all women become mothers, some researchers have emphasized life-affirming psychological and social sources—maternal or preservative thinking—stemming from female roles as mothers and nurturers. These are roles involving emphasis upon sustaining rather than acquiring, conserving the fragile rather than conquering, and holding on to and protecting the vulnerable rather than controlling and coercing.[3] Cynthia Enloe and others have emphasized the victimizing of women by militarization and war. These feminist approaches have added a new dimension to traditional concepts of political and economic roots of violence. They stress sexism—the misguided belief that men are biologically and intellectually superior to women—and resulting actions that subordinate and oppress women. These activities range from domestic to international violence and from vast masculine-emphasizing military systems to concepts of international relations mainly in terms of aggressive, threatening, potentially destructive behavior—namely, Realpolitik, Machtpolitik.[4]

In the first two decades of the twentieth century covered in this anthology, a number of documents reflect these concerns. Some illustrate the use of such goals and values, at the very least as metaphors, relating peace to women's roles and special characteristics or natures (see documents 13, 14, 50). Many offer evidence of the role of women in building and leading single-sex or nongender-specific organizations on behalf of peace and social justice (see documents 3, 13–15, 18, 20, 22, 24, 25, 27, 29, 30, 34, 38, 46–48, 50, 55, 57).

An important aspect of the role of women in the modern peace movement has been their contribution to the new concept of "positive" rather than "negative" peace. Jane Addams and many other women pacifists in the era of World War I argued that merely seeking to prevent war reflected a narrow and largely negative view of peace. In contrast, they espoused a broad and positive view of peace in which they sought to eliminate the courses of war that they variously identified as inequitable economic, social, and political conditions.

The denotation of negative peace represented a rejection of the narrow focus of conservative and male-dominated peace organizations and governments in the early twentieth century. The majority of these groups had at most attempted merely to restrict war, while accepting military and naval establishments as instruments of state policy. Indeed, some of the most conservative, business-dominated peace societies were somewhat suspicious of the reliability of mediation, arbitration, or adjudication through international commissions or a world court.

During the First World War, the more radical peace organizations in general and female pacifists in particular began to go beyond simply offering nations alternative mechanisms to use before resorting to war. Instead, these radical pacifists embraced ways of eliminating the underlying structural causes of such organized violence. Many of these women and their male associates were domestic reformers and social workers, and they drew on that experience as they advocated a far-reaching international program to eliminate war, poverty, and famine and to help achieve social justice for men, women, and children around the world (see documents 13, 14, 34, 46, 55, 57).

In the past decade, peace historians have increased the sophistication of their subfield of history. They have gone beyond the initial work in peace history—the biographies of pacifists and monographic studies of peace organizations—to begin to study in more detail the larger contexts of nonviolent movements for peace and social justice. Among the most promising are investigations of political culture, alternative foreign policies, and crisis behavior—that is, particularly case studies of crises in which war has been avoided.[5]

Our understanding of the norms, values, and power relationships in particular societies—as well as the resultant dilemmas of pacifists—can be enhanced by examining the relationship of peace movements to the larger political culture, as suggested by Charles Chatfield and Peter van den Dungen.[6] A recent and effective study of Wilhelmine Germany, for example, emphasized the powerful institutions of militant chauvinism—the government, the educational system, the army and navy. The author,

Roger Chickering, then focused on the unequal struggle between these chauvinistic institutions and the communal-oriented pacifist and socialist organizations as each sought to establish the dominant national attitude about Germany's relationship to other world powers. This study indicated that the victory of the advocates of *Realpolitik,* of international politics based on power and threat, suggested as much about the nature of German society in the early twentieth century as about the weakness of the peace movement there.[7]

The relationship in early twentieth-century America between pacifists and others engaged in defining dominant views of national interest and international relations—government officials, business, military, foreign policy elites, labor, radicals, ethnic group leaders, and the press—can suggest much about the nature of American society and culture in the Progressive Era. This edition of the anthology, therefore, includes several new documents that should increase the reader's understanding of the struggle for the dominant symbols and attitudes of the political culture in the United States (see, e.g., documents 5–7, 11, 14, 16, 17, 19, 21, 25–28, 31–39, 43–46, 49, 50, 52–58). Among these were concepts of national character, purpose and mission, secular and religious; of national security, whether best secured by arms and threat or by aid and understanding; and of national prosperity and the roles of public and private interests in achieving social harmony and economic progress.[8]

Historians of the Progressive Era are less concerned with the old debate over identity of the progressives, or whether they formed a true social movement, as they are over the context of the reforms of the Progressive Era—the changing structures of power, of politics, of ideas and values.[9] In this newly focused debate, the peace movement, like the so-called progressive movement, should be seen as a series of shifting coalitions rather than as a continuous unified social movement. It was also variously composed of radical, liberal, and conservative elements. More importantly, the peace movement can be better understood—and American society of the era more clearly perceived—if it is seen as part of the new domestic political context in which declining political parties were rapidly being supplanted by well-organized, issue-oriented pressure groups as well springs of policy influence. The modern pressure group, beginning with the prototypical Anti-Saloon League, was a creation of the Progressive Era. In military and foreign policy, the most important military-oriented and chauvinistic pressure groups included the Navy League, National Security League, Military Training Camps Association, and National Guard Association. These organizations were often opposed by more liberal and peace-oriented pressure groups, including the American Union Against Militarism (later the American Civil Liberties Union [ACLU]), the Woman's Peace party (later WILPF), and the National Council on Limitation of Armament. The Foreign Policy Association and the League to Enforce Peace (LEP) association occupied a middle ground.

Historians of the Progressive Era are concerned with how such pressure groups actually worked in the political process. Who joined them and who did not? Who led them? Who opposed them? How did they build coalitions? Most importantly, precisely how did they influence policy?[10] (For examples of how pacifist pressure groups worked, see documents 14, 15, 18, 20, 22, 23, 25, 27, 29, 30, 34, 38, 46–48, 54, 57; for the views of opponents of the pacifist pressure groups—such as Alfred Thayer Mahan, Elihu Root, Theodore Roosevelt, and Henry Cabot Lodge, see documents 2, 10, 16, 28, 37, 44, 53.) As in domestic politics of the Progressive Era, the most successful of these foreign-policy-oriented pressure groups conformed to the dominant ideas—or at least the rhetoric—of the period: a crusading sense of America's mission in the world; the increasing view of American society and even international relations as organic and interdependent; and an emphasis on democracy, political and moral purity, and social justice.

A valuable new idea by peace historians, shaped by the scholarship of crisis management, is to make detailed studies of instances of crises in which nations have *not* gone to war. As Michael Lutzker has stated, we can benefit from posing different questions and emphasizing other data than in traditional analyses.[11] War between the United States and Great Britain was avoided in the Venezuelan Crisis of 1895, and Lutzker argues that Britain's acquiescence in the crisis and her subsequent rapprochment with the United States shows that "a nation with worldwide commitments can strengthen rather than weaken itself by knowing when to draw back and where to relinquish its power" (although such a policy is not always appropriate, e.g., Britain's policy of appeasement in the 1930s). More recently, in the lessons drawn from two crises in 1954–1955 and 1958 between the United States and the People's Republic of China over Quemoy and Matsu, two islands between mainland China and Taiwan, the traditional emphasis has been on the United States' standing firm in the face of threats; but Lutzker's study suggests that policy analysts, because of the dominance of a frozen concept of deterrence, drew the wrong lessons from these crises. In fact, they missed opportunities to reduce tensions and instead wound up increasing the threat level—even daring the People's Republic of China to face nuclear war or back down—but leaving the final decision in the adversary's hands.[12] These were primarily studies in policy makers' perceptions, for the peace movement was greatly weakened in the 1950s.

In the Progressive Era, Lutzker's study of the crisis over the temporary occupation by U.S. troops of the Mexican port of Vera Cruz in the spring of 1914 concluded that President Wilson had already decided not to widen the war before the diverse peace movement could seek to mobilize popular reaction. But in another crisis with revolutionary Mexico in 1916 (see excerpts from several sources reprinted here as document 22)—this time over an alleged ambush and slaughter of U.S. soldiers at Carrizal in Chihuahua province—the radical wing of the American peace movement did play an influential role. By publicizing the true story of the incident (the Americans had attacked first), by mobilizing an antiwar coalition among influential groups in the United States, and by establishing links with the Mexicans for information and mediation, the American Union Against Militarism helped to counter demands from business interests, some religious organizations, and the jingo press, which had been pushing President Wilson, against his judgment, toward war with Mexico.

The prevention of war with Mexico in 1916 through effective mobilization of public opinion and the encouragement of alternative policies was a significant success by the peace movement in the Progressive Era. Peace advocates also enjoyed some additional gains, such as the creation and use of a Permanent Court of Arbitration (popularly known as The Hague Tribunal) for international arbitration and the calling of the Second Hague Peace Conference of 1907. Peace advocates were more successful in helping to achieve the eventual reduction in the rate of Theodore Roosevelt's naval arms buildup and in contributing to the defeat of national compulsory military training proposals in 1916 and 1920. The peace movement also played an important role in obtaining Wilson's pronouncements of liberal peace aims in 1917 and 1918. And pacifists helped to make wartime suppression of civil liberties a major issue and to create a lasting organization, the American Civil Liberties Union, to defend civil rights. Finally, the crowning achievement of the peace movement in this era was undoubtedly the enormous naval cutbacks adopted at the Washington Disarmament Conference of 1921–1922. (The conference actually produced nine treaties involving territorial aspirations and naval weapons in the western Pacific and East Asia. Those restricting naval armaments, the five-power treaties among the United States, Britain, Japan, France, and Italy, were known collectively as the Five-Power Naval Arms Limitation Treaty of 1922.)

The peace movement went through a cycle of growth, transformation, decline, and rejuvenation in the Progressive Era. Such a cycle is not uncommon given political realities. Indeed, the experience with the European peace movement in the 1980s contributed to examinations of exactly such cyclical phenomena in mass protest movements.[13] At that time the mass protests against the decision to deploy new U.S. short-range nuclear weapons, cruise missiles, and Pershing ballistic missiles on European soil generated rapid growth and enthusiasm for the peace movement but then a period of equally rapid public apathy. Some scholars suggest that the rise and fall of peace movements has little predictable relation to success or failure. Indeed, one Dutch student of the phenomenon has compared the peace movement to a leaping, diving whale. When it disappears it is not gone forever; it is operating in a different way than when it surfaces.[14]

The core of the peace movement, a number of ideological groups that have been called "prophetic minorities," are highly and continuously committed to drastic change. They form the undercurrent of the movement, and continue to exist even after the disappearance of the mass peace movements. Tending to remain relatively small in membership, they do not greatly profit from the periods in which the peace movement thrives, and their direct political impact may be limited. Nevertheless, they retain expertise and commitment, generate ideas, and act as a catalyst to the less radical groups that in particular periods become mobilized for peace. Peak activity comes with the mobilization of coalition peace movements as both existent and new organizations join behind specific issues and goals. These coalition movements seek to influence decision makers by exerting direct pressure upon political leaders and by attempting to change and mobilize public opinion, including both mass attitudes and the opinions of organized, active interest groups, not regularly directly involved in the movement for peace—groups such as business and professional associations, trade unions, women's groups, student organizations, and religious bodies.

The type of mass peace and antiwar mobilizations that occurred in Europe and in the United States in the late 1960s over the Vietnam War, and again in the early 1980s over the escalation of the nuclear arms race, are naturally viewed as products of particular historical episodes, tied to specific issues, and impossible to sustain for very long.[15] In the long run, however, the work of the peace movement is to create a climate of opinion favorable to peace. This means continuing commitment and work, obviously by a small number of groups, to develop new ideas, to educate the public about new facts and opportunities, and to lobby the attentive public and political leaders to implement policies for the reduction or elimination of the underlying causes of armament races, military intervention, and war.[16]

The experience of the peace advocates in the Progressive Era supports this view of the cyclical and dichotomous nature of the histories of peace movements. In terms of influence, public attention, and widespread legitimacy, the peace movement in those years probably reached its peak in the period between 1907 and 1914, when its efforts were directed at specific goals such as slowing the arms race and international arbitration while its more radical goals were concomitantly diluted.

The outbreak of World War I, the emergence of the "preparedness" movement, and efforts to pressure the Wilson administration into attempting to mediate a settlement before the United States was drawn into the war, all contributed, as the introductory essay indicates, to a transformation of the peace movement. More traditional and conservative organizations suspended operations or supported the Allies. In their place, came new, more radical core groups, such as the American Union Against Militarism and the Woman's Peace party, with new goals and methods. Pressure groups, the "prophetic minorities," rather than staid educative or deliberative bodies established a new agenda and worked to achieve it by building coalitions, seeking to mobilize public opinion, and actively lobbying political leaders (see documents 14, 15, 18, 20, 22–25, 29, 30). With U.S. entry into World War I, the core peace groups shrank but took on new tasks of defending civil liberties and pressing for liberal peace aims. During the postwar period a major rejuvenation of the peace movement focused on some kind of international organization as well as the curbing of conscription and the threatened naval arms race.

In the wake of the Washington Naval Arms Limitation Treaty, the mass movement of the immediate postwar period contracted once again to a number of core groups. Some of these, such as the War Resisters League, the Fellowship of Reconciliation, the American Friends Service Committee, the American Civil Liberties Union, the Women's International League for Peace and Freedom, and the Foreign Policy Association, were products of the wartime or immediate postwar period. Most of them later helped to provide leadership when mass peace movements burst forth again—first in the mid-1930s, then with the antinuclear movement beginning in the 1950s, and again in the anti-Vietnam War movement of the 1960s.

Significant developments have occurred in the field of diplomatic history—or international history as it has recently been called—since the first edition of this anthology. Emphasis remains on domestic influences on foreign policy. Indeed, in the first edition of this work, I sought to contribute to the discussion by stressing the influence of the peace movement, broadly conceived, upon U.S. foreign policy. There is now, however, an additional emphasis upon larger transnational forces and issues—economic, cultural, political—as well as a recognition of the realities of the international system itself. Thus scholars study aspects of balance of power or bipolar or other forms of international political-economic relations, including the impact of transnational concerns about scarcity of economic resources, unstable trade relationships, destabilizing arms races, and extensive inflation or economic contractions. Of particular concern is the interaction between international and domestic influences upon policy makers and those who help to shape governmental and public opinion.[17] Furthermore, there has been a call for greater attention to the national cultural predispositions that influence the way particular nations deal with specific other nations or regions of the world. As a much wider approach than simply the study of attitudes of elites and the attentive publics toward particular issues, this concept seeks a reconstruction of the long-term mentalités of entire peoples.[18] To that extent, the documentation of this edition of the anthology can contribute to an understanding of the ideas and assumptions employed by peace advocates, their adversaries, government officials, and others in the struggle to shape public opinion and influence policy. Such ideas and assumptions existed, of course, within the mentalités of the early 1900s, which contained both differences and similarities to predominant thinking today.

In regard to the World War I era, recent scholarship continues to explore the nature of the war experience, particularly the guilt of a reckless Germany driven by elites seeking to overcome internal divisions through external expansion and enrichment.[19] A few scholars have been intrigued by the strange duality of the pre-1914 years in which organized peace movements in Europe and America ascended to new heights of importance at the very time that the great powers of Europe were positioning themselves for conflict.[20] Leaders of the European great powers largely ignored the peace movements and accepted the idea of war as an instrument to expand their power, largely through additional territory. The military and some political leaders in Germany and Austria concluded that the crisis of July 1914 was the most propitious time to strike.[21] Historians have also provided an increasing number of studies of the effects of wartime mobilization on various aspects of society in all the major belligerent nations—Germany, Britain, France, Italy, the United States, and especially Russia and the revolutionary victory of the Bolsheviks.[22] Particularly fruitful has been the examination of the interrelationship between conservative domestic forces in the victorious Allied nations and the search for a stable, antiradical, postwar political, diplomatic, and economic order.[23]

Historians of U.S. foreign relations for that period have contributed to these trends, but they have also remained concerned with the degree to which the United States has been a nation-state like others, committed to its own prosperity and security (or more accurately those of its predominant elites) rather than being the exceptional and altruistic country that many Americans have believed that it was. The debate goes on between traditionalists and revisionists about what were the driving forces of U.S. foreign policy—economic prosperity, antiradicalism, an idealistic sense of mission, military security, political expediency, or simply the reaction to limited choices available. Current interpretations of Woodrow Wilson's foreign policy stress his growing commitment— influenced by economic, political, and idealistic forces—to a new open diplomacy with the goal of a liberal, capitalistic, democratic world order as an alternative to either conservative autarkic colonialism or to revolutionary communism.[24] This was also the general goal, despite differences on some aspects, of the liberal, middle- and upper-class men and women who comprised the majority of the organized peace movement, as can be seen in the documents in this anthology.

In the hope that the paperback of this new edition will be particularly useful in undergraduate college courses, especially in U.S. diplomatic history, foreign relations, international relations, twentieth-century U.S. history, peace studies, and women's studies, I have, as mentioned earlier, reduced the number of documents and, for brevity and clarity, have edited those that remain. I have also provided explanatory headnotes to identify each document and its author and to place it in proper historical context. I have included a variety of types of primary sources— from diary entries and confidential internal memoranda to newspaper accounts, official speeches, and formal treaties—to give the reader the opportunity to assess the credibility of such sources, a crucial aspect of the historical method.

In editing this anthology, I have tried to adhere to the high standards of analytical scholarly editing of historical documents. This means scrupulously preserving the precise wording and meaning of the original sources. Standard editorial indicators have been employed: ellipses indicate omitted material, and brackets enclose editorial notation and commentary. Those who wish to read these documents in their entirety or to examine additional documents on this topic are referred to the first edition of this anthology, which contained eighty-five unabridged documents, or to the original documents, the location of which is indicated in the source note at the beginning of each document.

I have not altered the introductory essay, except to insert references to particular documents and to make a few relatively minor changes. A chronology of key events as well as an index have been added for the reader's convenience. The selected bibliography has been updated to refer the reader to the latest relevant material as well as to classic works.

For this edition, I owe a debt of gratitude to a number of friends. Several historians of this period generously contributed their time, advice, and support, particularly in the formidable task of reducing the first edition of six hundred pages to this edition of two hundred pages (in which condensation *The Eagle and the Dove* became, as my friend from Wittenberg University put it, *The Eaglet and the Dovelet*). These advisers are Harriet Hyman Alonso of Fitchburg State College, Charles Chatfield of Wittenberg University, Thomas J. Knock of Southern Methodist University, and Michael A. Lutzker of New York University. I, of course, made the final decisions, and am solely responsible for any errors of fact or judgment. The members and guests in my graduate colloquium at Rutgers University on "Peace Movements in History" in the Fall 1989 semester contributed to the development of my thinking on this subject. I want particularly to thank my friend and colleague Dee Garrison, who participated in most of the weekly sessions. Lisa Baum did an excellent job of typing most of the abridged documents. This edition would not have been possible without the support and advice of the staff at Syracuse University Press.

I dedicate this book to the memory of two preeminent peace researchers, historians, and dear friends. The deaths in 1987 of Charles DeBenedetti of the University of Toledo and Warren F. Kuehl of the University of Akron were a great loss to many of us personally, to the historical profession, and to the cause of peace. Their productive lives, their valuable works, and their commitment to scholarship and to peace and justice can serve as models to us all.

JOHN WHITECLAY CHAMBERS II

New Brunswick, New Jersey
July 1, 1990

NOTES

1. See, e.g., Jill Conway, "Women Reformers and American Culture, 1870–1930," *Journal of Social History* 5 (Winter, 1971–1972): 164–77; and Barbara Sicherman, *Alice Hamilton: A Life in Letters* (Cambridge, Mass.: Harvard Univ. Press, 1984), 184–236. I am indebted to Kathryn Kish Sklar for this last reference. For other relevant works, see Paula Baker, "The Domestication of American Politics," *American Historical Review* 89 (June 1984): 620–49; Carroll Smith-Rosenberg, "The New Woman as Androgyne: Social Disorder and Gender Crisis, 1870–1936," in Smith-Rosenberg, *Disorderly Conduct; Visions of Gender in Victorian America* (New York: Oxford Univ. Press, 1985), 245–96; and Kathryn Kish Sklar, "Hull House in the 1890s: A Community of Women Reformers," *Signs* 10, no. 4 (1985): 658–77. Addams received a Nobel Peace Prize in 1931; Balch, in 1946.

2. Barbara J. Steinson, *American Women's Activism in World War I* (New York: Garland, 1982); see also Conway, 164–77; and Nancy F. Cott, *The Grounding of Modern Feminism* (New Haven: Yale Univ. Press, 1987).

3. Sara Ruddick, "Mothers and Men's Wars," in *Rocking the Ship of State: Toward a Feminist Peace Politics,* ed. Adrienne Harris and Ynestra King (Boulder: Westview, 1989), 75–92, and the other essays in this valuable anthology. For further indication that pacifism derives from women's social and political roles, not from innate biological characteristics, and that women have also been acculturated to be "Beautiful [complaisant] Souls" and even "Just Warriors," see Jean Bethke Elshtain, "On Beautiful Souls, Just Warriors, and Feminist Consciousness," in *Women and Men's Wars,* ed., Judith Stiehm (Oxford: Pergamon, 1983), 317–28; and Elshtain, *Women and War* (New York: Basic Books, 1987). The literature is surveyed in Micaela di Leonardo, "Morals, Mothers, Militarism: Antimilitarism and Feminist Theory," *Feminist Studies* 11, no. 3 (Fall 1985): 599–18. Jane Addams dealt extensively with the connection between women and peace in *The Long Road of Women's Memory* (New York: Macmillan, 1916).

4. See, e.g., the differing conceptualizations in Cynthia Enloe, *Does Khaki Become You?: The Militarization of Women's Lives* (Boston: South End Press, 1983); Enloe, "Feminist Thinking about War, Militarism and Peace," in *Analyzing Gender: A Handbook of Social Science Research,* ed. Beth B. Hess and Myra Marx Ferree (Newbury Park, Calif.: Sage Publications, 1987), 526–47; Betty A. Reardon, *Sexism and the War System* (New York: Teachers College Press, 1985); Birget Brock-Utne, *Educating for Peace: The Feminist Perspective* (Oxford: Pergamon, 1985); Carol Cohn, "Sex and Death in the Rational World of Defense Intellectuals," *Signs* 12, no. 4 (Summer 1987): 687–718; and Laurie Cashdan, "Anti-War Feminism: New Directions, New Dualities—A Marxist-Humanist Perspective," *Women's Studies International Forum* 12, no. 1 (1989): 81–86. For an insightful survey, see Berenice A. Carroll, "Feminism and Pacifism: Historical and Theoretical Connections," in *Women and Peace: Theoretical, Historical and Practical Perspectives,* ed. Ruth Roach Pierson (London: Croom Helm, 1987), 2–28. Frances H. Early, "Feminism, Peace, and Civil Liberties: Women's Role in the Origins of the World War I Civil Liberties Movement," *Women's Studies* 18 (1990): 95–115, is a particularly valuable case study in this regard.

5. Particularly illustrative of these new directions are Charles Chatfield and Peter van den Dungen, eds., *Peace Movements and Political Cultures* (Knoxville: Univ. of Tennessee Press, 1988); Lawrence S. Wittner, "Peace Movements and Foreign Policy: The Challenge to Diplomatic Historians," *Diplomatic History* 11 (Fall 1987): 355–70; and Michael A.

Lutzker, "Expanding Our Vision: New Perspectives on Peace Research," *Peace and Change: A Journal of Peace Research* 14, no. 4 (Oct. 1989): 444–60; and Kenneth E. Boulding, "A Proposal for a Research Program in the History of Peace," ibid.: 461–69. The status of peace history is particularly evident in three works by the late Charles DeBenedetti, "Peace History in the American Manner," *History Teacher* 18, no. 1 (Nov. 1984): 75–110; *The Peace Reform in American History* (Bloomington: Indiana Univ. Press, 1980); and DeBenedetti, ed., *Peace Heroes in Twentieth-Century America* (Bloomington: Indiana Univ. Press, 1986). See also the useful reference works, Warren F. Kuehl, ed., *Biographical Dictionary of Internationalists* (Westport, Conn.: Greenwood, 1983); and Harold Josephson, ed., *Biographical Dictionary of Modern Peace Leaders* (Westport, Conn.: Greenwood, 1985); and Charles F. Howlett, *The American Peace Movement: References and Resources* (Boston: G. K. Hall, 1991). The status of peace studies is summarized in George A. Lopez, ed., "Peace Studies: Past and Future," special issue of *The Annals of the American Academy of Political and Social Science* 504 (July 1989).

6. Chatfield and van den Dungen, xi–xx; the collection of essays illustrates this point.

7. Roger Chickering, "War, Peace, and Social Mobilization in Imperial Germany: Patriotic Societies, the Peace Movement, and Socialist Labor," in Chatfield and van den Dungen, 3–22; see also Chickering, *Imperial Germany and a World Without War: The Peace Movement and German Society, 1892–1914* (Princeton: Princeton Univ. Press, 1975); and Chickering, *We Men Who Feel Most German: A Cultural Study of the Pan-German League, 1886–1914* (London: Allen & Unwin, 1984). For a broader reach, see the forthcoming study of nineteenth century European peace movements by Sandi E. Cooper.

8. For an analysis of social conflict over the meaning of culture images and symbols, see Alain Touraine, "An Introduction to the Study of Social Movements," *Social Research* 52, no. 4 (Winter 1985): 749–89.

9. Excellent summaries are contained in Daniel T. Rodgers, "In Search of Progressivism," *Reviews in American History* 10, no. 4 (Dec. 1982): 113–32; Arthur S. Link and Richard L. McCormick, *Progressivism* (Arlington Heights, Ill.: Harlan Davidson, 1983); and John Whiteclay Chambers II, *The Tyranny of Change: America in the Progressive Era, 1890–1920*, 2d ed. (New York: St. Martin's, 1992). See the pathbreaking new work, Martin J. Sklar, *The Corporate Reconstruction of American Capitalism, 1890–1916: The Market, the Law, and Politics* (Cambridge: Cambridge Univ. Press, 1988). For reference, see John D. Buenker and Edward R. Kantowicz, eds., *Historical Dictionary of the Progressive Era, 1890–1920* (New York: Greenwood, 1988).

10. For studies of particular pacifist pressure groups in this period, see, e.g., Charles Chatfield, "World War I and the Liberal Pacifist in the United States," *American Historical Review* 75 (Dec. 1970): 1920–37; Blanche Wiesen Cook, "The Woman's Peace Party: Collaboration and Non-Cooperation," *Peace and Change: A Journal of Peace Research* 1 (Mar. 1972): 36–42; and Steinson. An excellent account of one of their adversaries is J. Garry Clifford, *The Citizen Soldiers: The Plattsburg Training Camp Movement, 1913–1920* (Lexington: Univ. Press of Kentucky, 1972). Although some of the more radical pacifists were sympathetic to the Socialists, the majority of liberal pacifists were wary of linking themselves too closely with the Socialists, a view reciprocated by many of the Socialists, particularly the left wing. The majority of cosmopolitan middle- and upper-class pacifists also kept themselves at a distance from leaders of farm and labor organizations, although the groups occasionally cooperated on particular issues. See, John Whiteclay Chambers II, *To Raise an Army: The Draft Comes to Modern America* (New York: The Free Press, 1987), 107–11.

11. Lutzker, "Expanding Our Vision," 444–60.

12. Michael A. Lutzker, "The Precarious Peace: China, the United States, and the Quemoy-Matsu Crisis, 1954–55, 1958," in *Arms at Rest: Peacemaking and Peacekeeping in American History,* ed. Robert L. Beisner and Joan R. Challinor (Westport, Conn.: Greenwood, 1987), 161–85; and Lutzker's other essays, including "Can the Peace Movement Prevent War?: The U.S.–Mexican Crisis of April 1914," in *Doves and Diplomats,* ed. Solomon Wank (Westport, Conn.: Greenwood, 1978), 127–53; and "How We Withdrew from Vietnam in 1965: The Search for an Alternative Past" (paper presented at the conference of the Society for Historians of American Foreign Relations, Williamsburg, Va., June 1989).

13. See, e.g., David S. Meyer, "Peace Movements and National Security Policy: A Research Agenda," *Peace and Change: A Journal of Peace Research* 16, no. 2 (Apr. 1991): 131–61; David Cortright, "Assessing Peace Movement Effectiveness in the 1980s," ibid., 16, no. 1 (Jan. 1991): 46–63; Nigel Young, "The Contemporary European Anti-Nuclear Movement: Experiments in the Mobilization of Public Power," ibid., 9, no. 1 (Spring 1983): 1–16; Young, "Why Peace Movements Fail: An Historical and Sociological Overview," *Social Alternatives* 4, no. 1 (1984): 9–16; Joanne Landy, "Can Summits Replace the Peace Movement?" *Tikkun* 3, no. 6 (Nov./Dec. 1988): 45–49, 105–9; Pam Solo, "The Reagan Era: The Freeze Campaign and Political Power," *Annual Review of Peace Activism, 1989* (Boston: Winston Foundation for World Peace, 1989), 1–9. I am indebted to Sandi E. Cooper of the City University of New York for this last reference.

14. Philip P. Everts, "Where the Peace Movement Goes When It Disappears," *Bulletin of the Atomic Scientists* (November 1989): 26-30, based on Everts and G. Walraven, *Vredesbeweging* (Utrecht, 1984). Everts is director of the Institute for International Studies, University of Leiden, The Netherlands. I am indebted to Professor Sherri West of Brookdale College for this reference.

15. On the antiwar and antinuclear movements in the United States in recent years, see Charles DeBenedetti, Charles Chatfield, assisting author, *An American Ordeal: The Antiwar Movement of the Vietnam Era* (Syracuse: Syracuse Univ. Press, 1990); Lawrence S. Wittner, "The Transnational Movement Against Nuclear Weapons, 1945–1986: A Preliminary Survey," in Chatfield and van den Dungen, 265–94; and Wittner, *Rebels Against War: The American Peace Movement, 1933–1983* (Philadelphia: Temple Univ. Press, 1984).

16. William Sloan Coffin, president, SANE/Freeze, letter to the editor, *New York Times,* Mar. 24, 1990; Everts, "Where the Peace Movement Goes," 26–30. For a perceptive recommendation, see Wittner, "Peace Movements and Foreign Policy," 355–70.

17. See the surveys of the field in "A Round Table: Explaining the History of American Foreign Relations," *Journal of American History* 77, no. 1 (June 1990): 93–180; and in Charles S. Maier, "Marking Time: The Historiography of International Relations," in *The Past Before Us: Contemporary Historical Writing in the United States,* ed. Michael Kammen (Ithaca: Cornell Univ. Press, 1980), 355–87. See also, Ole R. Holsti, "Models of International Relations and Foreign Policy," *Diplomatic History* 13, no. 1 (Winter 1989): 15–43. John R. Gillis, ed., *The Militarization of the Western World* (New Brunswick, N.J.: Rutgers Univ. Press, 1989) provides an excellent collection of relevant essays.

18. Akira Iriye, "The Internationalization of History," *American Historical Review* 94, no. 1 (Feb. 1989): 1–10; see also Iriye, "Culture and Power: International Relations as Intercultural Relations," *Diplomatic History* 3 (1979): 115–28; and Warren F. Kuehl, "Webs of Common Interests Revisited," ibid., 10 (Spring 1986): 107–20.

19. The debate over the thesis of Fritz Fischer and his students which emphasizes the role of domestic elites in pressing for German expansionism from 1890 to 1918 to resist

democratization at home is summarized in John A. Moses, *The Politics of Illusion: The Fischer Controversy in German Historiography* (New York: Barnes and Noble, 1975); Samuel R. Williamson, Jr., and Peter Pastor, eds., *Essays on World War I: Origins and Prisoners of War* (New York: Brooklyn College Press, distributed by Columbia Univ. Press, 1983); and more recently in David Blackbourn, "The Politics of Demagogy in Imperial Germany," *Past and Present*, no. 113 (Nov. 1985): 152–84.

20. Konrad Jarausch, "Armageddon Revisted: Peace Research Perspectives on World War One," *Peace and Change: A Journal of Peace Research* 7 nos. 1–2 (Winter 1981): 109–18; Lawrence E. Gelfand, "Through the Prism of Seven Decades: The World War, 1914–1918," *Diplomatic History* 14, no. 1 (Winter 1990): 115–21. For a critique of the leaders of the most conservative peace organizations in the prewar period, see Michael A. Lutzker, "The Pacifist as Militarist: A Critique of the Amerian Peace Movement, 1898–1912," *Societas* 5 (Spring 1975): 87–104.

21. James Joll, *1914: The Unspoken Assumptions* (London: Weidenfeld and Nicolson, 1968); David Stevenson, *The First World War and International Politics* (New York: Oxford Univ. Press, 1988).

22. James D. Shand, "Doves among Eagles: German Pacifists and Their Government During World War I," *Journal of Contemporary History* 10, no. 1 (Jan. 1975): 95–108; David M. Kennedy, *Over Here: The First World War and American Society* (New York: Oxford Univ. Press, 1980); M. Ceadel, *Pacifism in Britain, 1914–1945* (Oxford: Oxford Univ. Press, 1980); Francis Ludwig Carsten, *War Against War: British and German Radical Movements in the First World War* (London: Batsford Academic and Educational Publications, 1982); Jurgen Kocka, *Facing Total War: German Society 1914–1918* (Cambridge, Mass.: Harvard Univ. Press, 1985); Jean Jacques Becker, *The Great War and the French People* (New York: St. Martin's, 1986); Robert H. Ferrell, *Woodrow Wilson and World War I, 1917–1921* (New York: Harper and Row, 1985); J. M. Winter and R. M. Wall, eds., *The Upheaveal of War: Family, Work and Welfare in Europe, 1914–1918* (Cambridge: Cambridge Univ. Press, 1988); J. M. Winter, *The Experience of World War I* (New York: Oxford Univ. Press, 1989).

23. Arno J. Mayer, *The Politics and Diplomacy of Peacemaking: Containment and Counter-revolution at Versailles, 1918–1919* (New York: Knopf, 1967); Charles S. Maier, *Recasting Bourgeois Europe: Stabilization in France, Germany, and Italy in the Decade after World War I* (Princeton: Princeton Univ. Press, 1975).

24. Any study of Woodrow Wilson must begin with the works of his preeminent biographer: see, e.g., Arthur S. Link, *Wilson*, 5 vols. (Princeton: Princeton Univ. Press, 1947–1965), which goes through Apr. 1917; and Link, *Woodrow Wilson: Revolution, War, and Peace* (Arlington Heights, Ill.: AHM, 1979), which examines Wilson's foreign policy from 1913 to 1920. Of great value to any study of the period is Link et al., eds., *The Papers of Woodrow Wilson*, 65 vols. to date (Princeton: Princeton Univ. Press, 1966–), which makes available Wilson's papers and significant collateral material. In place of other, less accessible sources, I have usually cited this collection whenever a relevant document can be found there. Other important studies of Wilson's diplomacy are Ernest R. May, *The World War and American Isolation, 1914–1917* (Cambridge, Mass.: Harvard Univ. Press, 1959); N. Gordon Levin, Jr., *Woodrow Wilson and World Politics: America's Response to War and Revolution* (New York: Oxford Univ. Press, 1968); Carl P. Parrini, *Heir to Empire: United States Economic Diplomacy, 1916-1923* (Pittsburgh: Univ. of Pittsburgh Press, 1969); Burton I. Kaufman, *Efficiency and Expansion: Foreign Trade Organization in the Wilson Administration, 1913–1921* (Westport, Conn.: Greenwood, 1974); Patrick Devlin, *Too Proud to Fight: Woodrow Wilson's Neutrality* (New

York: Oxford Univ. Press, 1974); and Lloyd C. Gardner, *Safe for Democracy: The Anglo-American Response to Revolution, 1913–1923* (New York: Oxford Univ. Press, 1984); Frederick S. Calhoun, *Power and Principle: Armed Intervention in Wilsonian Foreign Policy* (Kent, Ohio: Kent State Univ. Press, 1986); Kendrick A. Clements, *Woodrow Wilson: World Statesman* (Boston: Twayne, 1987). See also John A. Thompson, *Reformers and War: American Progressive Publicists and the First World War* (Cambridge: Cambridge Univ. Press, 1987); and Lloyd E. Ambrosius, *Woodrow Wilson and the American Diplomatic Tradition: The Treaty Fight in Perspective* (Cambridge: Cambridge Univ. Press, 1987).

There were, of course, other perspectives. For a study of the leading champion of the nationalistic Right, see William C. Widenor, *Henry Cabot Lodge and the Search for an American Foreign Policy* (Berkeley: Univ. of California Press, 1980). For an examination of Wilson and the internationalist Left, see Thomas J. Knock, *To End All Wars: Woodrow Wilson and the Creation of the League of Nations* (New York: Oxford Univ. Press, 1992). Professor Knock graciously allowed me to read this work in manuscript.

Introductory Essay

Probably never in its erratic history has the American peace movement experienced a more volatile course than during the first two decades of the twentieth century. Within a single generation, it soared to heights of influence and expectation, then plunged like a roller coaster to the depths of impotence and despair during American belligerency in World War I, only to climb back to importance in the years following the armistice. It was an amazing performance by the conglomeration of individuals and groups known collectively as the peace movement.

Among the most dramatic aspects of the peace movement were not only its resiliency but also its diversity. Although this social movement sought to reduce or eliminate warfare in international relations, it was plagued by disagreement over both means and ends. The majority of adherents could be most appropriately called peace advocates. They wanted to move the world away from warfare; but although they sought other means of settling disputes, such as international law and a world court, they were willing in extraordinary conditions to employ some kind of force if necessary.

A more extreme minority was composed of pacifists—absolute non-resistants—who refused to sanction the use of collective violence in any case. Despite their differences, both peace advocates and pacifists considered themselves members of the peace movement and endeavored to redirect American foreign policy and international relations during this period.

As one aspect of the broad movement to reform American institutions in the Progressive Era, the peace movement met with both successes and failures in its campaign. Supported by some of the nation's most prestigious people, including the president of the United States, it established arbitration and conciliation as accepted methods for this country to settle secondary disputes. It won American participation in both Hague peace conferences and in the working of the Permanent Court of Arbitration, popularly known as The Hague Tribunal. Yet it was unable to achieve binding arbitration for all disputes, and it failed to establish the United States as chief mediator in a league of neutral nations during the European war that broke out in 1914. American participation in the World War splintered, drained, and radicalized the peace movement. Rebounding in the postwar period, the movement helped to defeat peacetime conscription and to achieve the first step toward comprehensive naval disarmament. However, it failed completely in its long-range goal of establishing the basis for lasting international peace.

The twisting history of the peace movement in these years can only be understood in relation to changing developments in the United States and the world. Industrialism, nationalism, and imperialism had brought immense changes by the turn of the century. Technological revolutions in transportation, communication, industry, and warfare had greatly increased the power and ambition of major nations. Provided with weapons by the new technology, the armies and navies of Britain, France, Germany, Italy, Russia, and Japan carried their nations' banners into Asia and Africa in a new surge of imperial expansion. Politically and economically, the face of the world changed within a few years. The aspirations and the forces of the expanding nations often clashed with those of indigenous peoples and those of other imperialist nations. Finally, in 1914, Europe itself marched to war initiating a conflict that, within three years, led to American military intervention across the Atlantic.

As the United States entered the twentieth century a burgeoning, urban-industrial giant in a rapidly changing world, Americans had already begun to reexamine and redefine many of the institutions that had been formed in years when the country had been more agrarian and isolated. Nowhere was that reappraisal more evident than in the field of international relations. The Venezuela controversy with Britain, the Spanish-American War, the acquisition of an island empire sweeping from Puerto Rico to the Philippines, and the extension of American interests to the Far East demonstrated that the United States was redefining its relations with other nations and exercising its increasing power.

The search for a proper foreign policy for the new industrial America in a world of arming and ambitious nations elicited a variety of proposed solutions. One was a reaffirmation of the traditional policies designed to avoid involvement in European dynastic conflicts and turmoil. Specific doctrines included political isolationism—the avoidance of permanent alliances that would restrict American freedom of action—and the policy of neutrality toward wars between other nations. The traditional isolationist program received much support. It was particularly popular in the rural South and Midwest. These agrarian regions, however, were not in favor of complete withdrawal from world affairs. They endorsed expanded trade, defense of the nation's shores, and prevention of any additional European colonies in the Western Hemisphere, the essence of the Monroe Doctrine. To the isolationists, Americans could continue to rely upon their traditional defense—the breadth of the Atlantic and Pacific oceans, the weakness of their Canadian and Mexican neighbors, the balance of power among major nations abroad, and the defense ability of the navy and the small regular army, supported by millions of Americans who would volunteer when needed.

Other Americans, however, sought to break with a tradition they considered inadequate for the new domestic and international circumstances. Militant expansionists like Theodore Roosevelt (see document 4), Admiral Alfred Thayer Mahan (see document 2), and General Leonard Wood sought to commit the United States to an active use of diplomatic, economic, military, and naval power in pursuit of broadened goals. Viewing continued expansion as inevitable and desirable, they concluded that this country should secure its strategic position in the Western Hemisphere and both vigorously pursue investment and trade throughout the world and ensure the shipping routes necessary to maintain that commerce. To support this foreign policy, they urged the building of a large modern navy and merchant marine, the establishment of far-flung coaling stations, naval bases, and entrepôts, and the creation of an efficient and expandable army and massive numbers of pretrained reservists. Additionally, they advocated a much more active diplomacy. The cornerstones of their policy were, first, active cooperation with Great Britain in maintaining the balance of power and freedom of the seas and, second, the prevention of threats to American interests in East Asia and the Western Hemisphere from powerful expanding nations like Germany and Japan.

A different suggestion for adjusting America's relationship with the world was made by those internationalists who also wanted the United States to play a more active world role economically and diplomatically, but who hoped to curtail or even eliminate the use of military and naval force. Unlike the militant expansionists, these people put their hope in arbitration, mediation, adjudication, and international cooperation rather than naked power to safeguard U.S. interests and security and world peace. This reform of the international order and American foreign policy was advocated most strongly in the first two decades of the twentieth century by members of the peace movement.

To a certain extent, these broad categories of foreign-policy attitudes are analytical devices imposed upon the past to help understand the processes of historical development. They are accurate only as general descriptions of broad tendencies. There was, in fact, considerable overlapping, especially as time progressed. Most members of the peace movement were reform internationalists; but when some specific issue, such as military or naval expansion or U.S. entry into World War I arose, some of them appealed to traditional isolationism. Conversely, some isolationists belonged to peace organizations because they saw the movement as a means of safeguarding U.S. interests without active intervention abroad. Some militant expansionists, like Theodore Roosevelt, were willing to support reform internationalism in minor matters while continuing to believe that expansion would ultimately generate conflicts that could only be resolved by force. Thus with considerable subtlety and complexity, these three broad strategies for foreign policy—isolationism, militant expansionism, and reform internationalism (organizationally expressed in the peace movement)—helped to shape American foreign policy during the first two decades of the twentieth century.

I
(1900–1914)

The American peace movement grew dramatically during the first decade and a half of the new century after years of relative lethargy. Since its inception during the reform outburst of the 1830s, the movement had been composed primarily of Quakers and other religious pacifists and a handful of New England reformers. Its foremost leaders, William Ladd, Elihu Burritt, Alfred Love, and Benjamin Trueblood, had advocated an international court, periodic congresses of nations, the use of arbitration, and the neutralization of zones of conflict. Yet they generated little enthusiasm. In 1900, even the largest and oldest group, the American Peace Society, remained a small, Boston-centered organization with an annual budget of less than six thousand dollars. Change, however, came quickly.

Beginning around 1905, the traditional peace movement began to be transformed under the pressure of events and changing attitudes. Central to this transformation were the imperialist rivalries among the major European powers, the growing naval arms race between Britain and Germany, the emergence of peace sentiments and organizations in many Western nations, the First Hague Peace Conference of 1899 (see documents 1, 2), and the increasing American attention to international events. More specifically, the pressure for a more effective peace movement came as a result of the Spanish-American War of 1898, the bloody American suppression of the Philippine insurrection between 1899 and 1902, the Russo-Japanese War of 1904–1905, and the call for a Second Hague Peace Conference.

Under pressure from a number of peace advocates, including several congressmen, President Theodore Roosevelt, during the 1904 election, called for another international conference to be held at The Hague in 1907. Alarmed by the enormous casualties of the Russo-Japanese conflict—the first war between major powers in thirty-five years and the first to be fought with rapid-firing artillery and machine guns—many Americans ardently supported Roosevelt's summons. The historian Warren Kuehl has suggested that the anticipation of the Second Hague Conference and the preparations for it contributed directly to the unprecedented activity and growth of the peace movement that began in 1905.

In the following decade, the ranks of the established peace groups swelled, and a number of new organizations were created. The American Peace Society grew from seven branch chapters in 1909 to thirty-one in 1914, an increase of 340 percent. By 1914, the society counted seven thousand dues-paying members, an increase of 600 percent in seven years. Furthermore, the expansion of the traditional peace groups was matched by the enlistment of new groups in the effort to eliminate war. C. Roland Marchand and Michael A. Lutzker have demonstrated that the assumptions of the peace movement about the need to restrain popular emotions that led to war and the necessity of achieving social and international harmony found favor with many American business and civic leaders (see documents 8, 10). Many of these men were already concerned about threats to American domestic peace and stability from new immigrants and from increasingly class-conscious groups like the Socialists. Thus concern about both external and internal disorder helped contribute to the growth of the peace movement and its programs in this period.

A number of alternative strategies were offered as the peace movement grew in strength and diversity in the early years of the twentieth century. Although not all adherents supported each with equal intensity, the methods were generally endorsed by the groups within the movement.

Many of the prestigious new peace advocates—lawyers, educators, and businessmen—sought to establish an international common law through a world court and its decisions. The number of international attorneys had been increasing with the growth of world trade and investment in the late nineteenth century. In 1905, a number of them, led by Dean George Kirchwey of Columbia Law School, founded the American Society of International Law. Five years later, James Brown Scott, the State Department solicitor, led another group in organizing the American Society for the Judicial Settlement of International Disputes. Viewing international arguments narrowly as specific grievances rather than broader clashes of economic and political interests, these legalistic peace advocates sought to substitute world law and an international judiciary for European-style power politics. It was in essence, a modest program, involving only slight constriction of national sovereignty and little change in the traditional reluctance of Americans to intervene politically or militarily in European affairs. The plan called for the United States to agree to submit justiciable disputes—which would not involve vital matters of self-defense—to a world court that would solve international disagreements through judicial action.

The growth of world trade and communications seemed to some Americans to be making war a wasteful anachronism. A number of peace-minded businessmen and publicists believed that economic growth and prosperity depended upon stable international conditions and uninterrupted trade. To them, the uncertainty produced by conflict and war scares disrupted economic conditions and jeopardized profits for most businessmen except unscrupulous speculators. Scholars like William Graham Sumner asserted that in the evolution of society, commerce and industry produced a more rationalized and less warlike world than the warrior-dominated societies of feudal times. The English writer Norman Angell contended in his influential book *The Great Illusion* that modern war was becoming so costly in life and property that it was unprofitable to wage it.

Peace advocates sought to educate the American public to the need for thinking in terms of international order and peaceful settlement of disputes. Among the most prominent businessmen joining this campaign were Edward Ginn and Andrew Carnegie. A wealthy Boston publisher, Ginn established the World Peace Foundation in 1910 with a gift of one million dollars, one-third of his fortune. It financed a massive promotional effort among young people on behalf of peace. Within a year, Carnegie, a retired steel magnate, dwarfed Ginn's gesture by creating the Carnegie Endowment for International Peace through a grant of ten million dollars. Headed by lawyers like Elihu Root and James Scott and educators like Nicholas Murray Butler, the president of Columbia University, the endowment promoted scholarly research into the causes of war and the peaceful settlement of international problems. It also subsidized most of the peace societies and soon became influential in determining their leadership and policies.

A multilateral approach to peace was attempted at the Second Hague Peace Conference, which met in 1907. Many peace advocates hoped the delegates from various nations would agree to limit armaments, codify international law, and create a permanent and effective international court. However, not all agreed. Elihu Root, then secretary of state, instructed the American delegates to avoid entangling alliances and to oppose disarmament because the U.S. Navy had not yet completed its new superbattleships. Although the Americans did work for extension of arbitration and a more precise statement of the rights and duties of neutrals in wartime, the conference was a disappointment to many. The Germans defeated a U.S. proposal for a permanent treaty of arbitration, and the British blocked American attempts to ensure greater protection of neutral rights in war. In the end, the conference merely urged represented governments to consider the problem of armaments. The delegates' chief accomplishment, an improved formula for a permanent court of arbitral justice, failed to be ratified.

Other suggestions for achieving world peace were put forward by bolder members of the peace movement. Proposals for disarmament ranged from suggestions for multilateral arms reductions to cries from nonresistants for unilateral abolition of armaments and the elimination of standing armies. Others called for some kind of federation of nations. One alternative was Andrew Carnegie's plan for a league of peace in which the major powers would use economic sanctions and an international police force against aggressors (see document 4). Another was the plan of Hamilton Holt, editor of *The Independent* magazine, for a world government that would include both a legislature to develop laws and procedures for peace and an executive to apply decisions to specific cases (see document 6).

An even more extreme alternative solution was advocated by a few pacifistic social reformers. Jane Addams, the founder of Hull House in Chicago, proposed the creation of an international welfare community as a substitute for war. As early as 1904, she suggested that the labor movement, with its ideal of human solidarity, and the social reform effort, with its trust in the masses, could serve as moral substitutes for international conflict. She offered these as alternative outlets for individual desires for patriotism, adventure, self-sacrifice, and glory. The idea greatly appealed to William James, the Harvard philosopher. Six years later, he called publicly for a different equivalent for war (see document 5). Concluding that martial tendencies were innate, James sought to redirect them into socially-useful purposes. As a consequence, he urged that young people be recruited into nonmilitary teams to help improve the conditions of life in the new industrial metropolises. Such direct alternatives to martial ventures were adopted by the Boy Scouts and a few other youth groups, but they did not become governmental programs until the Civilian Conservation Corps of the 1930s and the Peace Corps of the 1960s.

The peace movement, however, did have an influence on American foreign policy in the years before World War I. In part this was owing to the fear of the new technological warfare demonstrated in the Russo-Japanese War. To some extent, it was caused by the widespread belief that war had outlasted its usefulness and was wasteful and archaic. Partly, this influence was a result of the belief during this reform period that patterns of behavior—even international relations—could be improved through the application of human intelligence. And to a certain degree, it was a product both of the activity of the peace movement and of the location of a number of peace advocates in important positions in the government.

This influence was especially felt in the State Department. There, Secretaries of State Elihu Root (1905–1909), William Jennings Bryan (1913–1915), and Robert Lansing (1915–1920) had been, at other points in their careers, officers of peace groups. Furthermore, between 1906 and 1915, the department's chief legal officers—James Brown Scott, Chandler P. Anderson, John Bassett Moore, and Robert Lansing—had been members of the original executive committee of the American Society of International Law. Additionally, Presidents William Howard Taft and Woodrow Wilson were both partisans of the movement for international peace.

A number of Americans received Nobel Peace prizes during this period. Theodore Roosevelt won the prize in 1906 for his mediation of the Russo-Japanese War and his support of international conferences to reduce world tensions (see document 4). He accepted the prize in 1910 after leaving office. Elihu Root was awarded the prize in 1912 for his work on behalf of international law and arbitration; he did not deliver his acceptance speech until 1914 (see document 10). Woodrow Wilson was the recipient of the Nobel Prize for 1919 for his proposals for international peace in the postwar period, but because of his illness, was unable to journey to Norway to deliver an acceptance speech. A decade later, in 1931, two of the leading peace advocates of this period—Jane Addams and Nicholas Murray Butler—jointly received the Nobel Prize for their work for peace. There was no doubt that peace was popular with many citizens and political leaders during the first two decades of the twentieth century, but the various attempts to ensure peace produced mixed results.

The movement to establish a world court, which would construct an international common law, met with both success and failure. The First Hague Peace Conference in 1899 had established a Permanent Court of Arbitration (see documents 1, 2). Not a permanent sitting court, despite its name, this body consisted of a panel of more than one hundred potential arbitrators. Critics said that these jurists and diplomats often compromised and split differences regardless of law or equity, and that this action deterred nations with strong cases from using The Hague Tribunal.

Theodore Roosevelt and his secretary of state sought to invigorate this international agency. In an attempt to rescue it from inactivity, the president referred a minor American controversy with Mexico to it in 1902 and the following year persuaded Britain, Germany, and Italy to end their blockade of Venezuela and to submit their grievances over unpaid debts to the tribunal. From the State Department, Elihu Root tried to create a permanent court of sitting jurists that could substitute decisions based upon law for diplomatic compromises. In 1907, he played a key role in the creation of a Central American Court of Justice, and he instructed the American delegates to the Second Hague Peace Conference to work to convert The Hague Tribunal into a similar court.

A permanent international court with broad powers failed to come into existence until after World War I, however. The Second Hague Conference could not agree on the manner of choosing a small number of jurists because that restriction would eliminate some nations from representation. It was not until 1921 that a World Court was created by the League of Nations, with jurists chosen by a vote of the member nations. Despite the efforts to the peace movement and of President Wilson and Secretary Lansing, the Senate refused to allow the United States to join the court. Nevertheless, several American jurists were elected to it. Before it was succeeded by the International Court of Justice of the United Nations in 1945, the World Court rendered nearly three dozen judgments and over two dozen advisory opinions. The most important of these decisions was the disallowance in 1933 of Norway's claim to the north coast of Greenland and the affirmation of Danish sovereignty in that area.

Numerous attempts to establish arbitration as the basis for settling various types of difficulties between the United States and other nations were made under the impetus of peace advocates and in the wake of international events. In the nineteenth century, the United States had used the technique several times in regard to boundary disputes and property claims. The most famous of these was the 1872 award by an international arbitration board of fifteen million dollars in gold to the United States as a result of the damages caused by the British-built Confederate raider *Alabama* during the Civil War. Twenty-five years later, following a war scare between Britain and the United States over a Venezuelan boundary dispute, the administration of Grover Cleveland provided in the Olney-Pauncefote Treaty of 1897 for arbitration of several kinds of property and territorial disputes between the two nations if they should occur. Anglophobia and the Senate's own sense of prerogative, however, combined to prevent the two-thirds majority needed in the upper chamber to approve the treaty.

The popularity of the idea of arbitration grew slowly in succeeding years. It received the endorsement of the First Hague Peace Conference as the most effective and equitable means of settling legal questions. Further evidence of support came during the 1904 election year, when President Roosevelt sponsored a series of bilateral pacts requiring the United States to arbitrate certain classes of disputes. Once again, the Senate, cautious of its prerogative and American security, bridled at such suggestions. When it amended Secretary of State John Hay's treaties to such an extent that they became almost meaningless, except as general statements, the president refused to submit the modified treaties to the other signatory governments.

A compromise was worked out in the second Roosevelt administration. In the winter of 1908/1909, Secretary of State Root signed twenty-four bilateral arbitration treaties with other nations. In deference to the Senate, these treaties exempted disputes involving America's vital interests, independence, and national honor and, equally as important, upheld the Senate's authority to define the scope of arbitration in every case. Thus restricted, the five-year treaties were overwhelmingly approved. While Roosevelt and Root viewed arbitration as an occasionally useful, semijudicial device to settle minor international disputes or to allow a nation to retreat from an untenable or embarrassing position without loss of prestige, the succeeding Taft administration took a much bolder position.

William Howard Taft and his secretary of state, Philander C. Knox, wanted to make arbitration a vital tool in reshaping international relations into peaceful channels. They already encouraged private American investment in underdeveloped nations—the so-called dollar diplomacy—as a means of expanding American trade and avoiding instability and military intervention. In a bid to increase his sagging popularity, the chief executive in 1910 proposed to submit almost all international disputes relating to the United States—even those involving national honor—to judicial arbitration (see document 7). The program divided Americans and split the peace movement. Roosevelt and Root, for example, argued that the United States should not accept an arbitration decision against its vital interests. Despite an intensive educational and lobbying campaign by the White House and most of the peace groups, the Senate refused to accept Taft's treaties with Britain and France but rewrote them into general statements in favor of arbitration without compelling the United States to any specific action. Angrily, Taft rejected the Senate's amended treaties.

After three such clashes between the executive and the legislative branches in fifteen years, the limits of U.S. acceptance of the arbitral process had been clearly defined. Arbitration could be used only in regard to disputes of relatively minor importance. The Senate refused to jeopardize its power in foreign affairs; to endanger the Monroe Doctrine or U.S. security; to alienate southerners who feared the claims of foreign holders of Confederate bonds; to aggravate westerners concerned about Oriental immigration restriction; or to anger Americans, especially those of German or Irish ancestry, who feared that the treaties created a virtual Anglo-American alliance. The upper chamber determined that the U.S. government would not make sweeping promises in peaceful times that it would not fulfill in periods of crisis. Apparently, the Wilson administration agreed, for it did not adopt Taft's position but was content to renew Root's treaties in 1913 and 1914, when they approached expiration.

In the early years of the twentieth century, the United States did employ arbitration in at least three disputes with its neighbors. In 1903, it agreed to submit a Canadian-Alaskan boundary controversy that had flared after the discovery of gold in that area. With the support of the British and American delegates, a trinational panel decided in favor of the U.S. claims. Seven years later, The Hague Tribunal settled a dispute over American fishing rights off the Newfoundland Canadian fisheries through a compromise that gave some recognition to the position of both sides. Also in 1910, the United States and Mexico agreed to submit the contested Chamizal tract issue to a panel. Despite these cases, the U.S. government refused to arbitrate such important matters as Colombia's grievances regarding American support of the Panamanian revolution in 1903, the interpretation of the Hay-Pauncefote Treaty in the quarrel over the U.S. exemption from Panama Canal tolls in 1912, or the many differences between the policies of President Wilson and President Victoriano Huerta during the early stages of the Mexican Revolution in 1913 and 1914.

While the Wilson administration proved reluctant to arbitrate these issues, Secretary of State Bryan did seek to provide conciliation machinery to avert wars. Bryan had opposed American military conquest of the Philippines and had become a Christian pacifist after a visit with Count Leo Tolstoy in Russia in 1902. The leader of the agrarian wing of the Democratic party, Bryan found enthusiastic response in the rural South and Midwest to his religious rhetoric on behalf of peace. It was primarily the opinion makers in the metropolitan areas of the country who publicly belittled his aptitude for being secretary of state. During 1913 and 1914, Bryan negotiated thirty bilateral treaties that provided that every dispute, even those involving national honor, should be submitted to an international commission for investigation (see document 9). Uniquely, the signatory nations—including most major powers, except Germany and Japan—agreed to a one-year "cooling-off" period while the commission investigated such disputes. Even though he realized that the disputant nations could then reject the conciliating agency's recommendation, Bryan hoped that overheated tempers would cool in the waiting period and world opinion for peace would be mobilized. Although the conciliation treaties were never used, they did help to influence peace-keeping policies in the period after World War I.

And although peace advocates attempted to establish machinery that would eliminate war, they differed in their opinion over whether some degree of force might be necessary to ensure international order and whether the United States should, therefore, arm or disarm. Many of those like Ginn, Holt, and the Quakers Lucia Ames Mead (see document 3) and William I. Hull, who favored a world federation, wanted an international peace-keeping force with limited powers. They advocated national disarmament. On the other hand, international lawyers like Root, Moore, and Scott held national military power necessary for defense of vital interests. A number of peace society trustees were also affiliated with organizations that supported the expansion of American military and naval power, such as the Navy League and the National Security League. In Roosevelt's cabinet, Root had been secretary of war before he became secretary of state. While these people sought peace through arbitration, they were prepared to rely upon force if other means failed.

Many peace advocates urged disarmament, or at least arms reduction, rather than expansion. The idea was an old one; Americans had inherited a suspicion of large standing armies from their colonial period. During the nineteenth century, the United States, Britain, and Canada had averted a threatened arms race on the Great Lakes and along the Canadian border by demilitarizing the area during a fifty-four-year period between the Rush-Bagot Agreement of 1817 and the Treaty of Washington in 1871. Soon, however, the issue of the necessity of armaments arose from another area.

In the late nineteenth and early twentieth centuries, a naval arms race began among leading powers. Germany began to challenge British naval supremacy and triggered a naval building spree. Furthermore, the Japanese navy showed its prowess by demolishing the Russian ships in Far Eastern waters. In his first administration, President Roosevelt launched a major warship-building program. Naval appropriations leaped nearly 40 percent, from $85 million to $118 million a year, and the U.S. Navy became the second largest fleet in the world. Roosevelt's "Big Navy" program generated considerable opposition; and a coalition to stop it formed among many peace advocates, anti-imperialists, rural isolationists, and labor unionists. In Congress, a small but vocal bipartisan bloc criticized the shipbuilding program as a jingoistic and unnecessary waste of tax revenues fostered by the president, navalists, and the steel and munitions manufacturers. Led by Republican Senator Eugene Hale of Maine, the chairman of the Naval Affairs Committee, and Republican Congressman Theodore Burton of Ohio, the "Little Navy" group was able by 1906—in the middle of Roosevelt's second term—to trim the president's requests for new battleships. Taft continued the policy of naval expansion, but faced an increasingly hostile Congress. Between 1910 and 1913, the legislators balked several times in voting funds for more warships. Twice they adopted resolutions urging the chief executive to seek to limit the naval arms race through an international agreement. Despite this expression of opinion from Capitol Hill, however, the escalation of weaponry continued, except for a brief pause in the early years of the Wilson administration when the Democratic president curtailed the requests of the admirals.

In the first decade and a half of the twentieth century, the United States appeared a paradox as it emerged as an active world power.

During these years there occurred both an unprecedented peacetime naval building program and the dramatic revitalization of the peace movement as an important force in American foreign policy. The United States seemed to be represented by both the eagle and the dove.

Swollen in numbers, wealth, and prestige, the peace organizations in this period suggested alternative means of assuring national security and fulfilling what many saw as America's mission of redeeming the world through its liberal, democratic, capitalistic institutions. The peace strategists rejected involvement in European-style power politics and balance-of-power formulas. They also refused to continue traditional American political isolationism. Between 1900 and 1914, several proposals of the peace movement—arbitration, conciliation, disarmament, and the establishment of international peace conferences, international law, and a world court—reached the stage of national debate in the pages of the mass media and in the halls of the national government. Most of these proposals—except disarmament—were adopted to a limited degree as national goals, although U.S. foreign policy continued to be based in the short run primarily on the defense of expanding American interests through economic, diplomatic, and military measures.

The extent to which the United States relied upon nonforceful means of diplomacy represented both the strength of the peace movement and the belief in the sanctity of treaties and the pledged word of governments. Moreover, this was also a period in which neither American vital interests nor the world balance of power, which helped to protect them, was confronted by a major military challenge. The beliefs and circumstances of this period were abruptly confronted by dramatic new forces when the general European war broke out in August 1914.

II
(1914–1917)

War is a transforming event. The war that broke out in the summer of 1914 and raged for four bloody years had a profound impact upon the peace movement and U.S. foreign policy even before the nation joined the fray as a belligerent in 1917. Gradually, between 1914 and 1917, the world's most powerful neutral edged into the maelstrom across the Atlantic. As a result, the peace movement splintered into conservative and radical wings, each pursuing different strategies. Although many of the established peace societies became moribund or dormant under the changed circumstances, several new peace-oriented organizations emerged and pursued much more activist roles. In the meantime, the Wilson administration moved from attempts at mediation to the decision for American military intervention. The period of American neutrality during the first three years of the European war thus proved to be a time of reexamination of the attitudes and policies of the peace movement and of testing its influence upon American foreign policy.

Members of the peace movement had been shocked and dismayed by the bloodshed that began in 1914, but they divided in their response to the European war. Many of those in the prewar peace organizations came to support the Allied cause, especially after a German submarine sank the Cunard passenger liner *Lusitania* on its way from New York to Southampton. The brutality and recklessness of the U-boat campaign and the German challenge to British supremacy of the seas led some to condemn Kaiser Wilhelm II's actions as a threat both to American security and prosperity and to international law and order (see document 16).

A number of the more conservative prewar organizations suspended their major efforts for world peace until after the war. They advocated the defeat of Germany as essential to progress toward the establishment of international relations based upon cooperation and judicial principles; and many of them, therefore, supported increased military and naval spending by the United States. Led by its secretary James Brown Scott, the Carnegie Endowment for International Peace proved instrumental in persuading many peace groups not to try to stop the current war by mediation but to encourage an Allied victory or at least to concentrate on postwar plans. Subsidized organizations like the American Peace Society and the International Peace Bureau soon accepted that general position. So did many members of the American Society of International Law, the American Society for the Judicial Settlement of International Disputes, the New York Peace Society, and the World Peace Foundation.

Many of the more conservative peace advocates joined, however, in creating a new organization designed to work for a postwar league of nations that, if necessary, would use force to maintain peace and order. Under the impetus of President A. Lawrence Lowell of Harvard University, who had been a member of several peace organizations, these men founded the Association for a League to Enforce Peace. The idea of a league of nations was not entirely new. It had been advocated in various forms since the seventeenth century by people as disparate as the Duc de Sully, William Penn, and Immanuel Kant. The Holy Alliance and the First Hague Peace Conference had been steps toward it in the nineteenth century. In the early twentieth century, it was endorsed by Andrew Carnegie in 1905 (see document 4) and by Theodore Roosevelt in his Nobel Peace Prize Address in 1910. Yet these proposals had been largely ignored even by the peace movement. Not until the World War undermined the competing notion that nations could be restrained from going to war by public opinion or moral force did the concept of a league with sanctions begin to gain widespread support.

The 1915 proposal for a league to enforce peace combined the idea of deliberation and delay in times of crisis with the processes of arbitration and adjudication and the ultimate sanction of force. According to the association's proposal issued in January of that year, member nations would have to agree to submit justiciable questions to a world court and to abide by the result. All other questions—the most important ones—would be submitted to a council of conciliation, made up of the major powers, for recommendation. Economic and military force could be used against nations that refused to abide by these recommendations or that were judged guilty of aggression.

With deliberation and adroitness, the Association for a League to Enforce Peace put forward its program in an attempt to influence both the public and key governmental decision makers. Its distinguished leadership was headed by William Howard Taft, former president of the United States. Its program was widely publicized by a number of other prewar peace advocates, including Hamilton Holt (see document 12), Theodore Marburg, and John Bates Clark. Seeking broad-based mainstream support, the association emphasized the postwar nature of its program and shunned discussion of proposals to end the present war through compromise. It also avoided contact with the various new pacifist groups that emerged, and it advocated such a program after the outbreak of the European war. Although President Woodrow Wilson declined to endorse the League's program, he did address the group in May 1916 (see document 21) and made his first public declaration in favor of a postwar association of nations—the first such endorsement by a world leader.

Unlike the conservative peace advocates and the Association for a League to Enforce Peace, the new peace organizations that appeared after 1914 worked to conclude the bloody conflict as quickly and as fairly as possible. In fact, the new activist organizations that sprang up between 1914 and 1916 came into being to a great extent because the old-time and conservative peace societies refused to discuss proposals for ending the current war peacefully and, in a number of cases, even supported measures for increased military preparedness.

The new spectrum of groups virtually reconstituted the peace movement, at least one wing of it. Included were short-lived associations like the League to Limit Armaments and the Emergency Peace Federation and more enduring organizations like the Woman's Peace party and the American Union Against Militarism. This shifting coalition, as historians Charles Chatfield and Blanche Wiesen Cook have noted, was made up of action-oriented peace advocates who were also feminists, social workers, journalists, labor lawyers, and social-gospel clergymen. Although hostile to the kaiser's actions, they were also critical of many Allied policies as well.

Drawing upon liberal thought in both Europe and America, these pacifist progressives urged the United States to play an active but peaceful role in ending the war and preventing future conflagrations. They called upon the Wilson administration to summon a conference of neutral nations that would offer to mediate between the belligerents. They also advocated terms that they believed would ensure a just and lasting peace. The liberal peace proposals provided for no annexations or indemnities, an end to secret treaties and entangling alliances, elimination of trade barriers and colonial empires, and the reduction of large armies and navies. In their place, the liberal pacifists urged disarmament, neutralization of the sea lanes, self-determination of peoples, democratic governments, open diplomacy, and international machinery for the judicial settlement of disputes between nations.

The most lasting of the new liberal pacifist organizations was the Woman's Peace party, which soon became known as the Women's International League for Peace and Freedom (WILPF) and has continued to work for peace ever since. Founded in January 1915 by a score of women's groups, the organization represented forty thousand affiliated members (see document 14). It was led by American feminists such as Jane Addams, Carrie Chapman Catt, Anna Garlin Spencer, and Charlotte Perkins Gilman, and European feminists like Rosika Schwimmer of Hungary and Emmeline Pethick-Lawrence of Britain. They claimed that women had a special revulsion against war and a particular responsibility for the future of the human race. Endorsing mediation and the liberal peace proposals, they also recommended that the president appoint a commission to work to prevent war.

In April and May 1915, forty-five delegates from the Woman's Peace party attended an International Congress of Women at The Hague (see document 15). In conjunction with women from belligerent and other neutral nations, they formed the WILPF and elected Addams as its first chairperson. In a dramatic effort, the women called for a continuous conference of neutral nations to offer mediation to the belligerents. A delegation took the proposal directly to statesmen in the fighting countries; but because none of the men were willing to initiate proposals for peace, the conference was never organized.

A subsequent attempt to force the neutral governments to offer mediation to the belligerents ended in one of the most dramatic diplomatic episodes of 1915. It centered on the private initiative for peace launched by Henry Ford, the automobile manufacturer. A pacifist who believed war wasteful in both lives and property, Ford became convinced that the main stumbling block to ending the war had become the ineffectiveness of the diplomats. Psychologically and financially prepared to make a bold bid for peace, Ford was persuaded by Rosika Schwimmer to send a mission of distinguished persons across the Atlantic to join leading Europeans in compelling the neutral nations either to extend their good offices for mediation or, failing that, to offer suggestions for peace themselves.

Maladroitly promising to "get the boys out of their trenches and back to their homes by Christmas Day," Ford chartered the steamship *Oscar II* early in December 1915 to carry a peace mission to Europe later that month. Derided by the press, his effort was crippled before it began. Many public figures subsequently declined Ford's invitation to sail, and the auto magnate himself deserted the expedition as soon as the vessel landed in Scandinavia. Nevertheless, the "peace ship" mission did organize a Neutral Conference for Continuous Mediation at Stockholm. As historian Merle Curti has explained, the conference remained until 1917 a nongovernmental clearinghouse for suggestions for peaceful means to end the war.

Although some of the new peace groups emphasized the need for the United States to help mediate to end the war, the American Union Against Militarism (AUAM) was formed in New York City in November 1915 primarily to dissuade the U.S. government from expanding the army and navy. Originally, the new organization was established in response to the so-called preparedness campaign led by Theodore Roosevelt, General Leonard Wood, and groups like the National Security League, the Navy League, and the Military Training Camps Association. By the fall of 1915, these bodies and the international situation had convinced President Wilson to recommend an expansion of the armed services. In opposition, the AUAM was created by a number of progressives, including social workers like Addams and Lillian Wald; journalists like Oswald Garrison Villard of *The Nation* and the New York *Evening Post* and Max Eastman of *The Masses;* labor lawyers such as his sister Crystal Eastman, Amos Pinchot, and Hollingsworth

Wood; and social-reform clergymen like John Haynes Holmes and Rabbi Stephen Wise.

By the end of 1916, the American Union Against Militarism had become the largest antimilitarist organization in the country. With branches in twenty-two cities, it counted over six thousand members and had another fifty thousand sympathizers on its mailing list. Through its adherents and its propaganda campaign, it sought to build a coalition of aroused farmers, workers, pacifists, immigrants, and radicals against expansion of the military and the introduction of universal military training, which most of those supporting preparedness also advocated. On a budget of $35,000 a year, the AUAM sent out more than six hundred thousand pieces of literature and accurately claimed to provide the only active nationwide press service against militarism. It employed a full-time lobbyist on Capitol Hill, and its leaders met directly with President Wilson on several occasions (see documents 20, 23, 27, 29, 30).

Although not completely successful, the AUAM campaign against expansion of the armed forces was to some degree effective. And although it did not prevent the Congress from voting substantial increases in the military and naval services, it did aid in preventing the preparedness organizations from obtaining their full program, including conscription; and it even helped to modify the president's defense program. Furthermore, the antimilitarists obtained a congressional declaration that the United States approved in principle of reduction rather than expansion of armaments. Attached to the Naval Expansion Act of August 1916 was a rider introduced by Congressman Walter L. Hensley of Missouri that not only made such a statement of congressional opinion but also requested the president to invite an international conference on general disarmament and the creation of a true world court. If a disarmament agreement were reached, the chief executive was authorized to suspend the naval building program that Congress had just enacted (see document 25).

The American Union Against Militarism directed its efforts at international peace as well as at the prevention of the expansion of armaments. In a statement of principles entitled "Towards a Peace That Shall Last," the organization endorsed the liberal peace program. The leaders of the AUAM opposed war because it endangered the concepts of liberty and of the preciousness of human life. They also believed that war threatened to terminate the progressive movement's attempt to achieve social reform and to uplift humanity.

In the area of international peacekeeping, the AUAM's most significant historical accomplishment was in helping to prevent a war between

Mexico and the United States in 1916. Relations between the two nations, tense since the outbreak of the Mexican Revolution in 1910, had been further strained when irregulars led by Francisco ("Pancho") Villa crossed the border and killed a number of Americans in 1916. As a result, a punitive expedition under General John J. Pershing pursued Villa and his men several hundred miles into Mexico. Although the Americans failed to catch the irregulars, they came into conflict with Mexican federal soldiers.

On June 21, two troops of Pershing's cavalry encountered a detachment of 250 government troops near the town of Carrizal. A skirmish resulted in the deaths of nine Americans and thirty Mexicans. The next day, the New York Times and many other newspapers charged, under screaming headlines, that the American cavalry men had been treacherously ambushed (see document 22). War fever reached the government as well, and President Wilson prepared to ask for a full-scale invasion of northern Mexico.

Seeking to counter the pressure for war, the AUAM moved swiftly. It obtained a firsthand account of the Carrizal incident from an American officer that showed that the U.S. cavalry, not the Mexican troops, had initiated the fighting. In a number of advertisements, it reprinted the officer's testimony, asserted that the incident was not a valid cause for war, and urged people to write to the government (see documents 22, 25). Encouraged by this new information and by a flood of antiwar telegrams, Wilson reversed his initial judgment and worked to avoid a major conflict, as did Venustiano Carranza, the Mexican chief of state. Consequently, the AUAM helped to launch negotiations by convening a commission of conciliation, made up of several leading private citizens from both sides, which served as a transitional body while an official Joint High Commission was created. Through its quick initiative, the AUAM had helped to avert war, although relations between the two countries remained extremely tense until the worsening European situation caused President Wilson to remove Pershing's forces from Mexico and formally recognize Carranza's government in March 1917.

At the left wing of the peace movement in the years 1914 to 1917 stood the American Socialists. Although they sought to keep the United States out of the European war, the Socialists seldom worked with the peace societies. Nor did they share many of the assumptions or long-range goals of the liberal peace advocates. Indeed, the Socialists considered the peace groups thoroughly capitalistic and middle-class in orientation and generally held them in contempt. Unlike the liberals who believed the war had been caused by a combination of militarism, imperialism, nationalism, and the alliance system, the Socialists asserted the primacy of the economic motive. It was a businessmen's war, they argued, encouraged by the lust of merchants, manufacturers, and financiers for markets, trade, and colonies to exploit. Marxist-Leninist theory held that conflict between expanding capitalistic economies was an inevitable consequence of the profit seeking of wealthy elites (see document 17).

Socialists on both sides of the Atlantic proved ineffective in ending the war or in preventing the entry of the United States as a belligerent, although they offered a number of strategies to do both. With few exceptions, most European Socialist leaders endorsed their nation's war efforts, compromising their Marxist principles to retain the support of the trade unions, which generally were strongly nationalistic. American Socialists, with less strength in the labor movement, remained closer to Marx's principles of opposition to capitalist wars. To ensure U.S. neutrality, American Socialists like Eugene V. Debs, Allan Benson, Morris Hillquit, and Kate Richards O'Hare denounced preparedness, recommended an embargo against all belligerents, and urged that a national referendum be held before a declaration of war. William ("Big Bill") Haywood, leader of the Industrial Workers of the World (IWW), the radical wing of the Socialists, suggested that the workers should stage a general strike rather than fight in a capitalist war, but the proposal was not endorsed by the majority of Socialists. Neither the American Socialists nor the "Wobblies" (the popular term for the IWW) seems to have had much impact on the conduct of American foreign policy.

Woodrow Wilson had been influenced for some time by the growth of the peace movement and the ideas of international organization and world law. Although aware of the movement, he had largely ignored it until its transformation around the time of the Second Hague Peace Conference. In 1908, as president of Princeton, he had joined other leading educators in becoming an active member and speaker in the American Peace Society. Three years later, as governor of New Jersey, he had endorsed President Taft's arbitration treaties.

In the White House, Wilson continued to be attentive to the peace movement and its proposals. He endorsed Secretary of State Bryan's conciliation treaties. And in early 1914, he agreed to mediation by Argentina, Brazil, and Chile to avoid war between the United States and Mexico over U.S. nonrecognition of President Huerta and temporary American occupation of the ports of Tampico and Vera Cruz. Bryan remained in the cabinet until his resignation in the spring of 1915 over what he considered the harshness and partiality of the president's warning to Germany after the sinking of the *Lusitania*. Nevertheless, Wilson continued to learn of the views of representatives of various peace groups—the Association for a League to Enforce Peace, the Woman's Peace party, the American Union Against Militarism, the American Neutral Conference Committee (founded in June 1916), and others—through notes and proposals they submitted to him directly or through his confidant, "Colonel" Edward M. House. Although some urged increasing aid to the Allies to defeat Germany, others advocated mediation for a compromise peace. The divisions within the peace movement over both means and goals reduced the effectiveness of the peace advocates. Such differences in the peace movement, together with deep divisions within American society over preparedness, munitions trade with the Allies, and Germany's submarine warfare, allowed President Wilson greater freedom of action in pursuing his own foreign policy.

Wilson eagerly sought to maintain this freedom of action in his role as head of the most powerful neutral nation. His initial desire was for an early end to the fighting in Europe in a compromise peace settlement that would maintain the balance of power and thus protect U.S. security. While playing the peacemaker, the president pursued his own policies, not those of the pacifists. Within four months after the outbreak of the war, he sent Colonel House as an unofficial emissary on a secret mission to the foreign offices of both sides. In a series of visits in 1915 and 1916, House proposed a compromise solution in which Germany would be granted wider scope in colonial areas and overseas markets if it would end its challenge to British naval superiority.

In 1916, Colonel House signed an agreement with British Foreign Secretary Edward Grey (the House-Grey Memorandum) that stated that when and if the moment proved opportune for Britain and France, President Wilson would call for a peace conference. If the kaiser's government refused to participate, the United States in the words of the agreement "would probably enter the war against Germany." Because both sides believed they could still break the military deadlock and win the war, they did not respond to the Wilson administration's secret proposals for a negotiated peace. The House-Grey strategy was abandoned.

Wilson's cautious approach to America's policy was at odds with the dramatic proposals of the mediationists for U.S. leadership in ending the war. The keystone of their appeal was for the United States to take the lead in calling a convention of neutral nations to tempt the belligerents into peace negotiations. In view of German military dominance on the Continent and the emerging submarine issue that threatened to draw the United States into the war, the president refused to agree to such a proposal. Neutral mediation seemed a remote issue to most Americans, who were more concerned with Germany's submarine warfare, the president's policy of insisting on the right of Americans to travel on belligerent's ships (challenged by the unsuccessful Gore-McLemore Resolution in 1916 [see document 19]), the growing munitions trade with the Allies, and the controversy over military preparedness. Wilson, in several meetings with the mediationists, indicated a reluctance to participate in any joint mediation schemes (see document 23). His most important objections to American leadership in 1915 and 1916 in a neutral conference were, first, the unsettled difficulties with the German government over the submarine issue; second, the military situation on the Continent that was so unfavorable to the Allies that they would brand any American peace overtures as unneutral; and third, his belief that he should reserve judgment on the problem until the changing military situation made it fairly clear that both sides would accept American mediation. Wilson feared that if he committed himself prematurely to a specific mediation proposal, he might be rejected by the belligerents as a peacemaker and therefore lose whatever influence he might have for ending the war at an opportune moment.

Despite his vacillation for two years without publicly offering mediation, Woodrow Wilson did not alienate the majority of peace workers. He met with their delegations on more than a dozen occasions between 1914 and 1917, listened to their pleas, and answered their letters. He sincerely admired people like Jane Addams, Lillian Wald, Hamilton Holt, and Paul U. Kellogg and sympathized with their hopes for restoring peace in the world. He also hoped to bring an end to the war before the submarine controversy led to American belligerency. As a result, in the 1916 election, most of the mediationists supported him against the Republican nominee, Charles Evans Hughes, whose party had taken a more bellicose and nationalistic position on America's role in the war. Thus Wilson had skillfully pursued a foreign policy that did not alienate either the mediation advocates or those neutralist-isolationists who wanted to keep the United States aloof from Europe's problems. He won reelection in 1916 by campaigning on the slogans of peace and prosperity. Many liberal pacifists campaigned and voted for him (see document 24).

After his reelection, President Wilson began an intensive and public effort to mediate an end to the war based on the principles of the "new diplomacy"—open covenants and international cooperation. His note of December 18, 1916, asked both sides to state their war aims publicly. When the Germans refused and the Allies offered terms clearly unfavorable to the Central Powers—withdrawal from all conquered territories, payment of indemnities, and the breakup of the Austro-Hungarian Empire—Wilson announced his own program for a desirable peace. He had come increasingly to believe that mediation had to be tied to the goals of the liberal peace program in order to ensure not only the proper conclusion of the World War but also the prevention of its recurrence. In the spring of 1916, he had endorsed the idea of a postwar league of nations (see document 21) and asserted, in the Democratic party platform, that the United States had a duty to join any reasonable association of nations after the conflict. In a major address before the Senate on January 22, 1917, he called for a "peace without victory" and endorsed the liberal peace aims, including an international organization to guarantee world peace (see document 26). Although he dismayed those like Theodore Roosevelt who demanded unconditional surrender of Germany (see document 28), the president's call for mediation and a compromise peace to establish a new framework of international relations won the applause of reform internationalists and peace advocates in both Europe and the United States.

The influence of the peace movement upon the president's decision to attempt publicly to mediate the war was relatively slight according to historian David Patterson. Occasionally indecisive and often politically expedient, Woodrow Wilson nevertheless had strong personal opinions. It was his own assessment of the changing international circumstances in 1916, rather than the suggestions of his advisors or of the mediation workers, that led to Wilson's peace moves. He believed that jettisoning the House-Grey Memorandum and adopting a more favorable position toward Germany might persuade the belligerents to allow him to negotiate. At the same time, the Allies' increasing economic dependence upon the United States might enable him to force them to the conference table.

While the peace workers had little effect on the timing of Wilson's mediation attempt and failed to convince him of the usefulness of a conference of neutral nations, they did have significant influence on the president. Patterson has concluded that their persistent efforts between 1914 and 1916 helped nourish Wilson's interest in mediation even during the darkest hours, as they gave him emotional support and relayed reports of antiwar sentiment from the European nations. Thus they helped to convince him that his independent peace move would receive support from moderates in both the United States and Europe. Additionally, the peace workers also helped to stimulate Wilson's interest in the liberal program for the reform of international relations. The president consciously drew upon the resolutions of the International Congress of Women at The Hague and the pronouncements of British and American liberals in formulating his own maturing approach in 1916 to the postwar settlement (see and compare documents 12, 14, 26, 27, 39, 46).

Ironically, it was partly to achieve the principles of international reform that President Wilson took the United States into the World War in April 1917. His mediation proposals had failed to bring peace in the winter of 1916/1917. Instead, the German government, under the influence of the military, decided upon all-out submarine warfare beginning February 1 against neutral as well as belligerent shipping in an attempt to starve the British into suing for peace. Events followed each other in rapid and almost compelling order: the announcement of unrestricted submarine warfare, the American severance of diplomatic relations with Germany, the publication of the "Zimmerman telegram," sent by German Foreign Minister Arthur Zimmermann to the German ambassador to Mexico instructing him to propose a German alliance with Mexico against the United States. This was followed by the torpedoing and sinking of several American merchantships. On April 2, the president asked Congress to declare that a state of war already existed between the United States and Germany. He asserted that America would go to war to make the world safe for the spread of democratic principles (see document 31).

The most extreme crisis to confront the peace movement in the early decades of the twentieth century occurred during the period between February and April 1917. The drift toward American belligerency in those nine weeks increased the fragmentation within the movement and drove some activist groups toward even more intensive actions. Conservative organizations like the Carnegie Endowment and the American Peace Society, which had already decided against immediate peace efforts, concluded that U.S. intervention had become inevitable and even desirable to obtain world peace. Although divided, the more activist peace organizations refused to acquiesce. The Woman's Peace party, the American Union Against Militarism, and a newly formed coalition, the Emergency Peace Federation, tried to arouse the country. They staged antiwar demonstrations, prepared petitions, and lobbied in Washington. A delegation from the AUAM visited the president in February to encourage him to prevent the jingoes from pushing the United States into the war (see documents 29, 30).

Alternatives were offered to full belligerency. William Jennings Bryan spoke to mass audiences and urged that the submarine dispute be submitted to a joint high commission for investigation and recommendation for settlement following the war, just as the contested aspects of the British blockade had been relegated to postwar claims. In the meantime, he suggested that Americans be prohibited from sailing on ships carrying contraband and that perhaps all American ships should be ordered not to enter the war zone, a position taken unsuccessfully the previous year by a number of congressmen in the Gore-McLemore Resolution. If a declaration of war became inevitable, it should be submitted to the people in a referendum, Bryan argued, before the nation actually took up arms. A less extreme alternative to this acquiescence in the submarine blockade was offered by Carlton J. H. Hayes, a historian at Columbia University, who recommended armed neutrality. With its ships protecting themselves, the United States could uphold its rights while waging only defensive combat. Some argued that the United States should lead in forming a league of armed neutrals that would also include the Netherlands and the Scandinavian, Iberian, and Latin American countries. Such a coalition could provide the naval vessels needed to keep the sea lanes open to neutral trade.

President Wilson briefly employed independent armed neutrality in March, but he did not try to form a league of armed neutrals. He decided instead for full belligerency. His reasons, according to his preeminent biographer Arthur S. Link of Princeton University, included his complete mistrust of Germany, his desire to maintain as much domestic unity as possible, his underestimation of the military effort that would be required, and most importantly, his conviction that American intervention, guaranteeing a place at the peace conference, would be the most effective means of establishing an early peace and reform of international relations.

In Congress, the president faced the opposition of a midwestern and rural southern coalition of anti-interventionists led by Senators Robert La Follette of Wisconsin and George Norris of Nebraska and House majority leader Claude Kitchin of North Carolina. Ignoring their warnings that the United States was going to war to protect the investment of bankers and munitions makers in the Allied war effort, Congress passed the war resolution by a vote of 82 to 6 in the Senate and 373 to 50 in the House. On April 6, 1917, the United States officially entered the World War.

III
(1917–1918)

When the war came to the United States, it altered both the structure of the peace movement and its relationship to the government. Rapidly following the declaration of war in April came a dramatic change in the social and political environment. The range of acceptable debate narrowed as the nature of loyalty and the legitimacy of dissent were re-evaluated in a wartime context. Much of what had been permissible before became unwise or illegal in the wake of proscriptive new laws, such as the espionage and sedition acts and the increased power of governmental authorities. With victory over the kaiser's regime the proclaimed national goal, efforts for an immediate or compromise peace could be viewed as disloyal. Government officials, editorial writers, and irate mobs assailed the more activist dissenters, including many of those peace advocates who continued to work for an end to the European war even after it became an American war as well. The years 1917 and 1918 represented both the peak of dedication by a relative handful of pacifists and the nadir of the scope and impact of the peace movement as it withered under the forces of alienation and repression.

Confronted with the choice of supporting the war effort or challenging the government's policy, most of the leaders of the peace movement rallied behind the president's decision for belligerency. In his message to Congress, Wilson argued that Germany had thrust the war upon the United States and that this country, in entering the conflict, sought only to defend itself and to help ensure a just and lasting international peace. A few groups such as the Woman's Peace party took a neutral position and refused either to condemn or endorse American entry into the war. The government's decision, however, was upheld by most peace groups, including the American Peace Society, the Association for a League to Enforce Peace, the Church Peace Union, the American School Peace League, the World Peace Foundation, and the Carnegie Endowment for International Peace. These bodies pledged their loyalty and urged Americans to unite behind the war effort. To help demonstrate their patriotism, the directors of the Carnegie Endowment turned over the organization's offices to the government's main propaganda agency, the Committee on Public Information.

Most of these peace organizations spent the period of American belligerency working for a postwar settlement that they hoped would ensure permanent peace. Their members differed, however, over immediate aims and methods. Some, like John Spencer Bassett and journalist Norman Hapgood, advocated a federated world government. Others, like Nicholas Murray Butler and Elihu Root, favored conservative evolutionary legalism and supported organic growth through international law and a world court. William Howard Taft, president of the Association for a League to Enforce Peace, and a number of other people occupied a middle ground and sought a kind of limited internationalism. They urged collective security and order enforced by an association of nations with only partial abrogation of national sovereignty.

There were important differences over the use of force by an international organization. James Brown Scott of the Carnegie Foundation opposed the League of Nations because he doubted whether the United States would allow a combination of foreign countries to use military force against it. A majority of American peace leaders who met in May 1917 at the National Conference on Foreign Relations also opposed a commitment that bound members to use force against offenders or to concede that such coercion might be used against themselves. Although a few peace advocates like Root approved of the League as a coalition of the Allies, most wanted a universal association created after the war, one that would include Germany and not be another " Holy Alliance" of victors designed to maintain the settlement they had won. The Woman's Peace party and others also continued to advocate the liberal peace program, including disarmament and popular control of foreign policy as well as the election of some delegates to conferences to supplement the appointed governmental representatives (see document 38).

As the war continued, the peace advocates sought to win Woodrow Wilson's endorsement of their particular program. A combination of both foreign and domestic pressures and the president's own sense of leadership resulted in his endorsement of the liberal peace program. The Allies faced a growing demand in 1917 for a statement of war aims and for a negotiated peace. In the wake of the Russian Revolution in March and after an interim government under Prince Lvov, Alexander Kerensky's Social Democratic government assumed office in July, pledged to promote a peace based upon self-determination of peoples and without any annexations or indemnities. In August, Pope Benedict XV urged the belligerents to negotiate on a similar basis. He also urged the consideration of freedom of the seas, the substitution of arbitration for war, and the examination of territorial claims in a "spirit of equity and justice." The Wilson administration and the other Allied governments refused to deal with the kaiser, however, and the offer produced no results.

When in September 1917 President Wilson asked Colonel House to begin an investigation into the problems of a postwar peace conference and to recommend the appropriate policies for the United States, his unofficial adviser sought out the internationalist peace advocates for advice. Among those consulted were Taft, Lowell, and Hamilton Holt of the Association for a League to Enforce Peace; Fannie Fern Andrews of the American School Peace League and the Central Organization for a Durable Peace; and Nicholas Murray Butler and Elihu Root of the Carnegie Endowment for International Peace. Over a period of time, House conveyed their suggestions to Wilson. The president drew upon some of their recommendations and ignored others as he formulated his own ideas about the peace settlement.

Increased pressure for a statement of war aims occurred during the winter of 1917/1918. Following the November Revolution in Russia, the Bolsheviks published the secret Allied treaties (which called for punishing Germany and parceling her colonies among the victors) as evidence of the imperialistic nature of the war. Like a number of other groups on both sides of the Atlantic, the Woman's Peace party urged the meeting of an Inter-Allied Conference, composed of both selected and elected delegates, to formulate and announce new liberal peace aims, including a postwar league of nations. When governmental representatives at an Inter-Allied Conference in Paris met and failed to agree upon such a program, President Wilson assumed the leadership of the movement for a liberal peace settlement in a dramatic speech to Congress on January 8, 1918.

Wilson's "Fourteen Points" speech encapsulated the liberal alternative to the imperialism of the secret treaties and to the revolutionary restructuring proposed by V. I. Lenin and the Bolsheviks (see document 39). According to the president, the "only possible program" for peace as far as the United States was concerned would include open diplomacy, freedom of the seas, equality of trade, disarmament, impartial adjustment of colonial claims giving equal weight to the claims of the colonial power and the native population, withdrawal from territory conquered by the Central Powers, self-determination of autonomous peoples in Eastern Europe and the Turkish Empire, and finally a general association of nations to guarantee political independence and territorial integrity of all the member nations. Significantly, Wilson did not elaborate about the League at the time, for he had not decided upon its nature. In fact, he believed public discussion of it premature until the conclusion of the war.

Although the peace organizations that had supported American belligerency may have helped Wilson to arrive at this position, the antiwar groups in the peace movement after April 1917 became further alienated from the administration. They were also subjected to internal division and were suppressed by local, state, and national authorities.

The American Union Against Militarism, for example, had split over the proper course to follow after the declaration of war. Paul Kellogg, Lillian Wald, and Stephen Wise led a minority of the founders out of the organization when the majority decided to establish a National Civil Liberties Bureau (later the ACLU) to protect the civil rights of conscientious objectors and others who dissented from the government's war policies. Those who remained within the AUAM joined with remnants of the Emergency Peace Federation and antiwar Socialists to form the People's Council of America for Peace and Democracy.

Led by Roger N. Baldwin, a pacifist social worker; Louis Lochner, a journalist and internationalist; Emily Balch; Crystal Eastman; and Morris Hillquit, the People's Council campaigned for civil liberties during wartime, repeal of conscription, and the establishment of a quick peace that would include no annexations and no indemnities (see document 33). The pacifist-Socialist leadership tried to build a coalition of farm and labor groups behind their program of opposition to the war and support for dramatic economic and social change. Although large meetings were held in several cities, a grand Constituent Assembly planned for September was blocked by officials in several midwestern states.

The Socialist party took the most outspoken stand of any organization against the American war effort. Delegates to an emergency party conference in Saint Louis the day after the declaration of war adopted a report written by Morris Hillquit and Charles Ruthenberg that indicted both the war and U.S. belligerency. Declaring their "unalterable opposition" to the conflict, the antiwar majority urged the "workers of all countries to refuse to support their governments because wars of the contending national groups of capitalists are not the concern of the workers." Although a minority of important Socialists bolted the party and supported the administration, the majority recommended active opposition to the war through mass petitions, demonstrations, and "all other means within our power" (see document 32). The Socialist party also counseled resistance to many of the administration's war measures, such as conscription, war taxes, war bonds, and the curtailment of civil liberties. By a vote of approximately twenty-one thousand to eight thousand, Socialist party members supported the resolution in national balloting. The majority of Socialists joined with the Industrial Workers of the World and with Emma Goldman and Alexander Berkman of the anarchists to endorse active wartime dissent.

Socialist opposition to the war was demonstrated in a number of ways. Although no general strike took place, Socialists did encourage draft evasion and resistance. The only major incident of violence against the war came in the fields of Oklahoma, where many debt-ridden tenant farmers belonged to the IWW or the Socialist party. When drafting began in August 1917, a number of these sharecroppers shot a deputy sheriff and made plans to destroy a railroad bridge and cut telegraph wires to block the operation of conscription. The rebels planned a protest march to Washington, gathering support as they went and provisioning themselves enroute with barbecued steers and unripened corn. This so-called Green Corn Rebellion never matured, however, because a sheriff's posse galloped into a meeting of the protesters and scattered them before the march had begun. Within a week, some 450 men had been arrested.

Less violent but perhaps more significant were the impressive Socialist gains at the polls in the municipal elections in the fall of 1917. Capitalizing on antiwar sentiment, inflation, and other sources of discontent, Socialist candidates polled 22 percent of the total municipal vote in fifteen cities in the Northeast. In New York City, the Socialists elected ten state assemblymen, seven aldermen, and a municipal judge. Their candidate, Morris Hillquit, placed third—ahead of the regular Republican candidate—in a four-party race for the mayoralty.

The Socialists also sought to encourage international cooperation to end the war, but they were stopped by the U.S. government. In May 1917, delegates from the Socialist party of America sought to join other members of the Second International in Stockholm to discuss means of initiating peace negotiations and ending the war. But Hillquit and the other representatives were prevented from attending by the State Department. Agents seized their passports under the Logan Act of 1799, which prohibited private citizens from conducting diplomatic negotiations.

During the war, the government launched a major campaign to suppress the Socialists and other radicals who dissented against the military or economic policies of the administration. In his Flag Day speech in June 1917, President Wilson condemned the antiwar movement as treasonous and labeled its members as conscious agents or unwitting tools of the German militarists. New wartime legislation, including the espionage and sedition acts, gave the government extensive powers and made it a crime to obstruct the draft or enlistment or to criticize the government or its war policies.

Acting under these provisions, the federal government moved against radical dissenters. It was also joined by local authorities. By denying full mailing privileges, Postmaster General Albert S. Burleson suppressed a number of left-wing newspapers and magazines, including the New York *Call*, the Milwaukee *Leader*, *The Masses* (see documents 35, 36), and *The American Socialist*. Local district attorneys and the Justice Department obtained indictments and convictions of leading Socialists, such as Kate Richards O'Hare, Rose Pastor Stokes, and Eugene V. Debs, titular head of the party. Victor Berger and Max Eastman were indicted but acquitted. Federal agents, under orders from Attorney General Thomas W. Gregory, raided the offices of the IWW. More than one hundred "Wobbly" leaders, including Haywood, were convicted of antiwar activity in a mass trial in Chicago. Anarchist leaders like Goldman and Berkman, who had organized a No-Conscription League and held rallies against the draft, were convicted, imprisoned, and subsequently deported to Russia. Wartime suppression destroyed the Wobblies and anarchists as organized movements and left the Socialist party greatly weakened, its press impotent, and many of its leaders imprisoned.

The liberal pacifists who continued to criticize the war effort did not suffer the same degree of persecution as the radicals, but they were no more effective in influencing the foreign policy of the Wilson administration. They failed completely to block enactment of the espionage and sedition laws or to prevent or repeal conscription. Only in regard to conscientious objectors did they eventually have some success.

Sympathetic recognition of sincere objectors to military service was advocated by sects like the Quakers and the Mennonites and by new organizations like the National Civil Liberties Bureau, headed by Roger Baldwin, and the Fellowship of Reconciliation, a group of religious pacifists led by Norman Thomas, a Presbyterian minister. From the beginning, they urged that any draft law provide for recognition of not only religious but political objectors, who included a number of Socialists, individualists, and German and Austrian Americans. Despite their lobbying in Congress and personal appeals to President Wilson and Secretary of War Newton D. Baker, the pacifists were disappointed in the provisions of the draft act. The new law provided only for recognition of conscientious objectors who belonged to traditional pacifist sects and declared that they would be assigned to noncombatant work within the armed forces.

During the war, the liberal pacifists appealed to the administration to modify this initial decision, but Wilson and Baker were cautious until they determined that the number of objectors was limited. Draft boards recognized 57,000 men as C.O.s, and 21,000 of these had been inducted into the 3.5 million-man army by 1918. Segregated in camp under Baker's orders, nearly 80 percent of the C.O.s changed their minds. Out of a sense of isolation and rejection, they decided to rejoin their outfits. When only 4,000 men continued to refuse to train for combat, the administration advised camp commanders to treat them with tact and consideration. Nevertheless, many objectors were beaten with sticks, drenched with cold water, jabbed with bayonets, and starved on bread and water in solitary confinement. As many as eleven objectors died as a result. Vigorously protesting this treatment, the civilian pacifist groups obtained from the Wilson administration orders in 1918 that directed most of these objectors into noncombatant service or furloughed them to work on farms or in factories. Nevertheless, 500 "absolutist" conscientious objectors were court-martialed and imprisoned with sentences that averaged over ten years each (see document 40).

President Wilson had the greatest single influence in ending the fighting of World War I. Once again, Wilson's own sense of leadership and his desire to achieve a settlement that would not only protect American interests but also would ensure lasting world peace within a liberal, capitalistic, reform framework proved more important than the influence of particular groups. When the deteriorating military position in the fall of 1918 forced the German government to seek an armistice, it asked for peace negotiations based on Wilson's Fourteen Points rather than the Allies' war aims. The president made the decision to agree to an early and negotiated settlement. In so doing, he rejected the pleas of those like Theodore Roosevelt and General John J. Pershing, the commander of the American Expeditionary Force, who wanted to drive the Germans back across the Rhine and to obtain an unconditional surrender. In order to force the British and French governments to accept less than total victory, Wilson had to threaten to take the United States out of the war and make a separate peace with the Germans.

Wilson's pressure proved effective in obtaining an armistice. The British and French agreed to the cease-fire and negotiations based upon the Fourteen Points rather than their own secret treaties, with two exceptions. The British refused to endorse freedom of the seas, lest England be deprived of using a blockade in future wars. And the French demanded that Germany restore the territory it had conquered and pay reparation for war damages. Under these conditions, and with the abdication of the kaiser, with whom Wilson had refused to negotiate, a new German Republican government signed the armistice that ended the World War on November 11, 1918.

Because of Wilson's rejection of total military victory as the goal, the war ended a year earlier than most of the Allied officials and military leaders expected. As a result of his action, Germany was not forced to surrender unconditionally, and the Allied imperialistic war aims were not automatically achieved. Wilson had used the power of his office and of the United States to work for the general goals of the liberal internationalist peace movement. The end of the fighting, however, did not mean that he had accomplished those goals. In fact, the struggle had just begun.

IV
(1919–1922)

With the armistice and the end of the wartime strictures, the peace movement resumed its full range of activity. The immediate focal points of its work were the peace settlement for World War I, the creation of international machinery to reduce or eliminate the possibilities of such conflicts in the future, the demobilization of armies, and the reduction of wartime armaments. In the years between 1919 and 1922, the United States determined its postwar international position. This did not mean affiliation with the League of Nations, but it did include attempts to maintain both peace and national interest through the limitation of armaments and the establishment of multilateral regional agreements to protect the *status quo* in the Far East.

In regard to the shaping of the postwar settlement in the winter and early spring of 1919, members of the peace movement in general found themselves awaiting the outcome of the decision of the representatives of the big powers at Paris. President Wilson had seized the initiative by deciding to attend the peace conference himself, the first American chief executive to visit Europe while in office. As the leader of the hand-picked delegation, he exercised absolute personal control over the American position at the sessions. Wilson failed to sound out public or congressional opinion before leaving; but in the negotiations, he claimed to speak for the American people. The peace treaty hammered out in France was shaped by his conception of the needs of America and the world and the demands of the other major statesmen on behalf of Britain, France, Italy, and Japan. The peace movement had little direct influence in the formulation of its terms.

The Treaty of Versailles, which Wilson presented to the United States Senate in July 1919, departed significantly from the hopes of peace advocates. It was not a peace without victory but was a vindictive settlement. It forced Germany to accept sole guilt for the war, to disarm unilaterally, and to pay reparations ultimately fixed at $56 billion. It stripped the Germans of their colonies and concessions in Africa and

Asia and turned these over to the victorious Allies. It demilitarized the right bank of the Rhine, put the left bank under Paris's control for fifteen years, authorized the French to occupy the Saar for a similar period, and returned Alsace-Lorraine to France. In eastern Germany and in Russia, it reestablished Poland as an independent state with a corridor to the Baltic.

The peace treaty departed significantly from many of the Fourteen Points. It said nothing about freedom of the seas or reduction of tariffs. Under pressure from the European leaders, Wilson had sacrificed these to prevent an even more severe treaty, such as that proposed by the French, one which would have permanently dismembered the Rhineland.

In accepting deviations from the liberal peace programs such as these, Wilson hoped that the settlement would be ameliorated through the work of a League of Nations. He insisted that the League be made a part of the peace treaty. The covenant of the new international organization provided for a small but powerful executive council including the major Allied powers (the United States, Britain, France, Italy, and Japan), a large assembly in which each nation would have one vote, and a permanent secretariat in the neutral capital of Geneva. In the controversial ARTICLE X, member nations accepted the principle of collective security; pledged themselves to preserve each other's independence and territorial integrity against external attacks; agreed to submit all disputes that could lead to war to the League; and consented to employ military and economic sanctions against nations resorting to war; to reduce armaments; to cooperate in setting up a Permanent Court of International Justice; and to place the former colonies of the Central Powers under a mandate status in which the new colonial authorities would have to report to the League on steps being taken to prepare the native populations for self-government (see documents 41, 42).

The drafters of the covenant used some of the ideas of the peace movement, but they neglected many others. The preamble, expressing the aim of world cooperation, peace and security, and avoidance of war, echoed pacifist hopes. The covenant urged arbitration, advanced the principle of a continuous world conference, and achieved a congress of nations. Its provisions for force, however, seemed far removed from the mainstream of the peace movement and internationalist thought. Most peace advocates had rejected the possibilities of such open-ended use of force. The League of Nations also differed from the legalistic and procedural approach of internationalists like Root and Taft. Wilson's organization failed to have a court created as a co-equal body and lacked the machinery to create or determine international law. Furthermore, the association was clearly dominated by the great powers and tied to a vindictive peace settlement. It lacked a major focus on advancing democracy or justice, as pacifists like Addams and Villard had urged.

By 1919, the legalist wing of the American peace movement had achieved general agreement on a number of principles. Among those were the belief that a league should be established, but that it should be limited in its powers. International disputes should be settled peacefully through procedural action, but a new system for world order should evolve gradually. The legalists also believed that the use of force should be limited under strict safeguards.

As created, the League of Nations reflected this desire for a conference of nations, but it went far beyond these peace advocates' proposals. The Allies established the League upon a political rather than a legal foundation. Although the covenant recognized arbitration, it provided only peripherally for a judicial body. Wilson apparently did not envision the World Court as an integral part of the international machinery as had the legalistic peace advocates (see document 41). The more conservative internationalists were also shocked by Wilson's bold attempt to create a system of world government virtually overnight. They wanted to build upon previous experiences and achievements in a slower and more reassuring manner.

The majority of peace advocates were appalled by ARTICLES X and XVI, which obligated the signatories to use force if the association so determined. The idea that a league of states would defend the territory and independence of its members had appeared before 1919 in only a few plans for an association of nations. Even then its adherents, such as Hamilton Holt and Theodore Roosevelt (until his death in January 1919), qualified the concept by insisting that force be applied only in accordance with procedures involving law and justice. They envisioned an international judicial system that would prevent any autocratic action on the part of the organization. The position taken by President Wilson, who gave the League a political base and authority to compel military action, represented a minority view within the peace movement.

Many pacifists and liberals were disillusioned by the degree to which the covenant departed from democratic ideals, especially in its emphasis upon the council where big powers dominated, and the lack of legislative power in the assembly, which meant that no body of international law could be constructed by the organization. Thus the covenant failed to reflect the prevailing patterns of thought in the peace movement. The legalists wished to create a judicial system that would evolve into a world organization. Wilson created a world organization that he hoped would establish an international system under which peace and prosperity could be maintained.

When the details of the League of Nations were learned, the peace movement supported the general idea but urged various modifications. Advanced peace advocates like Holt, Marburg, and George W. Nasmyth wanted to strengthen and improve the League by creating a stronger world legislature, electing delegates by popular vote, and establishing an international police force to uphold disarmament agreements (see document 45). More moderate internationalists like Taft and Lowell and even some active pacifists like David Starr Jordan and Bryan, sought to protect traditional American policies by exempting immigration laws and the Monroe Doctrine from League consideration. A third group, led by Elihu Root, supported the League only reluctantly, fearing it endangered U.S. sovereignty and that it lacked detailed provisions for arbitration and a world court.

The Congress held in Zurich in the spring of 1919 by the Women's International League for Peace and Freedom was the first public body to protest against the terms of peace. It attacked the treaty as vindictive, and although gratified by the League, the WILPF criticized many of its aspects. Led by Jane Addams, Lillian Wald, and Emily Greene Balch, the Women's Congress urged immediate disarmament; free trade and travel; guarantees for the rights of minorities; full equality for women; abolition of child labor; abrogation of regional understandings, such as the Monroe Doctrine, when they were inconsistent with the Covenant of the League; free access to raw materials for all nations on equal terms; abolition of the protection of capital investments in foreign countries; and the abandonment of military action as a means of enforcing League decisions. They also urged an immediate end to the Allies' food blockade of Germany (see documents 46, 47, 48).

Many peace organizations found their membership divided over the proposed League of Nations. The Woman's Peace party split, some members supporting the League whole-heartedly, others only with reservations, and still others refusing to endorse the organization that they said approved of force to maintain a vindictive peace settlement. Within the Association for a League to Enforce Peace, most members wanted some modifications. A few, like Albert Shaw and John Bates Clark, were completely opposed to the proposal because of its failure to emphasize the judiciary. The organization could not agree on what changes to recommend. As a liberal alternative to the interventionist-oriented League to Enforce Peace, the League of Free Nations Association (later the Foreign Policy Association) was founded in 1918 by Paul U. Kellogg, publisher of *The Survey* magazine and a leading social reformer and pacifist-internationalist, as well as Lillian D. Wald and James T. Shotwell, a diplomatic historian and one of Wilson's advisers in Paris. The American Peace Society noted the lack of judicial processes in Wilson's League, called it authoritarian and coercive in emphasis, and refused to endorse it. The society suggested a Third Hague Peace Conference instead. Both the World Peace Foundation and the Carnegie Endowment also declined to take official stands on the League.

Even though Wilson obtained a number of modifications when he returned to Paris in the spring of 1919 for a second round of negotiations, the revised covenant still did not reflect those legal and procedural ideas that were held by most peace advocates (see documents 42, 43, 44, 46, 49). They wanted a court as an integral part of the League and its major agency, not as a derivative organ to be established sometime in the future. They desired separate but clearly defined bodies to hear different types of disputes. And they wished for a league with the power to formulate and codify international law.

On the other hand, those who supported Wilson's League used several arguments to counter this criticism. They praised the League as an outstanding advance toward world peace in the tradition of the Hague conferences and the arbitration treaties. Claiming that the majority of Americans supported U.S. membership in the League, they introduced resolutions passed by thirty-two state legislatures by the middle of 1919 as partial evidence. In their most emotional appeal, many advocates, including Wilson himself, argued that the League would be a bulwark not only against the return of German-style militarism but also against the spread of Bolshevik-sponsored revolution (see document 45).

The Versailles treaty was debated in the Senate as well as in the forum of public opinion in the United States in 1919 and 1920. The senators responded to the provisions of the covenant; the territorial, economic, and political aspects of the peace settlement; Wilson's leadership; and sectional and partisan advantage. A sizable Republican opposition existed, including a few who were irreconcilably opposed to U.S. membership in any league and a larger number who supported the demand of Henry Cabot Lodge, chairman of the Senate Foreign Relations Committee, for substantial modifications (see document 44). A militant expansionist and nationalist who wanted to maintain American freedom of action in foreign policy, Lodge had earlier insisted on safeguarding clauses in the Roosevelt and Taft arbitration treaties. In 1919 he feared that Wilson's League was an armed alliance that could control the forces of the United States and interfere in American domestic affairs.

The Association for a League to Enforce Peace and President Wilson sought to counter objections through a massive publicity campaign in favor of U.S. membership in the League of Nations. The president spoke out vigorously for the Treaty of Versailles. He refused to allow the Lodge reservations, which he argued, probably incorrectly, would destroy the League. During a ten-thousand-mile speaking tour, the health of the chief executive broke. Wilson's medical records, obtained in 1990 by Arthur S. Link, indicate that the president was already suffering from a disease of the carotid arteries that hindered blood flow to the brain and from hypertension, which worsened the condition. Wilson had suffered a stroke in 1906 that apparently triggered periodic episodes of internal bleeding. On July 19, 1919, the president may have suffered a minor stroke. Link concluded that by mid-August 1919 the disease had eroded Wilson's mental abilities and altered his behavior, making him confused, erratic, and completely unwilling to compromise. On September 25, Wilson suffered another stroke while on his speaking tour of the West. This stroke was followed on October 2 by a massive paralytic stroke that completely incapacitated him for nearly three months and rendered him a semi-invalid for the rest of his life. In November 1919, the Senate voted twice on the treaty. A combination of Democrats and moderate Republicans rejected the Lodge reservations. Then the irreconcilables and Lodge's supporters rejected Wilson's League without the reservations.

The peace movement does not appear to have played a major role in the Senate decision against the League. The verdict at that stage was in the hands of the president and the senators. The impotence of the peace movement at that critical moment seems to have been caused primarily by its failure to coalesce behind a single position. The peace advocates found themselves badly divided, and as a result, their influence was muted. It could be argued (and was at the time) that much of this disarray was a result of lack of leadership by Wilson. He had been unwilling or unable to take the lead in uniting them. Their former pilot had lost his own bearings on the politics of the issue, as the administration had supported domestic mobilization policies, curtailment of dissent, and a growing antiradicalism that divided and alienated many of those in the political center and on the liberal Left who might otherwise have been built into a strong constituency behind U.S. membership in the League of Nations.

The most effective action taken by the peace societies in regard to the League was a campaign arousing the American people to force the Senate to reconsider the treaty. For the first time in the treaty fight, the internationalists acted together. In January and February 1920, representatives of twenty-six groups that favored U.S. entry into the League and that claimed to represent fifty million people sent delegates to Washington to press for reconsideration. The Senate did take up the treaty a third time; but Wilson, Lodge, and the irreconcilables had not changed their positions. They were not willing to compromise, and the stalemate continued. Once again the treaty with the Lodge reservations failed to obtain the necessary two-thirds majority. And enough Democrats followed Wilson's orders and joined the irreconcilables to prevent passage (see document 53).

Ironically, President Wilson had contributed to the defeat of his own creation. With a stubbornness intensified by his illness and his own personal involvement in the definition of America's wartime and postwar aims, Wilson refused to compromise and accept the modifications Lodge demanded. Both Wilson's clash with Lodge and his lack of cooperation with the internationalists helped to prevent U.S. membership in the League.

Wilson had taken an advanced position on world organization, one far removed from prevailing thought. By March 1920, nearly all of the peace advocates favored reservations to the covenant. The struggle was not fought over whether the United States should join the League but what kind of a league the United States should join. Wilson's individualistic course, his failure to heed the internationalists who had spent years exploring the idea of a league of nations, and his inadequate knowledge of the pevailing American ideas on the subject all contributed to the defeat of his own League. Furthermore, Wilson himself helped to prevent the creation of Lodge's league. Historian Warren Kuehl has concluded that Wilson's real error lay not in his refusal to compromise on ARTICLE X, the commitment to force, but in including it at all. Neither the peace movement nor the majority of American people in those years was willing to bind the country to what was in essence a defensive alliance with the major countries of Europe and Asia.

In the wake of the Senate rejection, even the slightest American relations with the League of Nations came only gradually. In the summer of 1920, Congress terminated the state of war with Germany and Austria-Hungary through a simple joint resolution. After initially refusing any connection with the association in Geneva, the Republican administrations of the 1920s slowly increased American cooperation, at first in economic and social matters and later in diplomatic affairs. Without officially joining the League, the United States participated in its reparations commissions, the international opium conference of 1924, the conference on communication and transportation in 1926, and the conferences on trade and taxation in 1927 and 1928. By 1931, the United States had been represented at forty League meetings and had five officials at Geneva to represent American interests.

The World Court was created by the League in 1921 with judicial rather than the purely arbitral and diplomatic functions of the old Hague Tribunal. It had a permanent body of eleven sitting jurists. Numerous attempts were made by peace organizations to persuade the United States government to join the World Court. The Harding administration endorsed adherence to its protocol. Consequently, in 1925, Congress passed favorable resolutions; but the Senate included such reservations that the court rejected the American terms for membership. President Hoover submitted a formula for U.S. participation worked out by both Elihu Root and the members of the court. The irreconcilables in the Senate postponed consideration until 1935, however, when the formula was defeated by isolationists despite the support of President Franklin D. Roosevelt. Not until after World War II did the United States join an international association of nations—the United Nations—and a new World Court.

In the immediate postwar years, the peace movement was much more successful in its attempts to prevent expansion of the American military and naval establishments than it had been in its efforts to join the League of Nations and the World Court. Indeed, it helped to achieve limited disarmament in the army and navy. Some elements of the peace movement also worked in an additional campaign, one to obtain amnesty for imprisoned war resisters. Their efforts, which began after the armistice in 1918, eventually succeeded, but only after a long and sustained effort.

The Wilson administration resisted the postwar drive for amnesty for those pacifists, Socialists, members of the Industrial Workers of the World, and others convicted of resistance to the draft or violation of the Espionage or Sedition acts because they had spoken out against the war. Efforts to free several hundred such prisoners began almost immediately after the armistice. By early 1919, a number of organizations were carrying on an amnesty campaign in the metropolitan press, in liberal periodicals, in petitions, and in personal meetings with President Wilson and Secretary of War Baker. The American Civil Liberties Union (ACLU), created by the American Union Against Militarism, was especially active in the campaign, as were the League for Amnesty of Political Prisoners; the Washington, D.C., Citizens' Amnesty Committee; some labor unions; and liberal periodicals like the *Dial,* the *New Republic,* and the

Nation (see documents 51, 54). The movement gained increasing support as a result of newspaper and congressional investigations in 1919 into the equity of military justice.

Although the administration refused to grant a general amnesty, it did release some opponents of war on an individual basis. In 1919, one hundred conscientious objectors were released from Fort Leavenworth after a War Department Board of Inquiry found them to be sincere in their objection and judged that their sentences had been too harsh. But the president supported his attorneys general, Thomas Gregory and later A. Mitchell Palmer, in resisting pressure for the release of violators of the Espionage and Sedition acts, including the most prominent political prisoner, Eugene V. Debs, the Socialist presidential nominee then being held in the federal penitentiary in Atlanta.

Authorities even moved to curb the amnesty agitation itself. In the postwar fear of bolshevism, the Department of Justice indicted and obtained convictions, under wartime statutes, of three Syracuse men who were working for the release of political prisoners. The Espionage Act remained in effect until the war was officially declared at an end in November 1921. Police and patriotic groups broke up several amnesty meetings in 1919 and disrupted a parade on behalf of the prisoners held on Fifth Avenue in New York City on Christmas Day.

Although the fear of radicalism in 1919 and early 1920 militated against a general policy of amnesty, the Wilson administration released a number of political prisoners on an individual basis under growing pressure from the amnesty organizations; the American Federation of Labor; the press; and several congressmen, led by Senator William E. Borah, the progressive isolationist from Idaho. On November 23, 1920—two years after the armistice—Secretary Baker ordered the last thirty-three conscientious objectors released. But Debs and the more than one hundred other dissenters remained in prison.

With the arrival of President Harding and the Republican administration in Washington in March 1921, the amnesty committees obtained a more sympathetic hearing. The new chief executive listened to the pleas of Samuel Gompers of the American Federation of Labor and others. Following the approval of the formal peace proclamation on November 14, 1921, Harding freed Debs and twenty-three other political prisoners on Christmas Day. Despite the fact that additional individual inmates were pardoned or had their sentences commuted, 113 dissenters remained in federal penitentiaries in 1922, and hundreds more were still incarcerated in state prisons. At congressional hearings into the matter, Albert De Silver, the head of the ACLU, testified in favor of amnesty because wartime hysteria had prevented fair trials and because the laws under which these people had been convicted were no longer in effect. Many congressmen and others, however, continued to link the amnesty movement to socialism, bolshevism, and anarchism.

By 1923, the amnesty campaign had expanded dramatically and had produced significant results. Many prominent church leaders, governors, educators, journalists, and a number of national organizations joined the movement. In June, Harding offered conditional freedom to twenty-four IWW's, but they rejected his gesture because they said acceptance would amount to a confession of disloyalty. The last thirty-one federal political prisoners from World War I were released by Harding's successor, President Calvin Coolidge, on December 15, 1923. When Franklin D. Roosevelt became president in 1933, he issued a formal pardon to those who had been political prisoners in World War I, thus restoring their legal and political rights to full citizenship.

The peace movement achieved more immediate success in its postwar efforts to limit the military and naval establishments. Specifically, it helped to trim the army back to its prewar size, to prevent compulsory military training in peacetime, and to cut down the fleet and the naval building program. In these cases, it ran into opposition from the Wilson administration; the officer corps; and civilian support groups; such as the American Legion, the American Defense Society, the Military Training Camps Association, and the Navy League.

In his attempt to win American support for U.S. entry into the League of Nations, President Wilson had warned that the alternative to collective security would be a costly isolation for the United States. "If we must stand apart and be the hostile rivals of the rest of the world," he wrote to the Senate Foreign Relations Committee in 1919, "we must be physically ready for anything that comes.... We must see to it that every man in America is trained in arms." He proposed a dramatic increase in the army and navy in case the United States failed to join the League. In 1919, Wilson and Secretary Baker endorsed the General Staff's recommendations for a permanent regular army of 500,000 men (five times the prewar army) and civilian reserves prepared through compulsory universal military training of three months for each able-bodied young male citizen.

With the war over, however, the country was in no mood for such a departure in American military traditions. Old-line antimilitary groups, such as the American Federation of Labor, the National Farmers Union, and the National Grange, quickly came out against the proposal. So did many clergymen, educators, and liberal journalists. Coordinating the opposition to the administration's program for the army and conscription was a revitalized American Union Against Militarism, headed by publisher Oswald Garrison Villard (see document 52). Effectively, it united the opposition, especially in the South and West, against the scheme that it said would "Prussianize" America. In Congress, even most of the House Democrats revolted against the proposal of their president and party leader.

The National Defense Act of June 1920, which prescribed the postwar military, represented the will of Congress, not of the executive. It limited the regular army to 280,000 men (in fact Congress made appropriations for only 175,000 in 1920 and for 137,000 in 1922), rejected conscription in peacetime, and continued the traditional reliance upon the state militia—the National Guard—to provide trained reservists. The virtual return to the prewar model in this respect resulted from the resumption of peace and a demand for an end to wartime taxes and conscription. The adroit lobbying of the American Union Against Militarism played a key part in the decision.

The problems of disarmament and of militarism after World War I, however, involved the navy much more than the army. Although the three-year naval building program, adopted in 1916 to make the U.S. Navy equal to Britain's, had not yet been completed, President Wilson and Secretary of the Navy Josephus Daniels recommended in December 1919 an additional three-year construction program. In the immediate post-armistice period, the United States built more warships than the rest of the world combined. Considering Japan the next potential enemy, the United States also transferred half of its fleet to the Pacific and constructed naval bases there. Wilson seems to have been motivated not only by concern with increasing Japanese power and ambitions in the Far East but also by his desire to use the expansion program as a bargaining tool to coerce the British and the American public into supporting his concept of the League in exchange for a reduction of American warship building.

Once again, the American Union Against Militarism was in the forefront of opposition to the administration's proposals to expand the defense establishment. It coordinated the efforts of groups traditionally opposed to naval expansion. These included farmers, workers, clergymen, educators, and pacifists, and a number of important businessmen and financiers who had become convinced by wartime spending and postwar inflation of the necessity of cutting government spending and taxes. Faced with British acceptance of the League and with strong opposition from Congress and the American public to navalism, the administration withdrew its proposal in May 1919. In the Republican administration of President Harding two years later, the powerful new secretary of the treasury, Andrew Mellon, led in urging arms reductions. The resulting Appropriations Act of 1921 eliminated the proposed additional naval expansion and confined warship building to completion of the 1916 authorization, an action that reflected the growing sentiment against navalism and for disarmament.

Elements in the peace movement continued to press for international disarmament in the postwar period, and they scored probably their most dramatic success when the Naval Arms Limitation Treaty was signed in Washington in 1922. The international conference in that city resulted from both the Republicans' attempt to provide an alternative to the League and the increasing public pressure for disarmament even without U.S. membership in an association of nations. Despite the American rejection of membership, the League of Nations in the fall of 1920 invited the United States to take part in consultations regarding limitation of armaments. Public opinion supported disarmament, and even a number of leading military figures like Generals John J. Pershing and Tasker H. Bliss called for the United States to take the lead in arms reduction.

Within the Republican party, arms limitation found advocates among those who wanted to ensure America's security with less expense and without the departure from traditional unilateral action demanded by Wilson's proposal for collective security. Even before the Harding administration took office in March 1921, some congressional Republicans had seized the initiative. Replying to Geneva's invitation, Senator Borah, an irreconcilable opponent of the League, introduced a resolution on December 14, 1920, which revived the Hensley Amendment to the Naval Appropriations Act of 1916. It undercut the League's action by authorizing the president to call an American-sponsored naval disarmament conference. The Borah resolution served as the focus for the further mobilization of public opinion by advocates of disarmament and tax reduction (see documents 56, 57).

The movement for arms limitation at the Washington Disarmament Conference of 1921–1922 grew rapidly in 1921 on the basis of sensational disclosures and a powerful new coalition of interests.

Sentiment for disarmament was fueled by a number of important events. Already disillusioned by the war, many Americans were shocked by the apparent resumption of a naval race, this time by the United States, Britain, and Japan. Furthermore, in the summer of 1921, the bombers of General William ("Billy") Mitchell sank several unmanned

German battleships in target practice off the Atlantic Coast, a demonstration of how vulnerable even the largest naval vessels were to aerial bombardment. Antiwar sentiment was further exacerbated the same year by the publication of a startling book by the popular correspondent Will Irwin. Grimly entitled *The Next War—A Common Sense View,* it detailed War Department plans to use poison gas on a large scale in the next major conflict. A sermon by a rising young New York preacher named Harry Emerson Fosdick on the immorality of these military plans and others to employ germ warfare was also circulated nationally and helped to build the cry for disarmament and the abolition of war.

The movement received widespread support as the public came to believe that disarmament could be achieved in one conference that would result in not only an end to warfare but also a dramatic reduction in taxes. Disarmament committees sprang up in major cities. Catholic, Jewish, and Protestant leaders endorsed disarmament, as did the various peace groups. Two new organizations took the leadership in bringing public opinion to bear on Congress. One was the Women's Committee on World Disarmament, headed by the former suffragist leader Carrie Chapman Catt. The other was the National Council on Limitation of Armament, soon called the National Council for the Prevention of War. It was initiated by Philadelphia Quakers and led by Frederick J. Libby, a Maine-born educator and minister. Together, these two committees marshaled women's organizations; church and peace groups; and farm, labor, and educational associations behind the demand for disarmament. Most of the press vigorously endorsed the movement and exerted additional pressure upon the government to achieve results.

The campaign for arms limitation put the Harding administration in a difficult position. The president had been reluctant to call such a conference because of the warnings of Big Navy advocates, like Senator Lodge, who cautioned against the growing power of Japan. Additionally, the administration had its own plan for U.S. membership in an "association of nations" that would be less controlling than Wilson's League. This association would then work for disarmament, codification of international law, and the establishment of a world court. Opposition to immediate arms limitation had also come from the army and navy and some advocates of U.S. membership in the League of Nations who considered the renunciation of military force without alternative collective security to be unrealistic. Under public and congressional pressure for disarmament and tax cuts, however, and pressed by British and Japanese naval building, the administration endorsed Senator Borah's

Resolution. When the proposal was passed by Congress in July 1921, President Harding summoned an international conference to meet in Washington that winter.

Secretary of State Charles Evans Hughes startled the delegates on the opening day of the conference in November 1921 by proposing immediate disarmament and the scrapping of specific vessels. As delegates, including admirals from the major powers, sat bolt upright, Hughes proposed a ten-year moratorium on the construction of new major warships. He announced that the United States was willing to destroy thirty battleships, and he suggested that Britain and Japan sink thirty-six of theirs, so that the three nations would maintain the current ratio of capital ships at 5-5-3. Within thirty minutes, Hughes had demolished sixty-six battleships, totalling nearly two million tons, more than all the admirals of the world had sunk over the centuries (see document 58).

After much deliberation, the delegates on February 6, 1922, signed the Five-Power Naval Arms Limitation Treaty (actually a series of treaties dealing with different types of ships) between the United States, Britain, Japan, France, and Italy (see document 59). It represented the first voluntary acceptance by large nations of restrictions on their liberty to possess weapons of war. It was based on the principles of limiting the ratio to the *status quo* and of eliminating construction or continued existence of ships that would alter that balance. Shrewdly, Hughes had sought a defensive maintenance of the existing balance of power in the Far East. Combined with the other treaties signed at the Washington conference, the disarmament pact temporarily interrupted the naval race between the United States and Japan and replaced the Anglo-Japanese Alliance of 1902 with a regional nonaggression agreement that included all the major powers involved in East Asia (The Four-Power and Nine-Power treaties signed in February 1922).

The disarmament wing of the peace movement played an important role in the success of the deliberations at Washington. It helped to force the administration to summon the meeting, lobbied continually during the three-month conference, and conducted a drive for the ratification of the treaties. Despite the opposition of navalists and others who considered it unrealistic, the treaty won approval in the Senate on March 29, 1922, by an overwhelming vote of 74 to 1, clear indication of its popularity.

Nevertheless, the Five-Power Naval Arms Limitation Treaty was only a preliminary step. In succeeding years, the disarmament forces in the peace movement worked to extend its principles. The 1922 treaty applied only to capital ships, limiting battleships, battle cruisers, and aircraft carriers. Significantly cruisers, destroyers, and submarines were not included under the Washington restrictions. A separate agreement, also signed on February 6, 1922, tried to govern the operation of submarines, but it was not ratified by France and failed to go into effect.

Encouraged by the National Council for the Prevention of War, public opinion supported further attempts at naval arms limitation, but these efforts did not succeed. Between 1923 and 1925, Congress on three occasions asked the president to call a new conference to consider limiting cruisers. Even a three-nation meeting sponsored by the United States in 1927 failed to reach agreement; and in 1929, Congress authorized the country to enter the cruiser-building race already begun by Britain and Japan.

A final attempt to curb the growing naval arms race was made at the London Naval Arms Conference in 1930. The resulting treaty pledged the United States, Britain, and Japan to limit cruiser and submarine construction, but under a new ratio of 10:10:7, which proved more favorable to the Japanese than the 1922 agreements. The United States thus ensured its ability to achieve its goal of keeping naval parity with Britain while maintaining a 30 percent superiority over Japan, without having to pay for a huge building program. But the price of the agreement was a weak treaty that contained a number of escape clauses and that many contemporary observers saw would last no more than six years. Indeed, by the mid-1930s, the naval arms race had begun once again. Nevertheless, conditions and the naval arms limitation treaties of 1922 and 1930 had kept such a development restricted for more than a dozen years.

V
Conclusion

Analysis of these developments in the first two decades of the twentieth century indicates that the modern American peace movement first took shape in this period. Like many other collective efforts to reassess institutions effected by industrialization during that late nineteenth and early twentieth centuries, the attempt to reorient U.S. foreign policy and international relations became a powerful social movement. As with the women's movement and the labor movement, the peace movement represented collective action taken on behalf of social change. Although the mass public was roused by certain highly charged issues, the peace movement remained primarily an elite rather than a mass movement.

Some of the concerns of the pacifists could indeed have widespread domestic impact: peacetime universal military training, German assaults on American shipping and plots in Mexico, the League of Nations, and the possibility of a postwar naval arms race. But on the whole, the peace advocates' programs for a better world order did not directly affect most Americans and that fact helped keep it a restricted movement. Nevertheless, the peace movement did have some significant successes in the course of its growth.

The peace movement found unity in its discontent with the anarchy and warfare that characterized international relations at the turn of the century, when the United States emerged as a world power. The European arms race; the bloody Russo-Japanese War; and, in a different way, the First Hague Conference served as inducements to the internationalists. So did the peace advocates' belief in their ability to improve domestic and foreign institutions. Additionally, Theodore Roosevelt's mediation at Portsmouth and the call for a Second Hague Peace Conference served as the precipitating events that catalyzed scattered American discontent into action. A series of new organizations and leaders soon revitalized the remnants of the nineteenth-century peace movement. Aided by new and generous financing from prominent businessmen, the internationalists sought to apply what they considered America's unique institutions to its historic mission of offering an enlightened example to humanity. These peace advocates tried to achieve international peace and order, which would aid both the United States and the world.

Yet within this larger aim, a variety of lesser goals were attempted by various new American peace workers. The new leaders ranged from Elihu Root, a corporation lawyer and former secretary of war, to Jane Addams, a settlement house worker, social reformer, and suffragist. They included radicals and conservatives, businessmen, clergymen, journalists, feminists, educators, and politicians. A plethora of organizations, new and old, clustered in specific, issue-oriented movements that differed over the means for achieving world peace. The means included international law, world government, disarmament, and U.S. neutrality and mediation.

In general, the political strategy of these different groups was remarkably similar. Confident of their position and of the operation of the American political system, they placed primary reliance upon persuasion for achieving their goals. They sought to convince the decision-makers and the public of the desirability of peace and their means for achieving it. With the exception of some radicals, most of the peace advocates did this within the existing framework of nationalism (accepting the sense of America's uniqueness and mission) and within the structure of decision making in the United States. It was on the whole a movement moderate in its means. Most peace organizations, led by men and women of high prestige, supported in many cases by substantial funding and organizational and promotional skills, exuded confidence in the ultimate success of their educational campaign. They endeavored to awaken public opinion to the need to pursue their programs. Generally, they also tried to counter the influence of other groups that pressed for a more aggressive foreign policy backed up by expanded military and naval forces. Pacifists in particular portrayed these opponents as autarchic militarists, representing a danger to peace and to American institutions.

During the first twenty years of this century, the peace movement underwent a number of changes. Its development was strikingly cyclical, characterized by an intermittent pattern of growth, decline, and resumption. After a period of dramatic expansion, the peace movement, on the whole, went into hibernation in World War I, only to emerge once again in rejuvenated form after the armistice.

The peace movement had been transformed after 1905 by the influx of members, money, and new organizations dedicated to finding world order. The older peace societies had been overwhelmed and literally engulfed by the new enthusiasts. The movement gained the legitimation provided by affiliation with leading businessmen, educators, and political figures, including the president of the United States. With such leadership and financial support, the abolition of war had seemed to some to be within reach.

The outbreak of the European war in 1914 had proven a painful antidote to such optimism. Confronted with such a massive and bloody conflict, peace advocates redefined the aims and methods of their movement. The more conservative members decided to suspend activities or to work for the long-range achievement of peace rather than to try to stop the current war or to prevent American involvement in it. This decision split the movement. The more radical opponents of international conflict determined to confront the problems of the current war. They formed new, more activist, issue-oriented organizations, like the League to Limit Armaments and the American Union Against Militarism. They tried to prevent the expansion of the military establishment and American entry into the war. The activists worked to persuade the Wilson administration to play a major role in mediating among the belligerents. Unlike the more conservative peace organizations, these new groups endeavored not only to reduce the possibilities of future wars but also to end the current conflict.

American entry into full belligerency further fragmented the peace movement in 1917 and 1918. Only the most militant and dedicated pacifists proved willing to risk the charge of treason or subversion and to continue actively in opposition after the congressional declaration of war. Although moderates grew silent, radicals formed new organizations like the People's Council and the National Civil Liberties Bureau and, despite popular and governmental repression, worked to end the war and to curtail the erosion of civil liberties under the intensive wartime chauvinism. Nonpacifist, antiwar organizations, like the Industrial Workers of the World and the Socialist party, which had long incurred the hostility of more powerful groups, suffered such active persecution that they were virtually eliminated during the war.

In the postwar period, as the peace movement resumed its activities, its internal divisions remained. Conservative, legalistic organizations, like the Carnegie Endowment, continued to eschew mass-action campaigns. They preferred to concentrate on cooperation with governmental decision makers and on scholarly research into the causes of war. Their goals included codification of international law, American participation in the World Court, and the convocation of a third Hague Peace Conference. However, the newer, more activist organizations that had developed since the outbreak of war in 1914 continued to function in a different manner; and after the armistice, they were joined by a number of new organizations.

Much of the postwar peace movement differed from its predecessors in being more activist, more issue-oriented, and more successful in obtaining legislation in the 1920s and 1930s. It seemed to fit into the new interest-group bargaining arrangement that emerged in the nation's capital in the first third of the twentieth century as power shifted to Washington and additional groups organized on a national basis. Thus the League of Nations Non-Partisan Association and the Foreign Policy Association lobbied for American entry into the new international organization. They did not hesitate to seek to mobilize popular support and congressional and executive opinion behind specific programs aimed at rationalizing international relations. Similarly, the work of the Women's International League for Peace and Freedom and the National Council for the Prevention of War showed that public opinion could be aroused; activists coordinated; coalitions formed with labor, farm, business, education, and religious groups; and influence brought to bear on federal foreign and military policy. No longer merely educational devices, the organizations in the postwar peace movement worked as effective lobbies in the nation's capital. They remained so for the next two decades, until Pearl Harbor and U.S. entry into World War II.

The success of the peace movement in achieving its goals by influencing American governmental policy varied during the first two decades of the twentieth century. Its achievements were affected by changes in international and domestic circumstances, by the strength of counterpressures exerted by opposing organizations, by divisions within the peace movement itself, by public opinion, and by the receptivity of the president of the United States and the heads of other governments. The degrees of success also depended upon the specific immediate goal and strategy of particular elements of the peace movement.

Attempts by peace advocates to stop actual combat between the armed forces of the United States and other nations between 1900 and 1922 proved much less influential than military circumstances themselves. In addition to numerous uses of contingents of marines in Caribbean countries, the United States during this period was involved in substantial military operations in the Philippines, China (during the Boxer Rebellion), Mexico, France, and Russia during World War I. U.S. military successes or failures rather than the efforts of peace workers generally led to the termination of these hostilities. The antiwar movement seems to have been relatively ineffectual in concluding American conflicts during this period.

Somewhat more effective were those peace advocates who encouraged the mediation of international disputes that broke out during the first two decades of the century. President Theodore Roosevelt showed that the United States could play the role of mediator and peacemaker when he helped negotiate the settlement of the Russo-Japanese War at Portsmouth, New Hampshire, in 1905 and in acting as conciliator among the European nations at the Algeciras Conference in Spain in 1905 and 1906.

During World War I, peace activists urged President Wilson to play the role of mediator and employ a conference of neutral nations to initiate negotiations. Although the mediation movement failed to influence Wilson's efforts, it did bolster his hope and stimulate his interest in leading the world to abandon the old diplomacy of secret treaties and military alliances. Ironically, the president eventually concluded, in the face of the German submarine offensive, that only by going to war could he help achieve the new diplomacy of international cooperation to maintain a liberal, capitalist world order. Mediationists proved more successful in averting war between the United States and Mexico in 1916. Their talks among private citizens of the two countries helped lead to formal negotiations between the two governments and the easing of tensions.

Those members of the peace movement who sought to establish a world government proved somewhat less successful. They too fell short of obtaining their goal. They did, however, contribute to President Wilson's acceptance of the idea of an association of nations. Nevertheless, the League of Nations failed to embody the kind of unified world organization, with legislative, judicial, and executive powers, that these peace advocates desired. Despite their hope that it would lead to true world government, they were unable to obtain Senate approval for American membership in the League.

While opposing such a sweeping goal as world government, many legalistic internationalists supported arbitration, adjudication, and the construction of an international common law through a world court. These friends of peace were particularly successful in obtaining the adoption of their program for arbitration by the Roosevelt and Taft administrations. However, the Senate, jealous of its prerogatives and wary of compromising national interests, refused to allow the executive to commit the United States to arbitration of vital matters. In the Wilson administration, Secretary of State Bryan, one of the spokesmen of the peace movement, obtained less restrictive treaties of conciliation with a number of countries, but these treaties were never used and eventually expired.

The idea of a world court received much support by American presidents. The Roosevelt administration used The Hague Tribunal to settle several minor differences involving the United States and other countries, and the Wilson administration tried to establish an inter-American court of international justice. While Wilson also endorsed a world court, many peace activists were disappointed that it was not established simultaneously with the League but only later as a creature of the association of nations. Despite repeated efforts by internationalists, the United States never joined the World Court. Thus although highly successful in affecting the chief U.S. policymakers, the advocates of international arbitration and adjudication and a world court found themselves restricted by nationalism, isolationism, and political concern reflected within the United States Senate.

It was when both the executive and the legislative branches of government supported them that the peace advocates found themselves most effective. Such was the case in the Five-Power Naval Arms Limitation Treaty of 1922. Even then, however, the reduction applied only to the largest ships of the leading powers. Furthermore, the disarmament movement had not always been even that successful. It had exercised little constraint on the naval expansion encouraged by Theodore

Roosevelt. Nor did it prevent the massive construction program of 1916–1918 authorized during the Wilson administration. In the postwar period, however, arms limitation coincided with the attitudes of the majority in the country and Congress. Then disarmament advocates were able to block the efforts of the administration and the admirals and generals who sought to maintain a large naval and military establishment. Thus in 1919 and 1922, the peace movement proved perhaps most effective in obtaining its immediate goal of disarmament.

Study of the influence of the peace movement upon U.S. foreign policy between 1900 and 1922 also provides insights into both the operation of the American political system and the development of the United States as a world power. Our examination of one aspect of those phenomena suggests hypotheses about both the effectiveness of the peace movement and the nature of influence upon foreign policy within the American polity in the early years of the twentieth century.

From the preceding evidence, it appears that the peace movement was most effective when its goals coincided with public sentiment that was being shaped by other forces as well. The antipathy to war and armaments that followed World War I represented a dramatic example. Americans saw little justification for large defense expenditures in a period of little external danger and high domestic taxes. Within such a setting, peace advocates could provide both the arguments and the apparatus for catalyzing public opinion and channeling it into political action. The peace movement could become an especially effective lobby when it aimed at achieving limited and negative goals, such as reducing tax appropriations for armaments. In periods of little plausible danger to the national interest, peace workers could act as an effective counter to the recommendations of those who wished to maintain or expand large military and naval establishments.

Conversely, the peace movement seems to have been least effective during wartime, especially in the course of a relatively popular, short, and successful war, when public opinion and those who help to shape it were, on the whole, either apathetic or hostile to the pleas of peace activists. Pacifists appeal to people's hopes; the military appeals to their fears. At the outbreak of war, the military's arguments almost automatically gain legitimacy.

A declaration of war also provides increased power for the agencies of social control—the government, the judiciary, the clergy, and the mass media—to restrict those who continue to dissent from national policy. Persuasion by the authorities is enhanced by appeals to loyalty, patriotism, the symbols of national unity and history, and the ability to repudiate the more radical dissenters as people who willingly or unconsciously are aiding the enemy. Increased governmental control over the channels of information increases its power and, conversely, limits the means of these dissenters to extend their message. The government's ability to use sanctions also increases in wartime through both new enabling legislation and the acquiescence of the normally countervailing power centers, public or private. Authorities can, and in World War I did, prevent communications of some dissenters by breaking up meetings, denying mailing privileges, and confiscating printed publications. They can fine, imprison, or exile activist dissenters. They can encourage divisions within dissenting groups, and they can act to prevent American citizens from operating outside official channels in attempts to open private negotiations with other governments. As long as a particular war is supported by the overwhelming majority of the people, such constraints can curtail effective action by the peace movement. Such was the case during American belligerency in World War I.

Moments of suppression as in 1917–1918 or of achievements as in 1922, do not, however, appear typical of the peace movement during the first two decades of the twentieth century. The main function of the peace movement during that period seems to have been to present alternatives to American foreign policy makers and then to lobby for their acceptance and implementation. Not all of these options were accepted by the presidents, but a number were. Arbitration, the use of an international tribunal, and mediation of international disputes all became official U.S. policy. The chief executives, however, frequently failed to follow the specific advice of the peace organizations. Instead, the presidents tended to use the alternatives and support of the peace advocates when these coincided with their own thoughts or needs and to disregard them at other times.

Sometimes, the peace movement scored a dramatic tactical success, as in the prevention of war between the United States and Mexico over the Carrizal incident of 1916 or in the achievements of the Washington Disarmament Conference of 1922. At other times, it was able to help modify U.S. policy, as in the arbitration agreements of the Roosevelt administration and the conciliation treaties and the Treaty of Versailles of the Wilson administration.

It should be remembered, however, that the peace movement was not unified and that it was itself only one of the interest groups that sought to influence foreign policy in Washington. Business, agricultural, religious, military, and ethnic organizations were also active. Each of these jockeyed for influence upon Congress, the State Department, and the

White House. Furthermore, the peace movement was so broad that its constituent groups seldom worked together as they pursued their specific immediate goals. This heterogeneity of membership and diversity of immediate goals frequently hampered the effectiveness of the peace workers.

Like the other interest groups, the peace organizations operated on the whole between the decision makers and the media and members of an attentive public, in this case, those concerned with foreign policy. The peace activists tried to use the one to influence the other. As such, their political role was primarily communicative and educational. Their prestige and their arguments proved to be their major tools of persuasion, but they had their most significant effect when they could also demonstrate great popular support.

In retrospect, the most important trend of the period in the relationship of the United States to the rest of the world was the increased willingness of Americans to have the United States play the international role to which its economic strength and military potential entitled it. The first three presidents of the century, Roosevelt, Taft, and Wilson, led the country into new political, military, economic, and diplomatic involvement in international affairs.

The peace movement helped these presidents in their attempts to convince Americans to accept this increased international activity. Although many in the peace movement did not support the expanded military role, and some questioned the increased economic involvement, the majority of peace activists, through their educational campaigns, encouraged a more cosmopolitan world view among many Americans. Thus they helped to erode the traditional isolationism—more accurately, political unilateralism—that had characterized the American attitude toward the nations outside the Western Hemisphere. In some cases, such as the attempt to prevent American entry into World War I or the effort to achieve military and naval disarmament, elements of the peace movement reversed themselves and appealed to traditional isolationism. But overall, peace advocates urged an expanded American role and mission in the world. In their view, this would not be a military role but a political and perhaps economic one that would be in keeping with what they saw as America's unique destiny of bringing enlightened, humane, and just relations among peoples.

To peace advocates, as to many other Americans, the United States remained the world's last, best hope. They maintained their faith in that vision even through the agony of World War I. They coupled it with an intensive, new effort to bring lasting peace to the global community.

Their faith in America and in the pragmatic application of intelligence to human problems sustained them.

There has seldom been such a struggle waged, not just for particular policies, but for the mind and soul of America. Liberal internationalists pitted themselves against chauvinistic nationalism and pinched and narrow isolationism. As against the suspicions, fears, and pessimistic views of their opponents, peace advocates maintained a faith in human rationality and social progress. They offered a broad and soaring vision of a world without war, a world with liberty, peace, and justice for all humankind. It was a noble vision, offering much to their own time to the future.

PART ONE

Awakening of the Modern
American Peace Movement,
1899 to 1914

DOCUMENT 1

The First Hague Peace Conference, Arbitration Convention (1899)

Editor's Note: The International Peace Conference at The Hague in the Netherlands held in 1899 failed to reduce the arms race, its main announced purpose, but it did adopt a number of conventions concerning warfare and international relations. Most importantly, it adopted the following convention on July 29, 1899, which provided for a Permanent Court of Arbitration (popularly called The Hague Tribunal). The U.S. governmeant ratified this convention on April 7, 1900.

Convention for the Pacific Settlement of International Disputes

. . . . .

His Majesty the Emperor of Germany, King of Prussia; His Majesty the Emperor of Austria, King of Bohemia etc. and Apostolic King of Hungary; His Majesty the King of the Belgians; His Majesty the Emperor of China; His Majesty the King of Denmark; His Majesty the King of Spain and in His Name Her Majesty the Queen Regent of the Kingdom; the President of the United States of America; the President of the United Mexican States; the President of the French Republic; Her Majesty the Queen of the United Kingdom of Great Britain and Ireland, Empress of India; His Majesty the King of the Hellenes; His Majesty the King of Italy; His Majesty the Emperor of Japan; His Royal Highness the Grand Duke of Luxemburg, Duke of Nassau; His Highness the Prince of Montenegro; Her Majesty the Queen of the Netherlands; His Imperial Majesty the Shah of Persia; His Majesty the King of Portugal and of the Algarves etc.; His Majesty the King of Roumania; His Majesty the Emperor of all the Russias; His Majesty the King of Servia; His Majesty the King of Siam; His Majesty the King of Sweden and Norway; the Swiss Federal Council; His Majesty the Emperor of the Ottomans and His Royal Highness the Prince of Bulgaria

Animated by a strong desire to concert for the maintenance of the general peace;

Source: William M. Malloy, comp., *Treaties, Conventions, International Acts, Protocols and Agreements Between the United States of America and Other Powers, 1777–1909* (Washington, D.C.: GPO, 1910), 2: 2016–32.

Resolved to second by their best efforts the friendly settlement of international disputes;

Recognizing the solidarity which unites the members of the society of civilized nations;

Desirous of extending the empire of law, and of strengthening the appreciation of international justice;

Convinced that the permanent institution of a Court of Arbitration, accessible to all, in the midst of the independent Powers, will contribute effectively to this result;

Having regard to the advantages attending the general and regular organization of arbitral procedure;

Sharing the opinion of the august Initiator of the International Peace Conference [Nicholas II, tsar of Russia] that it is expedient to record in an international Agreement the principles of equity and right on which are based the security of States and the welfare of peoples.

Being desirous of concluding a Convention to this effect . . . .

TITLE I. ON THE MAINTENANCE OF THE GENERAL PEACE.

ARTICLE I.

With a view to obviating, as far as possible, recourse to force in the relations between States, the Signatory Powers agree to use their best efforts to insure the pacific settlement of international differences.

TITLE IV. ON INTERNATIONAL ARBITRATION.

CHAPTER I. On the System of Arbitration.

ARTICLE XV.

International arbitration has for its object the settlement of differences between States by judges of their own choice, and on the basis of respect for law.

ARTICLE XVI.

In questions of a legal nature, and especially in the interpretation of application of International Conventions, arbitration is recognized by the Signatory Powers as the most effective, and at the same time the most equitable, means of settling disputes which diplomacy has failed to settle.

． ． ． ． ．

CHAPTER II. On the Permanent Court of Arbitration.

ARTICLE XX.

With the object of facilitating an immediate recourse to arbitration for international differences, which it has not been possible to settle by diplomacy, the Signatory Powers undertake to organize a permanent Court of Arbitration [located at The Hague], accessible at all times and operating, unless otherwise stipulated by the parties, in accordance with the Rules of Procedure inserted in the present Convention.

． ． ． ． ．

ARTICLE XXIV.

When the Signatory Powers desire to have recourse to the Permanent Court for the settlement of a difference that has arisen between them, the Arbitrators called upon to form the competent Tribunal to decide this difference, must be chosen from the general list of members of the Court.

． ． ． ． ．

CHAPTER III. On Arbitral Procedure.

The said Convention was signed by the Plenipotentiaries of the United States of America under reservation of the following declaration:

"Nothing contained in this convention shall be so construed as to require the United States of America to depart from its traditional policy of not intruding upon, interfering with, or entangling itself in the political questions of policy or internal administration of any foreign state; nor shall anything contained in the said convention be construed to imply a relinquishment by the United States of America of its traditional attitude toward purely American questions."

． ． ． ． ．

DOCUMENT 2

Captain Alfred Thayer Mahan Cautions Against Arbitration (1899)

Editor's Note: Captain, later Admiral, Alfred Thayer Mahan, 1840–1914, author of the doctrine of sea power and a leading proponent of naval expansion and imperialism, was one of the U.S. delegates to The Hague Peace Conference of 1899. The following critique of the conference by Captain Mahan appeared in a national magazine in October 1899.

The Peace Conference and the Moral Aspect of War

. . . . .

The calling of the Conference of the Hague originated in an avowed desire to obtain relief from immediate economical burdens, by the adoption of some agreement to restrict the preparations for war, and the consequent expense, involved in national armaments; but before its meeting the hope of disarmament had fallen into the background, the vacant place being taken by the project of abating the remoter evils of recurrent warfare, by giving a further impulse, and a more clearly defined application, to the principle of arbitration, which thenceforth assumed preeminence in the councils of the Conference.

. . . . .

One of the most unfortunate characteristics of our present age is the disposition to impose by legislative enactment—by external compulsion, that is,—restrictions of a moral character, which are either fundamentally unjust, or at least do not carry with them the moral sense of the community, as a whole.

. . . . .

The resort to arms by a nation, when right cannot otherwise be enforced, corresponds, or should correspond, precisely to the acts of the individual man. . . . [A] State, when it goes to war, should do so not to test the rightfulness of its claims, but because, being convinced in its conscience of that rightfulness, no other means of overcoming evil remains.

. . . . .

Source: Captain A. T. Mahan, U. S. Navy, "The Peace Conference and the Moral Aspect of War," *North American Review* 169 (Oct. 1899): 433–47.

A concrete instance, however, is always more comprehensible and instructive than a general discussion. Let us therefore take the incidents and conditions which preceded our recent [1898] war with Spain. The facts, as seen by us, may, I apprehend, be fairly stated as follows. In the island of Cuba, a powerful military force,—government it scarcely can be called,—foreign to the island, was holding a small portion of it in enforced subjection, and was endeavoring, unsuccessfully, to reduce the remainder. In pursuance of this attempt, measures were adopted that inflicted immense misery and death upon great numbers of the population. Such suffering is indeed attendant upon war; but it may be stated as a fundamental principle of civilized warfare that useless suffering is condemned, and it had become apparent to military eyes that Spain could not subdue the island, or restore orderly conditions. The suffering was terrible, and was unavailing.

Under such circumstances, does any moral obligation lie upon a powerful neighboring State? Or, more exactly, if there is borne in upon the moral consciousness of a mighty people, that such an afflicted community as that of Cuba at their doors is like Lazarus at the gate of the rich man, and that the duty of stopping the evil rests upon them, what is to be done with such a case of conscience? Could the decision of another, whether nation or court, excuse our nation from the ultimate responsibility of its own decision? . . . For let us not deceive ourselves. Absolutely justifiable, nay imperative, as most of us believe our action to have been, when tried at the bar of conscience, no arbitral court, acceptable to the two nations, would have decided as our own conscience did. . . . Of the moral question the arbiter could take no account; it is not there, indeed, that moral questions must find their solution, but in the court of conscience. Referred to arbitration, doubtless the Spanish flag would still fly over Cuba.

. . . . .

Power, force, is a faculty of national life; one of the talents committed to nations by God. Like every other endowment of a complex organization, it must be held under control of the enlightened intellect and of the upright heart. . . . And this obligation to maintain right, by force if need be, while common to all states, rests peculiarly upon the greater, in proportion to their means. Much is required of those to whom much is given. So viewed, the ability speedily to put forth the nation's power . . . is one of the clear duties involved in the Christian word "watchfulness"—readiness for the call that may come, whether expectedly or not. Until it is demonstrable that no evil exists, or threatens the world, which cannot be obviated without recourse to force, the obligation to readiness must remain; and, where evil is mighty and defiant, the obligation to use force—that is, war—arises.

The great danger of undiscriminating advocacy of Arbitration, which threatens even the cause it seeks to maintain, is that it may lead men to tamper with equity, to compromise with unrighteousness, soothing their conscience with the belief that war is so entirely wrong that beside it no other tolerated evil is wrong.

· · · · ·

DOCUMENT 3

Lucia Ames Mead Endorses Arbitration
and an International Police Force (1903)

Editor's Note: Lucia Ames Mead, 1856–1936, pragmatic New England activist for peace, social reform, women's suffrage, and racial justice, helped found the Woman's Peace party in 1915 (see document 14) and became its national secretary. The following appeal by her appeared in a national magazine in July 1903.

International Police

"I believe in arbitration, of course, and in a stated International Congress —I have worked to promote that," said a Senator in the Massachusetts Legislature to me; "but when you peace people talk about ending war, I can't follow you. I think you will have to wait until the millennium; for so long as there is sin in the world there must needs be force." Doubtless there are some "peace men" who, like Tolstoi, decry all use of force; but the ordinary sensible man who is working to abolish national armaments, when the shrieks from [the killing in] Kishenev [Kishinev in Moldavia] and the Congo ring in his ears, calls for a strong hand, and no milk-and-water policy. As he remembers the

Source: Lucia Ames Mead, "International Police," The Outlook 74 (July 18, 1903): 705–6.

two thousand gangs of American anarchists [Mead refers to lynch mobs, not philosophical anarchists] who have torn open jail doors and hanged and burned untried men, and themselves gone unpunished, he believes there is still use in this world for the soldier.

But if he is a peace man who wants to make himself effective, he will not waste time in discussing the horrors of war and the beauties of peace. He will try to let in a light on a subject about which much sophistry has befogged the public's mind. His first proposition will be that the organized, authoritative force of this world is of two essentially different kinds. The one that we know most about is of comparatively recent origin; it is the police force. Time was, and not more than two or three centuries ago, when every man carried his own weapon and avenged his own wrong. To-day, in thoroughly civilized communities, he who avenges his own wrong becomes a criminal. The State has established a disinterested method of settling disputes according to evidence and justice. Force is employed, but not to settle the dispute. The policeman brings the contestants to a court. That is his function—to bring to court—and he uses only that modicum of force which is necessary to bring contestants to court. Often they come of their own accord, or, when brought, they usually venture little or no resistance.

. . . . .

. . . What would an international police do? It would bring stubborn nations to the World's Court with the same efficiency as the city police separate two men glaring at each other with murderous knives unsheathed, and drag them to the Police Court. Of what would the International Police be composed? Of a small body of armed men and battleships paid and organized by practically all the nations of the world and controlling them through a World Legislature which would make laws to be carried out by the Hague Court. We have the Hague Court. Next winter Congress will be asked to propose to the nations to establish an International Congress to meet at regular intervals to discuss international problems. This will not be a World Legislature, as its delegates will have, as at the Hague Conference, no power to do more than to refer questions to their nations for ratification. . . . It may be decades before it develops into a genuine Legislature with power. But a World Legislature is as definitely bound to come as the Isthmian [Panama] canal or the Cape to Cairo railroad. Not until it is established, and perhaps several decades after that, can we talk practically about forming an International Police; we must first, of course, all pledge ourselves to carry international differences to court. But though the period of complete national disarmament may be relegated to another century, it is of immense importance for the world to know that it is approximately near, that we need not wait until sin and quarrels have been banished from the earth before we find a rational way of treating them.

The police force will remain to bring men to court. The militia will remain to compel riotous mobs and lynchers to leave their quarrels and their vengeance to the courts. The international police will supplant the national, paid bodies of executioners who, under our present anarchic system of international relations, execute in absence of law, according to national whim or passion or prejudice. The reign of law has come in families, in cities, in the States, in the nations. It is coming between the nations. There is no new principle to be invented, simply the extension of an old and tried principle.

．　．　．　．　．

DOCUMENT 4

Andrew Carnegie and Theodore Roosevelt on International Peace (1905, 1906)

Andrew Carnegie Proposes a League of Peace (1905)

Editor's Note: Andrew Carnegie, 1835–1919, industrialist, philanthropist, anti–imperialist, pacifist, and internationalist, retired from business in 1901. He founded the Carnegie Endowment for International Peace with ten million dollars in 1910 and the Church Peace Union with two million dollars in 1914. In 1905, he presented the following proposal for a "league of peace."

A League of Peace

It may surprise you to learn that from the date of the Jay Treaty, one hundred and eleven years ago, no less than five hundred and seventy-

Source: Andrew Carnegie, *A League of Peace: A Rectoral Address Delivered to the Students in the University of St. Andrew, October 17, 1905* (New York: New York Peace Society, 1911), 32–37.

one international disputes have been settled by arbitration. Not in any case has an award been questioned or disregarded, except I believe in one case, where the arbiters misunderstood their powers. If in every ten of these differences so quietly adjusted without a wound, there lurked one war, it follows that peaceful settlement has prevented fifty–seven wars—one every two years. More than this, had the fifty–seven wars, assumed as prevented by arbitration, developed, they would have sown the seeds of many future wars . . . .

·   ·   ·   ·   ·

Much has been written upon the fearful cost of war in our day, the ever–increasing blood tax of nations, which threatens soon to approach the point of exhaustion in several European lands. . . .

The military and naval expenditure of Britain is fully half of her total expenditure; that of the other great Powers, though less, is rapidly increasing.

All the great national debts . . . are the legacies of war.

This drain, with the economic loss of life added, is forcing itself upon the nations concerned as never before. It threatens soon to become dangerous unless the rapid increase of recent years be stopped; but it is to be feared that not till after the financial catastrophe occurs will nations devote themselves seriously to apply the cure.

The futility of war as a means of producing peace between nations has often been dwelt upon. It is really the most futile of all remedies, because it embitters contestants and sows the seeds of future struggles. Generations are sometimes required to eradicate the hostility engendered by one conflict. . . . [In] the recent terrible war just concluded [the Russo–Japanese War of 1904–1905] . . . neither contestant obtained what he fought for. . . . Such considerations find no place, however, in the fiery furnace of popular clamor; as little do those of cost or loss of life. Only if the moral wrong, the sin in itself, of man–slaying is brought home to the conscience of the masses may we hope speedily to banish war. There will, we fear, always be demagogs in our day to inflame their brutal passions and urge men to fight, as a point of honor and patriotism, scouting arbitration as a cowardly refuge. All thoughts of cost or loss of human life vanish when the brute in man, thus aroused, gains sway.

It is the crime of destroying human life by war and the duty to offer or accept peaceful arbitration as a substitute which needs to be established, and which, as we think, those of the Church, the Universities, and of the Professions are called upon to strongly emphasize.

... Five nations cooperated in quelling the recent Chinese disorders and rescuing their representatives in Peking. [Actually, six nations—the United States, Great Britain, Germany, France, Russia, and Japan—sent troops in 1900 to Peking, now Beijing, to suppress the Boxer Rebellion.] It is perfectly clear that these five nations could banish war. Suppose even three of them formed a League of Peace inviting all other nations to join and agreed that since war in any part of the civilized world affects all nations, and often seriously, no nation shall go to war, but shall refer international disputes to the Hague Conference or other arbitral body for peaceful settlement, the League agreeing to declare nonintercourse with any nation refusing compliance. Imagine a nation cut off today from the world. The League also might reserve to itself the right, where nonintercourse is likely to fail or has failed to prevent war, to use the necessary force to maintain peace, each member of the League agreeing to provide the needed forces, or money in lieu thereof, in proportion to her population or wealth.... Further provisions, and perhaps some adaptations, would be found requisite, but the main idea is here.

. . . . .

Theodore Roosevelt Cautions of the Limits of Peace (1906)

Editor's Note: Theodore Roosevelt, 1858–1919, during his two terms as president, between 1901 and 1909, appeared to pursue various approaches to foreign policy in a world in flux. As an imperialist and warhawk, he vastly expanded the navy and engaged in high-handed interventions in the Caribbean. Yet as an apparent peacemaker, he mediated an end to the Russo-Japanese War of 1905, and supported limited arbitration treaties and The Hague conferences. In his 1910 speech accepting the Nobel Peace Prize, the former president advocated a league with force to uphold treaties and the decisions of a world court; but he later vigorously opposed Wilson's covenant for a League of Nations. In the following confidential letter to Andrew Carnegie in August 1906 explaining his position on the forthcoming Second Hague Peace Conference scheduled for 1907, Roosevelt revealed some of his core convictions about the underlying primacy of force in international relations and the duty of leading nations.

Theodore Roosevelt to Andrew Carnegie

Personal and private

Oyster Bay, August 6, 1906

My dear Mr. Carnegie:

... I hope to see real progress made at the next Hague Conference. If it is possible in some way to bring about a stop, complete or partial, to the race in adding to armaments, I shall be glad; but I do not yet see my way clear as regards the details of such a plan. We must always remember that it would be a fatal thing for the great free peoples to reduce themselves to impotence and leave the despotisms and barbarisms armed. It would be safe to do so if there was some system of international police; but there is now no such system; if there were, Turkey [the Ottoman Empire] for instance would be abolished forthwith unless it showed itself capable of working real reform. As things are now it is for the advantage of peace and order that Russia should be in Turkestan, that France should have Algiers, and that England should have Egypt and the Sudan. It would be an advantage to justice if we were able in some way effectively to interfere in the Congo Free State [governed harshly by King Leopold of Belgium] to secure a more righteous government; if we were able effectively to interfere for the Armenians in Turkey, and for the Jews in Russia [in both cases against government-sponsored pogroms]. But at present I do not see how we can interfere in any of these three matters, and the one thing I won't do is to bluff when I cannot make good; to bluster and threaten and then fail to take the action if my words need to be backed up.

. . . . .

... At The Hague I hope we can work hand in hand with France and England; but all three nations must be extremely careful not to get led off into vagaries, and not to acquiesce in some propositions such as those I am sorry to say Russia has more than once made in the past—propositions in the name of peace which were really designed to favor military despotisms at the expense of their free neighbors. I believe in peace, but I believe that as things are at present, the cause not only of peace but of what is greater than peace, justice, is favored by having those nations which really stand at the head of civilization show, not

Source: Theodore Roosevelt to Andrew Carnegie, Aug. 6, 1906, in The Letters of Theodore Roosevelt, ed. Elting E. Morison and John M. Blum (Cambridge, Mass.: Harvard Univ. Press, 1951–1954) 5:345–46.

merely by words but by action, that they ask peace in the name of justice and not from any weakness.

With warm regards to Mrs. Carnegie, believe me,

Faithfully yours
Theodore Roosevelt

DOCUMENT 5

William James Proposes a "Moral Equivalent of War" (1910)

Editor's Note: William James, 1842–1910, Harvard philosopher and psychologist, sought in this influential essay to reconcile the desire for peace with what he believed were the warlike nature of mankind and the positive values of the military tradition. His solution—conscripting young people into "armies" that would perform civic works rather than fight wars—later formed the basis, without the coercion and military emphasis, for several popular liberal programs involving youthful volunteers. Among these were the nongovernmental work of the American Friends Service Committee (which won the Nobel Peace Prize in 1947) and several federal governmental programs including the Civilian Conservation Corps, the Peace Corps, and the Job Corps. Although James had begun to develop his thesis earlier, his finished essay was published in 1910 by a peace organization, the American Association for International Conciliation.

The Moral Equivalent of War

The war against war is going to be no holiday excursion or camping party. The military feelings are too deeply grounded to abdicate their place among our ideals until better substitutes are offered than the glory and shame that come to nations as well as to individuals from the ups and downs of politics and the vicissitudes of trade.

. . . . .

Source: William James, *The Moral Equivalent of War* (New York: American Association for International Conciliation, 1910), leaflet no. 27.

Our ancestors have bred pugnacity into our bone and marrow, and thousands of years of peace won't breed it out of us. The popular imagination fairly fattens on the thought of wars. Let public opinion once reach a certain fighting pitch, and no ruler can understand it.... In 1898 our people had read the word WAR in letters three inches high for three months in every newspaper. The pliant politician [President William] McKinley was swept away by their eagerness, and our squalid war with Spain became a necessity.

At the present day, civilized opinion is a curious mental mixture. The military instincts and ideals are as strong as ever, but are confronted by reflective criticisms which sorely curb their ancient freedom. Innumerable writers are showing up the bestial side of military service. Pure loot and mastery seem no longer morally avowable motives, and pretexts must be found for attributing them solely to the enemy. England and we, our army and navy authorities repeat without ceasing, arm solely for "peace," Germany and Japan it is who are bent on loot and glory.

．　．　．　．　．

But, as things stand, I see how desperately hard it is to bring the peace-party and the war-party together, and I believe that the difficulty is due to certain deficiencies in the program of pacificism which set the militarist imagination strongly, and to a certain extent justifiably, against it.

．　．　．　．　．

One cannot meet them effectively by mere counter-insistency on war's expensiveness and horror. The horror makes the thrill; and when the question is of getting the extremest and supremest out of human nature, talk of expense sounds ignominious. The weakness of so much merely negative criticism is evident—pacificism makes no converts from the military party. The military party denies neither the bestiality nor the horror, nor the expense; it only says that these things tell but half the story. It only says that war is *worth* them; that, taking human nature as a whole, its wars are its best protection against its weaker and more cowardly self, and that mankind cannot *afford* to adopt a peace-economy.

Pacifists ought to enter more deeply into the esthetical and ethical point of view of their opponents. Do that first in any controversy . . . *then move the point,* and your opponent will follow. So long as anti-militarists propose no substitute for war's disciplinary function, no *moral equivalent* of war, analogous, as one might say, to the mechanical equivalent of heat, so long [will] they fail to realize the full inwardness of the situation. And as a rule they do fail. The duties, penalties, and sanctions pictured in the utopias they paint are all too weak and tame to touch the military-minded.

. . . . . .

. . . The fatalistic view of the war-function is to me nonsense, for I know that war-making is due to definite motives and subject to prudential checks and reasonable criticisms, just like any other form of enterprise. And when whole nations are the armies, and the science of destruction vies in intellectual refinement with the sciences of production, I see that war becomes absurd and impossible from its own monstrosity. . . . I look forward to a future when acts of war shall be formally outlawed as between civilized peoples.

All these beliefs of mine put me squarely into the anti–militarist party. But I do not believe that peace either ought to be or will be permanent on this globe, unless the states pacifically organized preserve some of the old elements of army-discipline. . . . We must make new energies and hardihoods continue the manliness to which the military mind so faithfully clings. Martial virtues must be the enduring cement; intrepidity, contempt of softness, surrender of private interest, obedience to command, must still remain the rock upon which states are built—unless, indeed, we wish for dangerous reactions against commonwealths fit only for contempt, and liable to invite attack whenever a centre of crystallization for military-minded enterprise gets formed anywhere in their neighborhood.

The war-party is assuredly right in affirming and reaffirming that the martial virtues, although originally gained by the race through war, are absolute and permanent human goods. Patriotic pride and ambition in their military form are, after all, only specifications of a more general competitive passion. . . . The war-function has graspt us so far; but constructive interests may some day seem no less imperative, and impose on the individual a hardly lighter burden.

Let me illustrate my idea more concretely. . . . It may end by seeming shameful to all of us that some of us have nothing but campaigning, and others nothing but unmanly ease. If now—and this is my idea— there were, instead of military conscription a conscription of the whole youthful population to form for a certain number of years a part of the army enlisted against Nature, the injustice would tend to be evened out, and numerous other goods to the commonwealth would follow. The military ideals of hardihood and discipline would be wrought into the growing fibre of the people; no one would remain blind as the luxurious classes now are blind, to man's real relations to the globe he lives on, and to the permanently sour and hard foundations of his higher life. To coal and iron mines, to freight trains, to fishing fleets in December, to dish-washing, clothes-washing, and window-washing, to road-building and tunnel-making, to foundries and stoke-holes, and to the frames of skyscrapers, would our gilded youths be drafted off, according to their choice, to get the childishness knocked out of them, and to come back into society with healthier sympathies and soberer ideas.

• • • • •

Such a conscription, with the state of public opinion that would have required it, and the many moral fruits it would bear, would preserve in the midst of a pacific civilization the manly virtues which the military party is so afraid of seeing disappear in peace. We should get toughness without callousness, authority with as little criminal cruelty as possible, and painful work done cheerily because the duty is temporary, and threatens not, as now, to degrade the whole remainder of one's life. I spoke of the "moral equivalent" of war. So far, war has been the only force that can discipline a whole community.

• • • • •

It would be simply preposterous if the only force that could work ideals of honour and standards of efficiency into English or American natures should be the fear of being killed by the Germans or the Japanese. Great indeed is Fear; but it is not, as our military enthusiasts believe and try to make us believe, the only stimulus known for awakening the higher ranges of men's spiritual energy.

• • • • •

DOCUMENT 6

Hamilton Holt Recommends a League of Peace (1911)

Editor's Note: Hamilton Holt, 1872–1951, a leading advocate of international arbitration and world organization, was managing editor of The Independent *magazine from 1897 to 1912 and editor and owner from 1913 to 1921. The following is a speech Holt made in the first week in May 1911 as president of the Third National Peace Congress in Baltimore, Maryland. The outbreak of war in 1914 led him to modify his views on force somewhat (see document 12), and he later became a champion of the League to Enforce Peace (see document 21) and Wilson's League of Nations (see document 45).*

A League of Peace

. . . . .

The peace movement, we have now come to realize, is nothing but the process of substituting law for war. The world has already learned to substitute law for war in hamlets, towns, cities, states, and even within the forty-six sovereign civilized nations. But in that international realm over and above each nation in which each nation is equally sovereign, the only way at the present moment for a nation to secure its rights is by the use of force. Force, therefore, or war as it is called when exerted by a nation against another nation—is at present the only legal and final method of settling international differences. The world is now using a Christian code of ethics of individuals, and a pagan code for nations, tho[ugh] there is no double standard of ethics in the moral world. In other words, the nations are in that state of civilization where without a qualm they claim the right to settle their disputes in a manner which they would actually put their own subjects to death for imitating. Thus the peace problem is nothing but the ways and means of doing *between* the nations what has already been done *within* the nations. International law follows private law. The "United Nations" follow the United States.

. . . . .

We may look with confidence therefore to a future in which the world will have an established court with jurisdiction over all questions, self-governing conferences with power to legislate on all affairs of common concern, and an executive power of some form to carry out the decrees of both. To deny this is to ignore all the analogies of private law and the whole trend of the world's political history since the Declara-

Source: Hamilton Holt, "A League of Peace," *The Independent* 70 (May 11, 1911): 995-99.

tion of Independence. As Secretary [of State, Philander C.] Knox has said in his great address delivered last June at the commencement of the University of Pennsylvania:

"We have reached a point when it is evident that the future holds in store a time when war shall cease: when the nations of the world shall realize a federation as real and vital as that now subsisting between the component parts of a single state."

The political organization of the world, therefore, is the task of the twentieth century.

. . . . .

How then can this movement be hastened? There are only two ways. First, by the education of the public opinion of the world so as to induce the governments to move at successive Hague conferences or at special international conferences, and second, by a few of the more enlightened nations organizing themselves together for peace in advance of the others. This latter method is already being adopted extensively. The Judicial Arbitration Court will be constituted by only a few of the nations at first. England and the United States will not wait for a general treaty of obligatory arbitration before establishing a model one between themselves [they were then negotiating a treaty requiring arbitration of disputes between the two nations]. Chile and Argentina did not delay for concurrent action on the part of the whole world before they commenced to disarm, as the status of the [giant statue of] Christ on the summit of the Andes so eloquently attests. Why, then, should not a few nations here and now form among themselves a League of Peace to hasten the ultimate world federation?

The idea of a League of Peace is not novel. All federal governments and confederations of governments, both ancient and modern, are essentially leagues of peace, even tho[ugh] they may have functions to perform which often lead directly to war.

. . . . .

The problem of the League of Peace is therefore the problem of the use of force. Shall the members of the League "not only keep the peace themselves but prevent by force, if necessary, its being broken by others," outside of the League, as ex-President [Theodore] Roosevelt has suggested? Or shall its force be exercised only within its membership and thus be on the side of law and order and never on the side of arbitrary will or tyranny? Or, rather, shall it never use force at all? Whichever of these three possibilities is ultimately adopted, I think that at first it would be unwise for a League of Peace to attempt to use force for any purpose whatsoever. Besides, the use of force will probably be found unnecessary. When nations arrive at that state of civilization in which they are ready to settle their differences by arbitration rather than by war, they are ready peaceably to abide by the decision of arbitral tribunals. The history of arbitration clearly demonstrates this. . . . We need a policeman to use force on criminals. But happily there is no such thing nowadays as a criminal nation.

[Holt then described a League of Peace which would hold regular conventions to draft rules for the league and in which member nations would refer all disputes to The Hague or other tribunals for arbitration. However, the league would not at first have its own international police force.]

Assuming, then, the desirability of such a League of Peace, how is it to be brought about?

Surely the first step is to conclude the arbitration treaty now being negotiated with Great Britain. Once this treaty is upon the international statute books, and as surely as daylight follows dawn it will be followed by similar treaties with other nations. Japan and France are said to be ready—even anxious—to negotiate similar treaties with us.

. . . . .

First, an unlimited arbitration treaty between Great Britain and the United States. Second, a League of Peace. Third, the Federation of the World.

. . . . .

DOCUMENT 7

President William Howard Taft Supports
General Arbitration Treaties (1911)

Editor's Note: William Howard Taft, 1857–1930, believed as a jurist in the ability of nations to achieve world peace through arbitration; international law; and ultimately, a world court and a system of collective security. While president between 1909 and 1913, Taft obtained general arbitration treaties between the United States and Britain and France in August 1911 and sought to obtain Senate ratification. The interview below was part of Taft's attempt to win Senate approval. However, opponents led by Senator Henry Cabot Lodge, a conservative nationalist from Massachusetts, largely vitiated the treaties through restrictive amendments before their ratification on March 7, 1912.

World-Peace and the General Arbitration Treaties

· · · · ·

Do you know that one of the most notable phenomena of the day is the swiftness with which belief in permanent international peace is growing?

Yes, this sentiment, comparatively new in the world, has made enormous strides within the past few years. Wherever I go I find the most eager interest in anything I say on the subject of war and peace. Crowds grow silent as I approach that theme; men put a hand behind the ear and stand on tiptoe leaning forward so as not to miss a word. There is astir a profound revolution in the popular thought on the subject of war, a moral awakening to the hideous wickedness of armed combat between man and man, and an economic perception of the wastefulness and folly not only of war but of the great armaments which the present jealousy of the powers makes it necessary to maintain.

Workingmen have brought it home to me as I have seen and talked with them in all parts of the country that they are against war. They have to pay the bills, and what do they gain? What interest have they in the common run of disputes between governments—matters of boundary, matters of dynasty, matters of so–called "honor"? And if they feel any interest in the dispute, they want to know why it can't be settled in some way less archaic, less barbarous, less wasteful, than the marching out of armies of men bent on killing one another.

· · · · ·

With this feeling in the mind of the workingmen, war to-day does not afford the glittering prospects it once did. It is, for instance, no longer advisable to resort to conflict with another country as a means of reuniting a country distracted by internal problems. On the contrary, war is distinctly dangerous to a country torn by internal dissensions.

Source: William Howard Taft (reported by William Bayard Hale), "World–Peace and the General Arbitration Treaties," *World's Work* 23 (Dec. 1911): 143–49.

The increased burden of taxation, the tightness of money, the inconvenience of living, the unpopularity of war, the absence of troops, abnormal conditions generally, and especially the vivid realization that the interests of the rulers are not the interests of the people—these things are likely to provoke and encourage domestic disaffection.

The birth and growth of this peace sentiment (and I tell you it is acquiring amazing strength) is not to be wondered at; it would have been a cause of wonder if it had not been born. We have advanced in everything else; we have lagged far behind in this serious and terrible matter of international disputes, allowing them to settle themselves according to the rude and savage methods of days long past. Now we have at last taken up that matter, I am inclined to think that we shall advance with it much more swiftly than some will believe.

I say boldly that what I look forward to is nothing less than a court of the nations—an Areopagitic court [a reference to the high tribunal in ancient Athens], to whose conscientious and impartial judgment peoples shall submit their disputes, to be decided according to the eternal principles of law and equity.

Civilization demands that, and it is coming. The treaties with Great Britain and France lately negotiated, will, if ratified by the Senate, mark a long step into the path along which the world must now advance.

Everyone recognizes that our existing treaties with England and France—which agree to arbitrate all questions except those which affect the vital interests or the national honor of the Powers concerned—make an advance in international relations. Yet, of course, when any question comes up, either nation might convince itself that its vital interests or its national honor were involved, and refuse to arbitrate. There are very few questions which might not be so construed in the opinion of one or the other nation. I mean to say that the exception in the present treaties is so phrased that it really leaves very little to be arbitrated; it leaves us definitely committed to very little indeed. In effect, we merely declare that we are in favor of arbitration, and that, when a question arises which we are willing to arbitrate, we will arbitrate it—if the other nation also is willing.

Now, that is all very well—but it doesn't go very far toward permanent peace—toward providing a means for the settling of those serious questions which lead to wars.

The new treaties do provide that means; the new treaties do really commit us, and the nations which sign with us, to seek a settlement of all disputes, even the most serious, without armed conflict. The new treaties do not leave it to the excited, momentary opinion of the countries involved to decide whether or not the question which has arisen is one that may honorably be arbitrated. The new treaties provide a judicial means of settling that initial question. They establish a Joint High Commission to pass on that question.

... These treaties establish such a tribunal; under the plan it will always be constituted of an equal number of citizens of the United States and of the other country involved—three of each. ... If five of the six members agree that it is capable of just settlement by the impartial principles of law and equity, then the Executive and the Senate are bound to take the steps necessary to submit the question to a board of arbitration.

We should not be forced to arbitrate anything, and, of course, on the other hand, we should not be able to secure arbitration for anything, unless two of our own three members agree on it.

. . . . .

Objection has been made, you know, that the ratification of these treaties would obligate us to submit to outsiders questions so vital as, for instance, the restriction of immigration, the Monroe Doctrine, and the payment of Confederate bonds. ... The treaties as they now stand do not contemplate the arbitration of any questions connected with immigration or the Monroe Doctrine. These are all domestic matters, matters of internal policy, which no other power could bring into question.

. . . . .

Now, those who object to these treaties in their hearts object to any arbitration; that is all there is about it.

. . . . .

Of course, a man who in his heart of hearts believes in war and likes it, who is convinced that it is a noble game, strengthening the body and elevating the soul—of course, that man can not be expected to support real arbitration treaties [a reference to Theodore Roosevelt who completely rejected Taft's treaties]. ...

Some of us really believe in arbitration—believe not only in talking about it, but also in practicing it. Some of us so hate war, while we so love the peace of righteousness, that we are willing to submit all our disputes to disinterested judges. ...

DOCUMENT 8

Lake Mohonk Conference on Business and International Law (1911)

Editor's Note: The Lake Mohonk Conference on International Arbitration, sponsored by the Religious Society of Friends (Quakers), was held at the resort near New Paltz, New York, each year from 1895 to 1916. The May 1911 meeting published this leaflet, "Business Men's Bulletin No. 10," which emphasized the interest of business in averting war through international arbitration and world law. The leaflet was signed by eight prominent business people from New York, Philadelphia, and Chicago, including George Foster Peabody, an investment banker, philanthropist, and peace activist.

The Business Man and International Law

There is at least one thing upon which business men agree. *Commercial endeavor is best served when law is certain.* This principle is universally recognized and of easy and usual application in domestic trade law. Its force is many times overlooked, however, in the broader fields of business activity even though there is infinitely greater reason for its recognition.

Whether or not one's business is large or small, domestic or foreign, it is affected by the uncertainty of international law. It works out this way. We manufacture and raise more goods and produce in eight months than we consume at home in twelve. The four months' surplus must be either exported or the home capacity for consumption greatly increased. Merchants who have secured foreign markets not only open the avenues to their own output, but by lessening the competition at home, materially assist the man whose business is local. Merchants who supply the home market are interested in an uninterrupted continuance of foreign exports, because any disturbance of foreign trade throws back upon this country goods which must be sold in direct competition with theirs. Therefore, whatever disturbs or embarrasses free commerce, such as war, internal revolution, fear of war or an uncertain international law is a detriment to all commercial activity. The wise business man has taken the cue; he is considering the to-morrows of trade as well as the to-days.

Source: Report of the Seventeenth Annual Lake Mohonk Conference on International Arbitration, May 24–26, 1911 (Lake Mohonk Conference, 1911), 188–89.

This tendency is best illustrated by comparing the texts of the two Hague Conferences. Read them. The first (1899) was dominated by the monarch and the moralist. Humane conventions predominated. But throughout the Second (1907) may be traced the influence of the business man. In defining and enlarging the rights of neutral nations and nations, their commerce and shipping, it achieved a work second to none in the field of national endeavor. There is not a business man on the corners who does not profit by some one of its provisions.

No matter how steady the hand, how cool the nerve, how well known the flag, commercial predominance that depends upon battleships, coaling stations and state secrets is at best a thing temporary, containing within itself the germs of its own possible destruction. Gunboat government tends to lawless law. Is it any wonder that our private international law which feebly attempts to harmonize the rules of nations upon such topics as contracts and their interpretation, agency, judgments, bankruptcy, patents, etc., is languishing?

Now that business men realize that the people of other lands are prospective if not actual customers, now that they are thinking in terms of hemispheres, now that they see that successful domestic business leans upon a constant export trade, it is for them to place international relations upon a safe foundation—one that will make possible a certain, universal law. This means that they must discredit the war game no matter who stands ready and willing to play it. War and commercial certainty, like disgruntled litigants, are not on speaking terms.

There are plenty of existing agencies about which to rally in support of international arbitration, treaties of arbitration, international courts, conferences and other forces making for a better and more certain law of nations. The main thing is active co-operation for the desired end.

DOCUMENT 9

Press Reaction to Secretary of State William Jennings Bryan
and His "Cooling Off" Treaties (1913)

Editor's Note: William Jennings Bryan, 1860–1925, was a lawyer, politician, and national leader of the predominantly rural, Jeffersonian wing of the Democratic party. After 1900, he championed morality, love, and

Christian brotherhood as the solution to international problems. As Woodrow Wilson's first secretary of state from 1913 to 1915, Bryan advocated arbitration, "cooling off" treaties, and neutralism if not pacifism in international affairs. In 1913, he negotiated treaties with thirty nations providing that in any dispute between them, they would agree to wait one year before increasing their armaments or resorting to war, while a bilateral commission investigated and made its report and, it was hoped, inflamed passions subsided. In May 1913, The Literary Digest, *a monthly summary of press opinion, printed the following reactions for and against Bryan's idea.*

A Pacifist in Charge of Our Foriegn Relations

In the brief time that he has held the portfolio of State, William Jennings Bryan has shown, in the felicitous words of a fellow speaker at a recent banquet, "that so far as he can, he is not going to permit humanity to be crucified on a cross of war, but instead, that he will work to have it crowned with the golden crown of peace" [allusions to Bryan's famous "Cross of Gold" speech at the Democratic National Convention in 1896]. Not that the universal recognition of the Secretary's stand means anything like a unanimous commendation of what he has said and done. His course "is winning him new and unaccustomed esteem," in the opinion of the New York *Evening Post*, which adds graciously that this is "not the least pleasing aspect of his peace policy." But other editors grumble at the sight of the Secretary of State "gadding about" to talk "generalities," and cannot find anything of practical merit in the plans he has announced. According to *The Army and Navy Journal's* way of thinking there is even danger that the Secretary of State may be hurting the nation's interest, at the present time, "by his attendance at peace meetings and his declarations that every question should be settled in a peaceful manner." Mr. Bryan evidently has no such misgivings.

. . . . .

The Secretary has offered a concrete plan for the promotion of peace which has compelled the newspapers to take it on its merits and to give it serious criticism or commendation. This proposition has been laid

Source: "A Pacifist in Charge of Our Foreign Relations," *Literary Digest* 46 (May 31, 1913): 1207–9.

before the Senate Foreign Relations Committee, and has been presented to the entire diplomatic corps, assembled expressly for that purpose. The Brooklyn *Eagle* sees in the Bryan plan simply an adaption to diplomatic purposes of the homely advice: "When angry, count fifty; when very angry, count a hundred."

. . . . .

This proposition "places the United States in the leadership of the peace movement," declares the Pittsburgh *Dispatch* (Rep[ublican]), and the Indianapolis *News* (Ind[ependent]), New York *Evening Post* (Ind.), Boston *Advertiser* (Rep.), and *Chicago Tribune* (Prog[ressive]) are equally confident of its value. The New York *Times* (Ind.) speaks of it as "one of those rare ventures in the field of world affairs of which it may be said that it can do no possible harm, and may do much good."

. . . . .

Yet the Brooklyn *Eagle* (Dem[ocratic]), which believes that nations would often find the "cooling–off" process of distinct value, notes this "serious objection" to the Bryan plan:

"It does not and can not prevent a nation secretly resolved on war from carrying on preparations for war during the whole period of investigation by the proposed international commission. . . . "

In a recent Sunday peace sermon in Washington, Secretary Bryan paid his respects to the business interests and the newspapers which he says are behind the "war-scare" talk [about bolder naval deployments and possible war in the Pacific with a Japan infuriated by California's discriminatory legislation against Japanese immigrants]. To quote from his remarks given in the press accounts:

"The world is learning that back of much of the furor for war, back of much of the stirring of the passions of the people, is the interest in armor-plate and in battle-ships on the part of corporations whose business it is to build those battle-ships and to make this armor-plate. It has even been found that men in one country will spend the money to stir up in another country a feeling against their own country. If you can think of a baser use of money than that you will have an inventive genius of which you may be proud.

"Not only that, but I believe that with a larger intelligence the people will begin to discriminate between patriotic newspapers and newspapers which are more interested in big headlines and sensational news than in the spread of truth."

The new and "refreshing thing" in all this, according to the New York *Evening Post*, "is to have a Secretary of State, especially concerned as he is in maintaining friendly relations with other countries, take the public into his confidence and courageously point out the selfish and insidious enemies of peace."

·　·　·　·　·

DOCUMENT 10

Elihu Root's Nobel Peace Prize Speech on the
Peace Movement and International Law (1914)

Editor's Note: Elihu Root, 1845–1937, a corporation and international lawyer, was one of the leading conservative, legal internationalists of the early twentieth century. The Wall Street attorney served as secretary of war, 1899–1904; secretary of state, 1905–1909; U.S. senator, 1909–1915; member, Permanent Court of Arbitration, 1910–1937; president, board of trustees, Carnegie Endowment for International Peace, 1910–1925; head of mission to revolutionary Russia, 1917; member of the advisory committee which drafted the plan for the World Court, 1920; and commissioner to the Washington Disarmament Conference, 1921–1922. In 1914, Root gave the following acceptance speech as the recipient of the Nobel Peace Prize for 1912, awarded for his support of The Hague peace conferences, his negotiation of a number of limited arbitration treaties, and his role in the creation of the permanent court for the Central American states in 1907 and defusing the war scare with Japan that same year. Root represented the most conservative elements associated with the American peace movement, as attested in his references in this speech to his beliefs in the innate aggressiveness of man, the social Darwinistic application of "survival of the fittest" to human society, and only the possibility of glacially slow progress in the improvement of international relations.

Nobel Peace Prize Address

. . . [T]he continual recurrence of war and the universally increasing preparations for war based upon expectation of it among nations all of

Source: Robert Scott and James Brown, eds., *Addresses on International Subjects by Elihu Root* (Cambridge, Mass.: Harvard Univ. Press, 1916), 153–74.

whom declare themselves in favor of peace, indicate that intellectual acceptance of peace doctrine is not sufficient to control conduct, and that a general feeling in favor of peace, however sincere, does not furnish a strong enough motive to withstand the passions which lead to war when a cause of quarrel has arisen. The methods of peace propaganda which aim at establishing peace doctrine by argument and by creating a feeling favorable to peace in general, seem to fall short of reaching the springs of human action and of dealing with the causes of the conduct which they seek to modify. . . .

. . . . .

. . . The limitation upon this mode of promoting peace lies in the fact that it consists in an appeal to the civilized side of man, while war is the product of forces proceeding from man's original savage nature. To deal with the true causes of war one must begin by recognizing as of prime relevancy to the solution of the problem the familiar fact that civilization is a partial, incomplete, and, to a great extent, superficial modification of barbarism. . . . War was forced upon mankind in his original civil and social condition. The law of the survival of the fittest led inevitably to the survival and predominance of the men who were effective in war and who loved it because they were effective. War was the avenue to all that mankind desired. . . . Nobody knows through how many thousand of years fighting men have made a place for themselves while the weak and peaceable have gone to the wall. Love of fighting was bred in the blood of the race, because those who did not love fighting were not suited to their environment and perished.

. . . . .

. . . To eradicate or modify or curb the tendencies which thus survive among civilized men is not a matter of intellectual conviction or training. It is a matter primarily of development of character and the shifting of standards of conduct—a long, slow process in which advance is to be measured, not by days and years but by generations and centuries in the life of nations.

The attractive idea that we can now have a parliament of man with authority to control the conduct of nations by legislation or an international police force with power to enforce national conformity to rules of right conduct is a counsel of perfection. The world is not ready for any such thing, and it cannot be made ready except by the practical surrender of the independence of nations, which lies at the basis of the present social organization of the civilized world. Such a system would mean that each nation was liable to be lawfully controlled and coerced by a majority of alien powers.

. . . . .

To help in the most practical and efficient way towards making peace permanent, it is needful to inquire with some analysis what are the specific motives and impulses, the proximate causes which, under the present conditions of the civilized world, urge nations to the point where the war passion seizes upon them. And then we should inquire what are the influences which naturally tend or may be made to tend towards checking the impulse, destroying the motive, preventing the proximate cause, before passion has become supreme and it is too late.

. . . . .

The first and most obvious cause for international controversy which suggests itself is in the field of international rights and obligations. . . . Upon all these there are continually arising controversies as to what are the true facts; what is the rule of international law applicable to the case; what is the true interpretation of the treaty; what is just and fair under the circumstances.

. . . . .

In this field the greatest advance is being made towards reducing and preventing in a practical and effective way the causes of war, and this advance is proceeding along several different lines. . . . There have been occasional international arbitrations from very early times, but arbitration as a system, a recognized and customary method of diplomatic procedure rather than an exceptional expedient, had its origin in the Hague Conference of 1899.

. . . . .

Plainly, the next advance to be urged along this line is to pass on from an arbitral tribunal, the members of which are specifically selected from the general list of the court for each case, and whose service is but an incident in the career of a diplomatist or a publicist, to a permanent court composed of judges who devote their entire time to the performance of judicial duties and proceed in accordance with a sense of judicial obligation, not to adjust or compromise differences, but to decide upon rights in accordance with the facts and the law.

Long steps in this direction were made in the Second Hague Conference by the convention for the establishment of a permanent international prize court [for cases involving confiscated ships and cargoes] and by the formulation and adoption of a draft convention relative to the creation of a general judicial arbitration court.

. . . . .

The second line of advance in this same field of international controversy is in pressing forward the development of international law and the agreement of nations upon its rules.

. . . . .

In this direction also great progress has been made within recent years. . . . That method has developed into the action of the two Hague Conferences of 1899 and 1907, which were really law–making bodies, establishing, by the unanimous vote of the powers, rules of conduct for the future, covering extensive portions of the field of international conduct.

. . . . .

Further Hague conferences should be insisted upon. They should be made to recur at regular periods without requiring the special initiative of any country. The process of formulating and securing agreement upon rules of international law should be pressed forward in every direction.

There is a third line of progress, little, if any, less important than the two already mentioned, and that is, the instruction of students and of the great bodies of the people of civilized countries in the knowledge of international law. Under the modern development of constitutional governments, with varying degrees of extension of suffrage, more and more the people who cast the ballots determine the issues of peace and war. No government now embarks in war without the assurance of popular support. It is not uncommon in modern times to see governments straining every nerve to keep the peace, and the people whom they represent, with patriotic enthusiasm and resentment over real or fancied wrongs urging them forward to war. . . . To meet this tendency there should be not merely definite standards of law to be applied to international relations, but there should be general public understanding of what those standards are. . . . To attain this end much has been done and much is in contemplation. Societies of international law have been formed. . . . Many journals of international law have been established and are rapidly increasing their circulation and influence.

. . . . .

There is, however, another class of substantive causes of war which the agencies I have described do not reach directly. This comprises acts done or demanded in pursuance of national policy, and ordinarily either for the enlargement or protection of territory or for trade or industrial advantage. . . . Illustrations of this kind of question are to be found in the protean forms of the Eastern question and of the balance of power in Europe, in the assertion of the Monroe Doctrine by the United States. . . . The independence of a state involves that state's right to determine its own domestic policy and to decide what is essential to its own safety.

It does not follow, however, that we are without opportunity to promote and strengthen specific influences tending to diminish or prevent causes of war of this description. In the first place, when there is a policy of intentional aggression, inspired by a desire to get possession of the territory or the trade of another country, right or wrong, a pretext is always sought. . . . The frank and simple days of the Roman proconsul and of the robber baron have passed, and three things have happened: first, there has come to be a public opinion of the world; second, that opinion has set up a new standard of national conduct which condemns unjustified aggression; and third, the public opinion of the world punishes the violation of its standard. It has not been very long since the people of each country were concerned almost exclusively with their own affairs, and, with but few individual exceptions, neither knew nor cared what was going on outside their own boundaries. All that has changed. The spread of popular education; the enormous increase in the production and circulation of newspapers and periodicals and cheap books; the competition of the press, which ranges the world for news; the telegraph, which carries instantly knowledge of all important events everywhere to all parts of the world; the new mobility of mankind, which availing itself of the new means of travel by steamship and railroad . . . ; the vast extension of international commerce; the recognition of interdependence of the peoples of different nations engendered by this commerce and this intercourse; their dependence upon each other for the supply of their needs and for the profitable disposal of their products, for the preservation of health, for the promotion of morals and for the increase of knowledge and the advance of thought;—all these are creating an international community of knowledge and interest, of thought and feeling. . . . True, we are but at the beginning but it is the beginning of a great new era in which the public opinion of mankind renders judgment . . . upon the just and unjust conduct of nations, as the public opinion of each community passes upon the just and unjust conduct of its individual members. The chief force which makes for peace and order in the community of individuals is not the police officer, with his club, but it is the praise and blame, the honor and shame, which follow observance or violation of the community's standards of right conduct.

. . . . .

Two conclusions from all these considerations are quite obvious: first, that the development and understanding of international law and the habit of submitting international controversies to judicial decision will continually tend to hinder wanton aggression, because it will tend to make it more difficult to find pretexts, excuses, or justification. Second, that quite apart from argument and exhortation concerning war and peace, there is a specific line of effort along which those who seek to promote peace may most usefully proceed; by insisting upon a willingness to do justice among nations, and this, not justice according to the possibly excited and warped opinion of the particular nation, but according to the general public judgment of the civilized world. . . .

. . . . .

Yet there are other influences tending in the same direction which may be usefully promoted. The self–interest which so often prompts nations to unjust aggression can no longer safely assume that its apparent profit is real; for a nation which has been built up by the industry and enterprise of its people, which depends upon its products and the marketing of them, upon its commerce and the peaceful intercourse of commerce for its prosperity, the prize of aggression must be rich indeed to counterbalance the injury sustained by the interference of war with both production and commerce. At the same time, freedom of trade regardless of political control is diminishing the comparative value of extension of territory. The old system of exploitation of colonies and the monopolization of their trade for the benefit of the mother country has practically disappeared. The best informed men are coming to understand that, under modern conditions, the prosperity of each nation is enhanced by the prosperity of all other nations; and that the government which acquires political control over new territory may gratify pride and minister to ambition, but can have only a slight effect to advance the welfare of its people.

. . . . .

Prejudice and passion and suspicion are more dangerous than the incitement of self-interest or the most stubborn adherence to real differences of opinion regarding rights. In private life more quarrels arise, more implacable resentment is caused, more lives are sacrificed, because of insult than because of substantial injury. And it is so with nations.

The remedy is the same. When friends quarrel we try to dissipate their misunderstandings, to soften their mutual feelings, and to bring them together in such a way that their friendship may be renewed. Misunderstanding and prejudice and dislike are, as a rule, the fruits of isolation. There is so much of good in human nature that men grow to like each other upon better acquaintance, and this points to another way in which we may strive to promote the peace of the world. That is, by international conciliation through intercourse . . . the intercourse of real acquaintance, of personal knowledge, of little courtesies and kindly consideration; by the exchange of professors between universities, by the exchange of students between countries; by the visits to other countries on the part of leaders of opinion . . . ; by the spreading of correct information through the press; . . . by cooperation in the multitude of causes which are world–wide in their interest; . . . and by constant pressure in the right direction in a multitude of ways—a slow process, but one which counts little by little if persisted in.

．　．　．　．　．

There are many reasons to believe that progress toward the permanent prevalence of peace may be more rapid in the future than in the past.

Standards of conduct are changing in many ways unfavorable to war.

Civilized man is becoming less cruel. Cruelty to men and to the lower animals as well, which would have passed unnoticed a century ago, now shocks the sensibilities and is regarded as wicked and degrading. The severity of punishments for minor offenses which formerly prevailed now seems to us revolting. The torture of witnesses or of criminals has become unthinkable. Human life is held in much higher esteem and the taking of it, whether in private quarrel or by judicial procedure, is looked upon much more seriously than it was formerly. . . . The Hague Conventions to regulate the conduct of war and the Geneva Conventions to ameliorate its horrors have a significance which goes beyond their professions. . . . The growth of modern constitutional government compels for its successful practice the exercise of reason and considerate judgment by the individual citizens who constitute the electorate. The qualities thus evoked in the training schools of domestic affairs are the qualities which make for national self–restraint and peace in international affairs. History is being rewritten, and the progress of popular education is making men familiar with it. . . . Taken all in all the clear and persistent tendencies of a slowly developing civilization justify cheerful hope.

. . . . .

yet this before bloodiest century in history!

PART TWO

Responding to War in Europe and Revolution in Mexico, 1914 to 1917

DOCUMENT NO. 11

The Reverend John Haynes Holmes on War and the Jeopardy to Social Reform (1914)

Editor's Note: John Haynes Holmes, 1879–1964, was a Harvard trained Unitarian minister, social-gospel clergyman, radical religious pacifist, and pastor of New York's Church of the Messiah from 1907 to 1919. He helped found the National Association for the Advancement of Colored People in 1909, the American Union Against Militarism in 1915, the American Civil Liberties Union in 1917–1920, became a leading champion of Gandhian nonviolent struggle beginning in the 1920s, and much later participated in the first protests against the U.S. involvement in the Vietnam War in 1963. The following article was published in September 1914 in The Survey, *a magazine of social work and social reform.*

War and the Social Movement

In the storm and stress of the stupendous conflict now raging in Europe, it is inevitable that our attention should be absorbed by the more obvious horrors of the situation. Captured cities, burning harvest fields, desolate homes, bleeding men, weeping women and children— these are the things which are holding our interests to the exclusion of everything else. Yet there must be quiet moments, now and then, when we see more clearly and think more deeply than is possible in the hours of reading newspapers and watching bulletin boards.

Then it is that we begin to understand that there is a calamity in this warfare which is more permanently terrible than any of the surface incidents of the struggle. I refer to the awful fact that suddenly, as in the wink of an eye, three hundred years of progress is cast into the melting-pot. Civilization is all at once gone, and barbarism come. . . .

As Harold Begbie [an American poet] put it recently, "Already now civilization stops—stops dead. . . . Religion, philosophy, literature, painting, and, chief of all perhaps, science, with its torch at the head of our human hosts, are suddenly flung backward; they become of no moment. . . . Who bothers about books and pictures? Who is ready to

Source: John Haynes Holmes, "War and the Social Movement," *Survey* 32 (Sept. 26, 1914): 629–30.

endow a laboratory or listen to the chemist and the biologist?" And who, we may add here, cares a fig about the social movement?

．　．　．　．　．

For who is talking in England today about national insurance, woman suffrage, or the breaking of the land monopoly? Who is interested in the enactment of the plural voting bill? What chance has Lloyd-George [David Lloyd George, 1863–1945, liberal chancellor of the exchequer in Great Britain, 1908–1915; prime minister, 1916–1922] of living to complete his program of social legislation? Where is the campaign for franchise reform in Germany? Who cares about co-operation in Belgium, or syndicalism in France, or socialism anywhere? Is there an international labor movement any longer; and if there can be said to be such a movement, what does it amount to?

Nor is it only in the countries immediately concerned in this awful struggle that the social movement has vanished. We are three thousand miles away from the smoke and flame of combat, and have not a single regiment or battleship involved. And yet—who in these United States is thinking at this moment of recreation centers, improved housing, or the minimum wage? Who is going to fight the battle for widows' pensions, push the campaign against child labor, or study exhaustively the problem of unemployment?. . . What are the suffragists going to do to stir a ripple of interest in their cause? . . .

Nor can we hope for any revival of the social movement with the conclusion of the war. If, as now seems probable, the nations fight to the point of exhaustion, the question facing the world at the conclusion of peace will not be that of social progress at all, but simply and solely that of social survival!

．　．　．　．　．

The situation is terrible! And yet, may it not be that this calamity, like every calamity, will work at last to final and universal good?

．　．　．　．　．

From this moment on, every lover of civilization and servant of human kind—the social worker first among them all—must be a *peace fanatic*. He must seek for nothing before this, care for nothing above this, strive for everything through this. He must fight war as Cato fought Carthage, as Voltaire fought *L'enfame*, as [William Lloyd] Garrison fought slavery.

Nor must he be content to urge this fight in the dilettante, academic, pink-tea, high-brow way too much practiced hitherto by the organized peace movement. He must join forces, without apology or reserve with Labor, and strike straight and sure not so much at war, as at the things which make war—first, militarism; second, political autocracy; and third, commercialism. The axe must be laid at the roots of the tree—which are armaments, dynasties, and exploitation.

. . . . .

DOCUMENT 12

Hamilton Holt Urges U.S. Leadership
in Creating a League of Peace (1914)

Editor's Note: After the outbreak of World War I, Hamilton Holt added to his earlier proposals for disarmament and a League of Peace (see document 6) a need for collective security against aggressor nations and a plea for U.S. leadership in creating a league after the war. As a result, Holt helped create the association for a League to Enforce Peace in 1916 (see document 21) and championed Woodrow Wilson's covenant for a League of Nations in 1919 and 1920 (see document 45).

The Way to Disarm: A Practical Proposal

In his famous essay, *Perpetual Peace,* published in 1795, Emmanuel Kant, perhaps the greatest intellect the world has ever produced, declared that we never can have universal peace until the world is politically organized and it will never be possible to organize the world politically until the people, not the kings, rule.

If this be the true philosophy of peace then when the Great War is over, and the stricken sobered peoples set about to rear a new civiliza-

Source: Hamilton Holt, "The Way to Disarm: A Practical Proposal," *Independent* 79 (Sept. 28, 1914): 427–29.

tion on the ashes of the old, they cannot hope to banish war from the earth unless they are prepared to extend democracy everywhere, and to organize the international realm on a basis of law rather than force.

The question of the extension of democracy is a domestic one. It can hardly be settled by joint action of the nations. World organization and disarmament, however, can be provided for in the terms of peace or by international agreement thereafter. As the United States seems destined to play an important part in the great reconstruction at the end of the war, this is perhaps the most important question now before American statesmanship.

The only two powers that ever have governed or ever can govern human beings are reason and force—law and war. If we do not have the one we must have the other.

. . . . .

But now the Great War has come upon us. "When the storm is spent and the desolation is complete; when the flower of the manhood of Europe has past into eternal night; when famine and pestilence have taken their tithe of childhood and age," will then the exhausted and beggared that live on be able to undertake the task of establishing that World Government . . . ?

If it can be done at all it can only be done in one of two ways.

First. By building on the foundations already laid at The Hague the Federation of the World.

Second. By establishing a Great Confederation or League of Peace, composed of those few nations who thru political evolution or the suffering of war have at last seen the light and are ready here and now to disarm.

It is obvious that the time is scarcely ripe for voluntary and universal disarmament by joint agreement. There are too many medieval-minded nations still in existence. The Federation of the World must still be a dream for many years to come. It must be developed slowly, step by step.

The immediate establishment of a League of Peace, however, would in fact constitute a first step toward world federation and does not offer insuperable difficulties.

. . . . .

The problem of the League of Peace is therefore the problem of the use of force. Force internationally exprest [*The Independent* used a particularly idiosyncratic "simplified" spelling style] is measured in ar-

maments. The chief discussion which has been waged for the past decade between the pacifists and militarists has been over the question of
armaments. The militarists claim that armaments insure national safety.
The pacifists declare they inevitably lead to war. Both disputants insist
that the present war furnishes irrefutable proof of their contentions.

As is usual in cases of this kind the shield has two sides. The confu-
sion has arisen from a failure to recognize the threefold function of
force:

1. Force used for the maintenance of order—police force.
2. Force used for attack—aggression.
3. Force used to neutralize aggression—defense.

Police force is almost wholly good.

Offense is almost wholly bad.

Defense is a necessary evil, and exists simply to neutralize force
employed for aggression.

The problem of the peace movement is how to abolish the use of
force for aggression, and yet to maintain it for police purposes. Force
for defense will of course automatically cease when force for aggression
is abolished.

The chief problem then of a League of Peace is this: Shall the members of the League "not only keep the peace themselves, but prevent by
force if necessary its being broken by others," as ex-President [Theodore]
Roosevelt suggested in his Nobel Peace Address delivered at Christiania,
[Oslo, Norway] May 5, 1910? Or shall its force be exercized only
within its membership and thus be on the side of law and order and
never on the side of arbitrary will or tyranny? Or shall it never be used
at all? Whichever one of these conceptions finally prevails the Great
War has conclusively demonstrated that as long as War Lords exist
defensive force must be maintained. Hence the League of Peace must be
prepared to use force against any nations which will not forswear force.
Nevertheless a formula must be devised for disarmament. For unless it
is a law of nature that war is to consume all the fruits of progress
disarmament some how and some way must take place. How then can
the maintenance of a force for defense and police power be reconciled
with the theory of disarmament?

In this way: Let the League of Peace be formed on the following five
principles:

First. The nations of the League shall mutually agree to respect the
territory and sovereignty of each other.

Second. All questions that cannot be settled by diplomacy shall be
arbitrated.

Third. The nations of the League shall provide a periodical assembly to make all rules to become law unless vetoed by a nation within a stated period.

Fourth. The nations shall disarm to the point where the combined forces of the League shall be a certain per cent higher than those of the most heavily armed nation or alliance outside the League. Detailed rules for this pro rata disarmament shall be formulated by the Assembly.

Fifth. Any member of the League shall have the right to withdraw on due notice, or may be expelled by the unanimous vote of the others.

The advantages that a nation would gain in becoming a member of such a league are manifest. The risk of war would be eliminated within the League. Obviously the only things that are vital to a nation are its land and its independence. Since each nation in the League will have pledged itself to respect the territory and the sovereignty of every other, a refusal to do so will logically lead to expulsion from the League. Thus every vital question will be automatically reserved from both war and arbitration. All other questions are of secondary importance and can readily be arbitrated.

By the establishment of a periodical assembly method would be devised whereby the members of the League could develop their common intercourse and interests as far and as fast as they could unanimously agree upon ways and means. As any law could be vetoed by a single nation, no nation could have any fear that it would be coerced against its will by a majority vote of the other nations. By such an assembly the League might in time agree to reduce tariffs and postal rates and in a thousand other ways promote commerce and comity among its members.

As a final safeguard against coercion by the other members of the League, each member will have the right of secession on due notice. This would prevent civil war within the League. The right of expulsion by the majority will prevent one nation by its veto power indefinitely blocking all progress of the League.

But it will be said that all these agreements will have no binding effect in a crisis. A covenant is a mere "scrap of paper" [the term Germany had used in dismissing its treaty with Belgium when it invaded that country in 1914] whose provisions will be violated by the first nation which fancies it is its interest to do so. In order to show that their faith is backed up by deeds, however, the nations on entering the League agree to disarm to a little above the danger point, and put all their defensive power under a federal authority. This is the real proof of their conversion to the peace idea.

Thus the nations which join the League will enjoy all the economic and political advantages which come from mutual cooperation and the extension of international friendship and at the same time will be protected by an adequate force against the aggressive force of the greatest nation or alliance outside the League. The League therefore reconciles the demand of the pacifists for the limitation of armaments and eventual disarmament and the demand of the militarists for the protection that armament affords. Above all the establishment of such a League will give the liberal parties in the nations outside the League an issue on which they can attack their governments so as sooner or later to force them to apply to the League for membership. As each one enters there will be another pro rata reduction of the military forces of the League down to the armament of the next most powerful nation or alliance outside it; until finally the whole world is federated in a brotherhood of universal peace and armies and navies are reduced to an international police force.

This is the plan for a League of Peace. Is the hour about to strike when it can be realized?

. . . . .

It would seem to be the manifest destiny of the United States to lead in the establishment of such a League. The United States is the world in miniature. The United States is the greatest league of peace known to history. The United States is a demonstration to the world that all the races and peoples of the earth can live in peace under one form of government, and its chief value to civilization is a demonstration of what this form of government is.

Prior to the formation "of a more perfect union" our original thirteen states were united in a confederacy strikingly similar to that now proposed on an international scale. They were obliged by the articles of this confederacy to respect each other's territory and sovereignty, to arbitrate all questions among themselves, to assist each other against any foreign foe, not to engage in war unless called upon by the confederation to do so or actually invaded by a foreign foe, and not to maintain armed forces in excess of the strength fixed for each state by all the states in congress assembled.

It is notable that security against aggression from states inside or outside the American Union accompanied the agreement to limit armaments. Thus danger of war and size of armaments were decreased contemporaneously.

. . . . .

When the Great War is over and the United States is called upon to lead the nations in reconstructing a new order of civilization, why might not Woodrow Wilson do on a world scale something similar to what George Washington did on a continental scale?

Stranger things than this have happened in history. Let us add to the Declaration of Independence a Declaration of Interdependence.

DOCUMENT 13

Emmeline Pethick Lawrence Addresses Americans
on "Motherhood and War" (1914)

Editor's Note: Emmeline Pethick Lawrence, 1867–1954, English suffragist and pacifist leader, was in frequent contact with Americans on these issues—as were many British reformers. She made several visits to the United States on behalf of these causes, and her speeches and writings received considerable attention among liberal activists. Her ideas on the special relationship of women and peace, reprinted below from a prominent American magazine in December 1914, were widely echoed among feminists and other reformers in the United States.

Motherhood and War

From time to time the current of the world's life is quickened by some new stream that is poured into it. The emergence of the middle class into political life wrought a commercial revolution in Great Britain. The emancipation of the working classes changed the national outlook upon many industrial and social questions. Today the new force that is entering into the woman's life is that of an awakened and still rapidly awakening womanhood.

At the very moment that this new force has been generated, the whole world is standing aghast at the contemplation of its own disruption. We are witnessing in the present European War something that resembles a "twilight of the gods" the passing away in blood and fire of

Source: Emmeline Pethick Lawrence, "Motherhood and War," *Harper's Weekly* 59 (Dec. 5, 1914): 542.

an epoch. It is from the ruins that a new civilization will have to be built up.

. . . . .

But what kind of peace will it be when it comes? That is the question. Who is going to determine it? Who will arrange its conditions? Everything depends upon that. If the same people who by secret diplomacies brought war upon Europe, without the consent, without even the knowledge of their respective democracies, settle in this same way the conditions of peace, then the new peace will only be once again the prelude of a new war, which will ensue some generations hence and will be vaster and more destructive even than the present colossal conflict.

It has been claimed that the aim of the present war is to end war. But war cannot end war, neither can militarism destroy militarism. The only thing that can end war is the birth of a new spirit, embodied in a constructive peace hitherto new to the world. It is possible that even now, amongst the non-combatants of the world, a new spirit may find embodiment in some great organization that may bring influence to bear upon this question when the opportune moment comes.

There are only two forces that can withstand the force of the war's spirit when it seizes upon the world. The one is the force of an independently thinking, free, and articulate democracy. The other is the force of an instructed and enlightened public opinion.

But the democracies, one and all, are utterly impotent in present conditions to inspire, or to criticise, or to direct the foreign policy of their respective nationalities. This condition of things must be brought to an end and some constitutional machinery must be found for the future exercise of democratic control of foreign policy. International treaties and alliances should not be ratified without the consent of the peoples whose destinies they control. In this, and in many other respects, the new epoch must see the rise of a reinforced democracy.

The new force of the woman's movement should be seized upon to further this end. It is vital to the deepest interests of the human race that the mother half of humanity should now be admitted into the ranks of the articulate democracies of the world, in order to strengthen them and to enable them to combine the more effectively in their own defense against the deadly machinery of organized destruction that threatens in the future to crush the white races and to overwhelm civilization.

The bed-rock of humanity is motherhood. The solidarity of the world's motherhood, potential or otherwise, underlies all cleavages of nationality. Men have conflicting interests and ambitions. Women all the world over, speaking broadly, have one passion and one vocation, and that is the creation and preservation of human life. Deep in the hearts of the women of the peasant and industrial classes of every nation, there lies beneath their readiness to endure their full share of their nations' toll of sacrifice and suffering, a denial of the necessity of war. There is a rooted revolt against the destruction of the blossoming manhood of the race. This revolt is now for the first time finding expression, as the race soul of the womanhood of the world comes in this twentieth century to consciousness. The woman's movement has awakened women to their great responsibilities as the natural custodians of the human race. It is vital to the interests of the human race itself that the mother half of humanity should now be admitted to articulate citizenship. The emancipation of women must be included in the program of those who would lay a broad foundation of constructive peace for the rebuilding of the modern world.

It would be a great thing if the woman's movement all over the world should enter now upon a great organized campaign of preparation for peace, allying itself with all the other forces now at work in the same direction and setting itself the task, first, in the great neutral nation of America, and then, in all other countries, of awakening and educating public opinion with regard to the supreme value of human life and of racial evolution. Peace movements in the past have been negative. That is where they have failed.

Since public opinion cannot be educated solely by words, such a campaign, if started, should be linked with certain definite propositions to be decided upon in conference between the men and women who should initiate it. These propositions should be urged as some of the conditions of constructive peace. I tabulate by way of illustration the following suggestions that civilized peoples should unite in demanding from their respective countries:

First, the broadening and strengthening of the democracies by the admission of the mother-half of the human race into the body politic.

Second, the creation, where none already exists, of some adequate machinery for insuring democratic control of foreign policy.

Third, the assurance that no treaty arrangement or undertaking be entered upon, in the name of the country, without the sanction of the people concerned expressed through their representatives.

Fourth, that the manufacture of armaments and ammunition be taken over by the nation itself, and that the export of armaments to other countries be prohibited.

Fifth, that at the termination of the war, the influence of the nation be used to discourage the transfer of any of the European provinces from one government to another without the consent by plebiscite of the population of such province, and that the plebiscite should include the women who have borne the burden of suffering equally with the men.

Sixth, that there should be some representation of women at the Hague conference.

In addition to such concrete proposals as these, public opinion has to be enlightened and organized towards the ideal of international agreement. "We must labor," as says ex-President [Theodore] Roosevelt, "for an international agreement among the great civilized nations which shall put the full force of all of them, back of anyone of them, and of any well-behaved weak nation which is wronged by any other power."

By the initiation throughout the [United] States of a popular campaign carried out upon lines indicated by these suggestions, led by influential men and women, aided by the President, reinforced by great public meetings, America would give a much needed lead to the democracies of Europe.

The better, happier world that we hope for in the future must be built up by the people themselves, upon the foundations of a constructive, lasting peace. This task cannot be left to the detached and secret agencies of Governments. It should be begun now. There is not a moment to lose.

DOCUMENT 14

Formation and Platform of the Woman's Peace Party (1915)

Editor's Note: The Woman's Peace party (WPP) was organized on January 10, 1915, in Washington, D.C., by representatives of more than a dozen women's groups, including suffragist, social work, educational, genealogical, temperance, trade union, and peace organizations. Critical of seemingly ineffectual male-dominated traditional peace societies, the women formed the WPP in direct response to pleas by two visiting foreign feminists and peace activists, Emmeline Pethick Lawrence of Britain and Rosika Schwimmer, 1877–1948, of Hungary. The two visitors, one from the Allies and one from the Central Powers, urged the American women to organize a group which could discuss reasonable peace terms, promote a conference of neutral nations to call for peace and perhaps help mediate an end to the war, and protest against war as a means of settling international disputes.

The leaders of the conference were Carrie Chapman Catt, 1859–1947, the preeminent leader of the American suffragist movement in the first two decades of the twentieth century and an active if moderate peace activist in the 1920s and early 1930s; and Jane Addams, 1860–1935, founder of Hull House in Chicago, leader of the settlement house and social work movement in the United States, and prominent pacifist. The conference elected Addams president of the WPP and adopted a platform similar to that of the liberal British Union for Democratic Control. The WPP platform adopted at the January 1915 meeting called for neutral mediation, limitation of armaments, democratic control of foreign policy, elimination of the economic causes of war, and extension of the vote to women.

Addresses Given at the Organization Conference of the Woman's Peace Party

MRS. CARRIE CHAPMAN CATT, of New York, presided over this meeting, which she opened with the following statement:

"This meeting has been called as a part of a conference of women held in Washington to review the general situation concerning the great problem of peace, and looking to a national, and probably international, organization among women. The women of this country were lulled into inattention to the great military question of the war by reading the many books put forth by great pacifists who had studied the question deeply and who announced that there never could be another world war. But when the great war came, and the women of this country waited for the pacifists to move, and they heard nothing from them, they decided all too late to get together themselves and to try to do something at this eleventh hour."

MRS. ANNA GARLIN SPENCER [educator and ordained minister, representing the American Peace Society] then presented the preamble with the platform.

Source: *Addresses Given at the Organization Conference of the Woman's Peace Party, Washington, D.C., January 10, 1915* (Chicago: Woman's Peace Party Headquarters [1915]), pamphlet located in the Woman's Peace Party Papers, Swarthmore College Peace Collection.

Preamble

WE, WOMEN OF THE UNITED STATES, assembled in behalf of World Peace, grateful for the security of our own country, but sorrowing for the misery of all involved in the present struggle among warring nations, do hereby band ourselves together to demand that war be abolished.

Equally with men pacifists, we understand that planned-for, legalized, wholesale, human slaughter is today the sum of all villainies.

As women, we feel a peculiar moral passion of revolt against both the cruelty and the waste of war.

As women, we are especially the custodians of the life of the ages. We will not longer consent to its reckless destruction.

As women, we are particularly charged with the future of childhood and with the care of the helpless and the unfortunate. We will not longer endure without protest that added burden of maimed and invalid men and poverty stricken widows and orphans which war places upon us.

As women, we have builded by the patient drudgery of the past the basic foundation of the home and of peaceful industry. We will not longer endure without a protest that must be heard and heeded by men, that hoary evil which in an hour destroys the social structure that centuries of toil have reared.

As women, we are called upon to start each generation onward toward a better humanity. We will not longer tolerate without determined opposition that denial of the sovereignty of reason and justice by which war and all that makes for war today render impotent the idealism of the race.

Therefore, as human beings and the mother half of humanity, we demand that our right to be consulted in the settlement of question concerning not alone the life of individuals but of nations be recognized and respected.

We demand that women be given a share in deciding between war and peace in all the courts of high debate—within the home, the school, the church, the industrial order, and the state.

So protesting, and so demanding, we hereby form ourselves into a national organization to be called the Woman's Peace Party.

. . . . .

PLATFORM

THE PURPOSE of this Organization is to enlist all American women in arousing the nations to respect the sacredness of human life and to abolish war. The following is adopted as our platform:

1. The immediate calling of a convention of neutral nations in the interest of early peace.

2. Limitation of armaments and the nationalization of their manufacture.

3. Organized opposition to militarism in our own country.

4. Education of youth in the ideals of peace.

5. Democratic control of foreign policies.

6. The further humanizing of governments by the extension of the franchise to women.

7. "Concert of Nations" to supersede "Balance of Power."

8. Action toward the gradual organization of the world to substitute Law for War.

9. The substitution of an international police for rival armies and navies.

10. Removal of the economic cause of war.

11. The appointment by our Government of a commission of men and women, with an adequate appropriation, to promote international peace.

The following speakers were introduced by Mrs. Catt:

MRS. CHARLOTTE PERKINS GILMAN, [1860–1935, leading feminist and socialist author and lecturer] of New York:

I think we are all of one mind as to the general purpose or purposes of this convention, but it is of even more importance that we settle upon some single immediate definite possible action, and that we then set in motion large, carefully planned, efficient measures to promote that one action. . . . [that is] the calling of an international conference and calling it quickly. . . . We want it done nationally, officially, governmentally. If at present it is not so done, it remains in the hands of the American people by millions and millions to express their definite will in the matter. To that end, the thing that I want to leave before this house is a suggestion as to active propaganda in the interests of our already established purpose. It is an interesting thing in this country to watch the nation-wide, swift, confident, efficient action of a political party when it wishes to influence public opinion, whether it is on free silver or a gold standard, or any other subject. There is an organized body whose business it is to distribute information, and not only information, but emotional appeal. That sort of work is what has to be done now; to get together and start the definite machinery for distribution through the press, the platform, the pulpit, the college, the school, through every medium of reaching the public that is open to us of as much of this program as they will take, and most especially to have before them all one simple, definite and concrete proposition that no one can object to. Surely that proposition is the one that stands first with us all—the calling of the international conference to discuss measures for the ending of this war and the prevention of further wars. . . . Now, if this simple proposition can be brought before the American public all up and down the land, laid before the women's clubs and the men's associations, and all the great bodies of people, and backed up by the alliance of body after body, having for its signatories not merely individuals, but representative groups; if we can roll up millions upon millions of organized public opinion in America, then surely a representative government will express the will of the people and call as soon as it is humanely possible that conference of representative delegates which alone can take the further measures to promote the end for which we are all gathered here.

. . . . . .

MRS. KATE WALLER BARRETT, President, National Council of Women [a sociologist and philanthropist from Virginia, also national chair of the Congress of Mothers and the Parent-Teacher Association]:

As you know, the National Council of Women of the United States was represented at the international conference at Rome last summer, at which were represented thirty-six national councils, representing all the nations that are now at war, and many of the neutral nations; and it has been my privilege in the last few weeks to receive letters from every one of those organized groups of women. . . . I bring to you the desire expressed by the National Council of Women of the Netherlands that the women of the United States join with them in trying to bring about a federation of Europe similar to the federation of the United States of America. I bring to you an expression of opinion from the women of Switzerland that we do everything possible to bring about the least possible suffering among the women and children and non-combatants and foreigners in the countries that are now at war with each other. I bring to you a plea from the women of Austria, from the women of Hungary, that we unite with them in an effort to stop this war, to end the needless suffering of women and children and non-combatants in the war zone. . . .

MADAME ROSIKA SCHWIMMER, of Budapest, Hungary:

... I wonder whether you realize how great this gratitude is which we feel for the American women who have taught us European women.... By adopting this platform of peace, then by adopting this program for action—for active, not theoretical peace—you have laid down the foundations for a new Europe, for a Europe which seemed to many of us European people as hopelessly broken down....

Our old-fashioned idea was that a man must have the courage to face death, not only for something that is worth dying for, but even for a whim. It is a wonderful thing that you women of the United States are teaching us of the old world, teaching the men of the world that there is a greater courage than the physical one—the courage to stand for a principle, the high human courage.

· · · · ·

MISS JANE ADDAMS, of Chicago:

... [T]here are certain things now being destroyed by war in which from the beginning of time women, as women, have held a vested interest, and I beg to draw your attention to three or four of them.

One thing war is now destroying, and which is being "thrown back" in the scientific sense, is the conception of patriotism gradually built up during thousands of years. Europe has had one revolution after another in which women as well as men have taken part, that a patriotism might be established which should contain liberty as well as loyalty.

At the present moment, however, thousands of men marching to their death are under compulsion, not of this higher type of patriotism, but of a tribal conception which ought to have left the world long since.

A state founded upon such a tribal ideal of patriotism has no place for women within its councils, and women have a right to protest against the destruction of that larger ideal of the state in which they had won a place, and to deprecate a world put back upon a basis of brute force—a world in which they can play no part.

Women also have a vested right in the developed conscience of the world. At this moment, because of war, the finest consciences in Europe are engaged in the old business of self-justification, utilizing outgrown myths to explain the course of action which their governments have taken.

And last, shall we not say that sensitiveness to human life so highly developed in women has been seriously injured by this war....

I do not assert that women are better than men—even in the heat of suffrage debates I have never maintained that—but we would all admit that there are things concerning which women are more sensitive than men, and that one of these is the treasuring of life. I would ask you to consider with me five aspects concerning this sensitiveness, which war is rapidly destroying.

The first is the protection of human life. The advanced nations know very accurately, and we had begun to know in America, how many children are needlessly lost in the first years of infancy. Measures inaugurated for the prevention of infant mortality were slowly spreading from one country to another. All that effort has been scattered to the winds by the war. No one is now pretending to count the babies who are dying throughout the villages and countrysides of the warring nations.

The second aspect is the nurture of human life. From the time a soldier is born to the moment he marches in his uniform to be wantonly destroyed, it is largely the women of his household who have cared for him. War overthrows not only the work of the mother, the nurse and the teacher, but at the same time ruthlessly destroys the very conception of the careful nurture of life.

The third aspect is the fulfillment of human life. Every woman who cares for a little child, fondly throws her imagination forward to the time when he shall have become a great and heroic man. Every baby is thus made human and is developed by the hope and expectation which surrounds him. But no one in Europe in the face of war's destruction can consider any other fulfillment of life than a soldier's death.

The fourth aspect is the conservation of human life; that which expresses itself in the state care of dependent children, in old age pensions, the sentiment which holds that every scrap of human life is so valuable that the human family cannot neglect the feeblest child without risking its own destruction. At this moment, none of the warring countries of Europe can cherish the aged and infirm. The State cannot give care to its dependents when thousands of splendid men are dying each day. Little children and aged people are dying too; in some countries in the proportion of five to one soldier killed on the field; but the nation must remain indifferent to their suffering.

And last of all is that which we call the ascent of human life; that which leads a man to cherish the hope that the next generation shall advance beyond the generation in which he lives; that generous glow we all experience when we see that those coming after us are equipped better than we have been. We know that Europe at the end of this war will not begin to build where it left off; we know that it will begin generations behind the point it had reached when the war began.

If we admit that this sensitiveness for human life is stronger in women than in men because women have been responsible for the care of the young and the aged and those who need special nurture, it is certainly true that this sensitiveness, developed in women, carries with it an obligation.

Once before in the history of the world, in response to this sensitiveness, women called a halt to the sacrifice of human life, although it then implied the abolition of a religious observance long believed to be right and necessary. In the history of one nation after another, it was the mothers who first protested that their children should no longer be slain as living sacrifices upon the altars of the tribal gods, although the national leaders contended the human sacrifice was bound up with the traditions of free religion and patriotism and could not be abolished.

The women led a revolt against the hideous practice which had dogged the human race for centuries, not because they were founding a new religion, but because they were responding to their sensitiveness to life. When at last a brave leader here and there gave heed to the mother of the child, he gradually found that courage and religion were with the abolition of human sacrifice, and that the protesting women had anticipated the conscience of the future.

Many of us believe that throughout this round world of ours there are thousands of men and women who have become convinced that the sacrifice of life in warfare is unnecessary and wasteful. It is possible that if women in Europe—in the very countries which are now at war—receive a message from the women of America solemnly protesting against this sacrifice, that they may take courage to formulate their own.

DOCUMENT 15

Alice Hamilton's Account of the International Congress
of Women at The Hague (1915)

Editor's Note: More than forty American women, most of them members of the Woman's Peace party, met with European feminists, suffragists, and pacifists from more than a dozen countries at an International Congress of Women at The Hague, Holland, April 28 to May 1, 1915.

As a prominent neutral citizen, Jane Addams was elected presiding officer. The conference adopted twenty resolutions, endorsing international arbitration, a society of nations, a peace settlement based on the principle of territorial integrity. The most controversial resolution (submitted by Rosika Schwimmer of Hungary and Julia Grace Wales of the United States) recommended the immediate creation of a continuous conference of neutral nations that would encourage the warring powers to clarify their war aims and that would actively seek to mediate a negotiated peace. Delegations took the resolutions to neutral and belligerent leaders during the next two months. Because they were received kindly at most capitals, the women became convinced that neutral mediation was possible; and several of them later tried, without success, to convince Woodrow Wilson to adopt their mediation plan (see document 18).

Alice Hamilton, 1869–1970, physician, medical professor, reformer, and one of the leading authorities on occupational hazards and industrial diseases in the early twentieth century, was a Hull House resident and a close friend of Jane Addams. In the letter below, she offered first hand reflections on The Hague conference to Addams' closest friend, Mary Rozet Smith.

Alice Hamilton to Mary Rozet Smith

Den Haag
May 5th [1915]

Dear Mary,

I am sitting in the parlor of this very pleasant hotel, surrounded by a crowd of Dutch people, whose language is guttural but whose voices are full and agreeable.

The Congress is over and since Sunday Miss [Jane] Addams has been in sessions of the Resolutions Committee, making the final draft. I wonder how much has been reported to you in the American papers. The Dutch papers are mostly contemptuous, the English sometimes quite nasty. To me it was intensely interesting and sometimes very moving. People are saying now that the German note predominated, that it was a pro-German Congress, but that is true only in the sense that the German women were there in goodly numbers and were an unusually

Source: Letter of Alice Hamilton to Mary Rozet Smith, May 5, 1915, in Barbara Sicherman, *Alice Hamilton: A Life in Letters* (Cambridge, Mass.: Harvard Univ. Press, 1984), 189–90.

fine lot of women, so able and so fair and so full of warmth and generosity. I wish Miss [Amalie] Hannig [of Hull House] could hear them talk, not only the real Germans, but the Hungarians and Austrians. The English were only three, and not even a united three, for Mrs. [Emmeline] Pethick Lawrence was ignored by the two legitimate suffragists, Miss [Kathleen D.] Courtney and Miss [Chrystal] Macmillan. There was a fine Canadian girl there, a niece of Sam Hughes, the Major-General of the Canadian forces. We expected the English delegation to welcome her with joy as an addition to their small numbers, but they were very thoroughly English and evinced no enthusiasm over a Colonial. The Norwegian and Swedish women impressed one very well, but they were the most cautious of all, being in fear all the time lest they do something to violate the neutrality of their countries. Finally there were the Poles and Belgians who were very moving and yet seldom overemotional. Indeed what I felt all the time was the deep undercurrent of emotion, but an admirable self-control. Only Madam [Rosika] Schwimmer could sweep the Congress off its feet and she did it several times, notably at the end when she succeeded in having them pass the resolution which filled most of us with dismay and which you will have seen in the papers, that the resolutions passed by the Congress be presented by a committee to the various Powers. As you will have seen, J. A. [Jane Addams] is one of the delegates to visit all the countries except Russia and Scandinavia. She wants me to go with her and of course I will. To me it seems a singularly fool performance, but I realize that the world is not all Anglo-Saxon and that other people feel very differently.

J. A. was simply wonderful as president. She could not have been better. And Grace Abbott and Miss [Sophonisba] Breckinridge helped her as nobody else could have. I was really lost in admiration of their ability, their clearness and quickness. They are with her in Amsterdam tonight.

· · · · ·

Yours ever
A.H.
[Alice Hamilton]

DOCUMENT 16

Theodore Roosevelt and Woodrow Wilson Differ
over the Proper U.S. Response to the Sinking
of the *Lusitania* (1915)

Editor's Note: On May 7, 1915, the giant British passenger liner,
Lusitania, *was torpedoed by a German submarine off the Irish coast.
The ship sank within eighteen minutes. (It was rumored at the time that
the ship carried munitions, and this was confirmed fifty years later when
the manifest was released showing that the cargo included shrapnel,
fuses, and four million rounds of ammunition). The sudden death of
nearly 1,200 passengers and crew, including 128 U.S. citizens, in the*
Lusitania *disaster brought home to Americans the brutality of modern
war. Although former president Theodore Roosevelt and a few others
wanted the United States to enter the war immediately, the public re-
acted more with shock than anger.*

*Woodrow Wilson decided to respond with diplomatic protests rather
than threats of force. In a speech to newly naturalized citizens in
Philadelpha, he inserted an impromptu paragraph indicating that the
United States should be guided in its response by its moral rectitude and
desire for world peace. The press and the president's hawkish critics,
however, focused on one of Wilson's phrases about a man being "too
proud to fight." From a different perspective, pacifist Secretary of State
William Jennings Bryan resigned over what he considered Wilson's
unneutrality in insisting on Americans' rights to travel on belligerents'
ships in the war zone and in failing to hold the British surface naval
blockade to the same "strict accountability" of the German submarine
blockade. Subsequently, Wilson replaced him with State Department
counselor Robert Lansing. The German government eventually pledged
to stop sinking passenger ships without warning, apologized for the
deaths of the Americans on the* Lusitania, *and paid an indemnity; but
it continued to protest the British blockade of foodstuffs as well as
munitions.*

Roosevelt's Accusation
"Pure Piracy" Statement to Press, May 9, 1915.

Murder on the High Seas

The German submarines have established no effective blockade of the British and French coast lines. They have endeavored to prevent the access of French, British *and neutral* ships to Britain and France by attacks upon them which defy every principle of international law. . . . Many of these attacks have represented pure piracy; and not a few of them have been accompanied by murder on an extended scale. In the case of the *Lusitania* the scale was so vast that the murder became wholesale.

A number of American ships had already been torpedoed in similar fashion. In two cases American lives were lost [one on a British liner and three on an American oil tanker]. When the *Lusitania* sank some twelve hundred non-combatants, men, women and children, were drowned, and more than a hundred of these were Americans. Centuries have passed since any war vessel of a civilized power has shown such ruthless brutality toward non-combatants, and especially toward women and children. The Moslem pirates of the Barbary Coast behaved at times in similar fashion, until the civilized nations joined in suppressing them; and the other pirates who were outcasts from among these civilized nations also at one time perpetrated similar deeds, until they were sunk or hung. But none of these old-time pirates committed murder on so vast a scale as in the case of the *Lusitania*.

The day after the tragedy the newspapers reported in one column that in Queenstown there lay by the score the bodies of women and children, some of the dead women still clasping the bodies of the little children they held in their arms when death overwhelmed them. In another column they reported the glee expressed by the Berlin journals at this "great victory of German naval policy." It was a victory over the defenseless and the unoffending, and its signs and trophies were the bodies of the murdered women and children.

· · · · ·

In the teeth of these things, we earn as a nation measureless scorn and contempt if we follow the lead of those who exact peace above righteousness, if we heed the voices of those feeble folk who bleat to high heaven that there is peace when there is no peace. For many

Source: "Murder on the High Seas" Statement to the press, May 9, 1915, in *Theodore Roosevelt: His Life, Meaning, and Messages,* ed. William Griffith (New York: Current Literature, 1919) 3: 847–52.

months our government has preserved between right and wrong a neutrality which would have excited the emulous admiration of Pontius Pilate—the arch-typical neutral of all time.

· · · · ·

Unless we act with immediate decision and vigor we shall have failed in the duty demanded by humanity at large, and demanded even more clearly by the self-respect of the American Republic.

· · · · ·

[A few days later, Roosevelt gave to the press a specific program of action.]

Without 24 hours' delay this country should and could take effective action. It should take possession of all the interned German ships, including the German warships, and hold them as a guarantee that ample satisfaction shall be given us. Furthermore it should declare that in view of Germany's murderous offenses against the rights of neutrals all commerce with Germany shall be forthwith forbidden and all commerce of every kind permitted and encouraged with France, England, Russia, and the rest of the civilized world.

I do not believe that the firm assertion of our rights means war, but, in any event, it is well to remember there are things worse than war.

Let us as a nation understand that peace is worth having only when it is the hand-maiden of international righteousness and of national self-respect.

· · · · ·

Wilson's Response:
"Too Proud to Fight" Speech, May 10, 1915.

An Address in Philadelphia

... Americans must have a consciousness different from the consciousness of every other nation in the world. I am not saying this with even the slightest thought of criticism of other nations. You know how it is with a family. A family gets centered on itself if it's not careful and

Source: Woodrow Wilson, "An Address in Philadelphia to Newly Naturalized Citizens," May 10, 1915, in *The Papers of Woodrow Wilson,* ed. Arthur S. Link et al. (Princeton: Princeton Univ. Press, 1966–), 33: 149.

is less interested in the neighbors than it is in its own members. So a nation that is not constantly renewed out of new sources is apt to have the narrowness and prejudice of a family, whereas America must have this consciousness—that on all sides it touches elbows and touches hearts with all the nations of mankind. The example of America must be a special example. The example of America must be the example, not merely of peace because it will not fight, but of peace because peace is the healing and elevating influence of the world, and strife is not. There is such a thing as a man being too proud to fight. There is such a thing as a nation being so right that it does not need to convince others by force that it is right.

DOCUMENT 17

The Socialist Party of America, Position Against the War (1915)

Editor's Note: The Socialist party of America, which in the Progressive Era was a broad protest-based political body advocating the achievement through the ballot of democratic socialism in the United States, had won nearly a million votes in the 1912 presidential election, 6 percent of the total cast. At its annual meeting, May 13 to 18, 1915, the party's National Committee publicly deplored the Lusitania *disaster and warned the American people against being stampeded by "jingoes" and "militarists" into a war that it said was "the logical and inevitable outcome of the forces of the capitalist system." The committee also issued the following peace program.*

Peace Program of the Socialist Party

· · · · ·

The immediate causes of the war are obvious. Previous wars and terms of settlement which created lasting hatreds and bred thoughts of

Source: Peace Program of the Socialist Party's National Committee, May 1915, in *The American Socialists and the War*, ed. Alexander Trachtenberg (New York: Rand School of Social Science, 1917), 14–19.

revenge; imperialism and commercial rivalries; the Triple Alliance and the Triple Entente dividing all Europe into two hostile camps; secret intrigue of diplomats and lack of democracy; vast systems of military and naval equipment; fear and suspicion bred and spread by a vicious jingo press in all nations; powerful armament interests that reap rich harvests out of havoc and death, all these have played their sinister parts. But back of these factors lie the deeper and more fundamental causes, causes rooted in the very system of capitalist production.

Every capitalist nation on earth exploits its people. The wages received by the workers are insufficient to enable them to purchase all they need for the proper sustenance of their lives. A surplus of commodities accumulates. The capitalists cannot consume all. It must be exported to foreign countries.

In every capitalist nation it becomes increasingly difficult for the capitalists to re-invest their accumulated profits to advantage in their own country, with their people destitute and their resources fully developed and exploited. The capitalists are constantly forced to look for new and foreign fields of investment.

. . . . .

. . . Hence arise the strategy, the intrigues of secret diplomacy, till all the world is involved in a deadly struggle for the capture and control of the world market.

Thus capitalism, inevitably leading to commercial rivalry and imperialism and functioning through the modern state with its vast armaments, secret diplomacies and undemocratic governments, logically leads to war.

. . . . .

For more than half a century the Socialist movement has warned the world of this impending tragedy. With every power at their command the Socialists of all nations have worked to prevent it. But the warning has gone unheeded and the Socialist propaganda against imperialism, militarism and war has been ignored by the ruling powers and the majority of the people of all nations.

. . . . .

To the Socialist and labor forces in all the world and to all who cherish the ideals of justice, we make our appeal, believing that out of the ashes of this mighty conflagration will yet arise the deeper internationalism and the great democracy and peace.

As measures calculated to bring about these results we urge:

I. Terms of Peace at the Close of the Present War
MUST BE BASED ON THE FOLLOWING PROVISIONS:

1. No indemnities.
2. No transfer of territory except upon the consent and by vote of the people within the territory.
3. All countries under foreign rule be given political independence if demanded by the inhabitants of such countries.

II. International Federation—The United States of the World:

1. An international congress with legislative and administrative powers over international affairs and with permanent committees in place of present secret diplomacy.
2. Special Commissions to consider international disputes as they may arise. The decisions of such commissions to be enforced without resort to arms.
3. International ownership and control of strategic waterways such as the Dardanelles, the Straits of Gibraltar and the Suez, Panama and Kiel Canals.
4. Neutralization of the seas.

III. Disarmament.

1. Universal disarmament as speedily as possible.
2. Abolition of manufacture of arms and munitions of war for private profit, and prohibition of exportation of arms. . . .
3. No increase in existing armaments under any circumstances.
4. No appropriations for military or naval purposes.

IV. Extension of Democracy.

1. Political democracy.
   (a) Abolition of secret diplomacy and democratic control of foreign policies.
   (b) Universal suffrage, including woman suffrage.
2. Industrial democracy.
Radical social changes in all countries to eliminate economic causes for war, such as will be calculated to gradually take the industrial and

commercial processes of the nations out of the hands of the irresponsible capitalist class and place them in the hands of the people, to operate them collectively for the satisfaction of human wants and not for private profits in co-operation and harmony and not through competition and war.

V. IMMEDIATE ACTION.

Immediate and energetic efforts shall be made through the organizations of the Socialist parties of all nations to secure universal co-operation of all Socialist and labor organizations and all true friends of peace to obtain the endorsement of this program.

DOCUMENT 18

Two Representatives from the International Congress of Women
Contact President Wilson about Mediation and Peace (1915)

Woodrow Wilson to Juliet Barrett Rublee, June 2, 1915.

Editor's Note: Juliet Barrett Rublee, pacifist and wife of George L. Rublee, coauthor with Louis D. Brandeis of the Federal Trade Commission Act, had recently returned to Washington, D.C., from the International Congress of Women at The Hague (see document 15). The delegates had adopted resolutions endorsing democratic foreign policy, including the participation of women; international arbitration; a society of nations; and a peace settlement that would be based on principles of territorial integrity. In the most controversial resolution, the delegates proposed a conference of neutrals that would "without delay offer continuous mediation," invite the belligerents to offer terms for settlement, and submit to all of them simultaneously "reasonable proposals as a basis of peace."

Source: Woodrow Wilson to Juliet Barrett Rublee, June 2, 1915, in Link et al., The Papers of Woodrow Wilson 33: 314.

Juliet Barrett Rublee's letter of June 1, 1915, to Woodrow Wilson about the Women's Congress is missing from the president's papers. However, the following copy of Wilson's reply suggests his general admiration for the women's efforts, even though, as evident in the letter from Aletta Jacobs to Jane Addams (following) and his subsequent discussion with members of the American Neutral Conference Committee in August 1916 (see document 23), Wilson avoided any effort to create a league of neutral nations as an instrument to mediate an end to the war.

[The White House] June 2, 1915

My dear Mrs. Rublee:

I thank you sincerely for your very interesting and informing letter of June first. Its contents interest me deeply.

I followed as best I could the action of the women at the Hague and the other day read the resolutions adopted with the greatest interest and admiration.

Cordially and sincerely yours,
Woodrow Wilson

Aletta H. Jacobs to Jane Addams, September 15, 1915.

Editor's Note: Aletta Henriette Jacobs, 1854–1929, Dutch physician, social reformer, feminist, pacifist, and president of the Dutch [Women's] Suffrage Society, had been one of the main initiators of the International Congress of Women at The Hague. Afterwards, Aletta Jacobs and Jane Addams personally presented the congress's resolutions to the heads of government of a number of nations. During Jacobs's visit to the United States in August and September 1915, Jacobs, Carrie Chapman Catt, Emily Greene Balch, and Jane Addams discussed at different times with Secretary of State Robert Lansing, presidential adviser Edward M. "Colonel" House, and President Wilson himself the proposal of the Women's Congress for a "League of Neutral Countries" to serve as a mediating force to bring an end to the war. The following is Jacobs's account of her meeting with the president:

Source: Aletta H. Jacobs to Jane Addams, Sept. 15, 1915, in the Jane Addams Papers, Swarthmore College Peace Collection.

Sept. 15, 1915

Dear Miss Addams,

I saw the President at noon. I told him what I had to say and asked him the several questions. He was very kind and manlike as well as gentleman-like. His answers were very diplomatical. In short it was: "The U.S. were now in such great difficulties with the belligerents that a definite answer in one way or another was impossible. The Pres. was very thankful for the information I brought, but about his attitude towards peace he could not say a word. Every-day that attitude could be changed, according to the circumstances and even a quite unofficial statement in one way or another could bind him in a certain degree. He wants to remain free to act in the best way as he sees the things himself."

. . . . .

I hope to hear soon from you and if there is an opportunity to meet you before I return to Europe. Please give my kind greetings to Miss [Mary Rozet] Smith, Miss [Lillian] Wald will be in N.Y. now, where I hope to meet her soon.

With my best wishes for your health,

Cordially yours,

[signed]   Aletta H. Jacobs

DOCUMENT NO. 19

The Gore-McLemore Resolution Against Americans Traveling on Armed Belligerent Ships, and Wilson's Reply (1916)

Editor's Note: Continued submarine warfare and the risk raised by Wilson's policy of defining Americans' neutral rights to include unlimited commerce and travel—even voyage into the blockade zone on armed enemy merchant ships—stirred isolationist fears in Congress that further loss of American lives at sea might draw the United States into the war. The Gore-McLemore Resolution, introduced on February 17, 1916, by Congressman A. Jefferson ("Jeff") McLemore (D., Tex.) and in slightly different form on February 25, 1916, by Senator Thomas P. Gore (D., Okla.), challenged Wilson's policy and sought to ban Americans from traveling into the war zone on armed merchant vessels of belligerent nations. Wilson publicly denounced the move, and Congress, under pressure from the White House, tabled the measure by a vote of 68 to 14 in the Senate and 276 to 142 in the House.

The Gore-McLemore Resolutions

Resolved. . . .That it is the sense of the Congress, vested as it is with the sole power to declare war, that all persons owing allegiance to the United States should in behalf of their own safety and the vital interest of the United States, forbear to exercise the right to travel as passengers on any armed vessel of any belligerent power, whether such vessel be armed for offensive or defensive purposes, and it is the further sense of Congress that no passport should be issued or renewed by the Secretary of State, or anyone acting under him, to be used by any person owing allegiance to the United States for the purpose of travel upon any such armed vessel of a belligerent power.

President Wilson to Senator William J. Stone (D., Mo.), chair of the Senate Foreign Relations Committee, February 24, 1916

The White House February 24, 1916

My dear Senator:

· · · · ·

. . . No nation, no group of nations, has the right while war is in progress to alter or disregard the principles which all nations have agreed upon in mitigation of the horrors and sufferings of war; and if the clear rights of American citizens should ever unhappily be abridged or denied by any such action, we should, it seems to me, have in honour no choice as to what our own course should be.

For my own part, I cannot consent to any abridgement of the rights of American citizens in any respect. The honour and self-respect of the nation is involved. We covet peace, and shall preserve it at any cost but

Source: U.S. Congress, Senate Concurrent Resolution 14, *Congressional Record,* 64th Cong., 1st sess. (Feb. 25, 1916), 3120.

Source: Woodrow Wilson to Senator William J. Stone, Feb. 24, 1916, in Link et al., *The Papers of Woodrow Wilson* 36: 213–14.

the loss of honour. To forbid our people to exercise their rights for fear we might be called upon to vindicate them would be a deep humiliation indeed. It would be an implicit, all but an explicit, acquiescence in the violation of the rights of mankind everywhere and of whatever nation or allegiance. It would be a deliberate abdication of our hitherto proud position as spokesmen even amidst the turmoil of war for the law and the right. It would make everything this Government has attempted and everything that it has achieved during this terrible struggle of nations meaningless and futile.

It is important to reflect that if in this instance we allowed expediency to take the place of principle, the door would inevitably be opened to still further concessions. Once accept a single abatement of right and many other humiliations would certainly follow, and the whole fine fabric of international law might crumble under our hands piece by piece. What we are contending for in this matter is of the very essence of the things that have made America a sovereign nation. She cannot yield them without conceding her own impotency as a nation and making virtual surrender of her independent position among the nations of the world.

. . . . .

Faithfully yours,
[Woodrow Wilson]

[Wilson's letter was widely reprinted in the press; for example, *New York Times*, Feb. 25, 1916.]

DOCUMENT 20

A Discussion Between President Wilson and Leaders
of the Peace and Antimilitarism Movements (1916)

Editor's Note: A "preparedness" movement to modernize and increase greatly the size of the military and naval establishments and to adopt a system of short-term universal military training (UMT) was organized in the spring of 1915 under the sponsorship of wealthy individuals and corporate interests. It was encouraged by Republican leaders and some military officers. In the fall of 1915, Wilson announced his conversion to a less extreme program of military expansion, but even this encountered strong opposition in Congress. In November 1915, concerned with what they considered a growing spirit of militarism being fostered in the country, a group of pacifists and social reformers founded the American Union Against Militarism (AUAM).

After holding public meetings in New York City and throughout the isolationist Middle West, AUAM representatives met with Wilson on May 8, 1916, and reported on the widespread public sentiment against UMT, a greatly enlarged military establishment, and U.S. involvement in the war. Among the major spokespersons at that meeting were Lillian D. Wald, 1867-1940, nurse, social reformer, feminist, pacifist, and the founder of Henry Street Settlement House in New York City and of modern public health nursing; and Max F. Eastman, 1883-1969, author, lecturer, and radical leftist editor of the Socialist monthly magazine The Masses *from 1912 to 1917. The following transcript, which was confidential, also provides a valuable account of Woodrow Wilson's thinking in 1916 on military establishments and their role in international relations.*

(A month after this meeting, following a threat of war with revolution-torn Mexico, Congress, on June 3, 1916, adopted the compromise National Defense Act, which rejected UMT but enlarged the regular army from 108,000 to 175,000; created a Reserve Officers Training Corps (ROTC); and expanded the National Guard to 450,000 reservists. In August 1916, Congress authorized a huge construction program for the navy to make it the largest and most modern in the world.)

Meeting in the White House, May 8, 1916

[Lillian D. Wald] [The president's stenographer put the speaker's name in brackets in the transcript, and his use is continued here.]: Mr. Wilson, the American Union against Militarism was organized some months ago as a protest against the spirit of militarism, which some of us felt very deeply was imperiling the democracy of our country. We felt that it was in the intention to promote the expansion of the army and navy that the propaganda was started that went deep into our life—the life of the nation—that touched our schools, attempting conscription and [military

Source: Transcript of the meeting of May 8, 1916, made by Wilson's personal stenographer, Charles L. Swem, printed in Link et al., The Papers of Woodrow Wilson, 36: 634-46.

training] exercises. And those true Americans, who would gladly lay down their lives for the America that is the America of democracy, the America of opportunity and the land of promise, believed that it was their duty to stand out against militarism insofar as we believed that it would imperil our democratic institutions.

. . . . .

[Max Eastman] It is a special privilege, Mr. President, to take the place of an official representative of organized labor. Mr. Maurer [James H. Maurer, president of the Pennsylvania State Federation of Labor and a socialist member of the Pennsylvania legislature] also can tell you of the workingman's—the so-called common man's—opposition to any increase in the military aspects of our civilization. As you know, the working people have no distinct voice in the press. . . . Therefore, it is only by noting certain rather insignificant incidents that their wishes can be taken allowance of in one or two of these incidents. The United Mine Workers, which is the biggest labor union in the country and perhaps the greatest in the world, unanimously adopted the report of their president that not only were they opposed, but it was their belief, that organized labor all over the country was opposed to the whole preparedness program. And when you get a response from other classes to the proposal to increase our military branch, it misleads you as to the true sentiment of the country. If it could happen, by some extraordinary accident, for instance, that, instead of addressing the Daughters of the American Revolution, or the Women's Section of the Navy League, you had come to New York to address such a representative body as the 60,000 boat workers now on strike. I am sure that you would get a response far different from this military excitement which seems to have possessed our upper and leisure classes since the European war, and more particularly since the profits of the European war began to accumulate.

. . . . .

[Lillian Wald] . . . We feel, Mr. President, as a result of all this militaristic talk, that the attention of the masses is being concentrated upon the militarists' method of settling our international questions, such as you are dealing with, rather than on the possibility of such adjustment and conciliation as, after all, we ought to be bent upon making possible.

. . . . .

... [W]hat it [the Middle West] is concerned about, too, is this—and we are deeply concerned about it, Mr. President, as we know that you are—we feel that the acceptance by the American people now of a big army or a big navy program would simply neutralize and annul the moral power which our nation ought, through you, to exercise when the day of peace negotiations has come.

I think that moral power has always counted, and, without making any new, explicit references, such as would be confusing, that moral power still counts. We have had one recent revelation of the definiteness with which that moral power counts. We are opposed to the militarists. We feel that we have the right to call it a militarist rather than a preparedness program because we want to go—we want to go into the peace negotiations, so that we go morally in such a way that we shall have a part with our hands clean—with our hands clean, with our hands undefiled. We want to count in justice to ourselves and in good-will to the world. We want America, yours and our own, to count for the things worthwhile, for the things of America.

[Wilson] I want to say this, Miss Wald: I don't think I have been deceived about the mind of the country. I have never dreamed for a moment that America, as a whole, or its rank and file, had got any military enthusiasm or any militaristic spirit. And I think it is very necessary, in order that we should work this thing out wisely, that we should carefully discriminate between reasonable preparation and militarism. . . .

I think it would be a disservice not to recognize that there is a point of reasonable preparation, and that you can go to that point without changing the spirit of the country or violating the traditions of the country, considering that the traditions of the country have not been those of a military helplessness, though they have been those of a distinct antimilitarism.

The currents of opinion, or rather the bodies of opinion, in this country are very hard to assess. For example, Mayor [John Purroy] Mitchel of New York City and a group of gentlemen associated with him [in the "preparedness" movement] made a tour not unlike that which you made, and had meetings. And they came back and reported in the most enthusiastic terms a unanimous opinion, not for universal military service, but very distinctly for universal military training, which, of course, is a very different thing.

. . . . .

Now, as to the general thing we are all most profoundly interested in, and that is peace. We want the peace of the world. . . . But a nation which, by the standards of other nations, however mistaken those standards may be, is regarded as helpless, is apt in general counsel to be regarded as negligible. And when you go into a conference to establish foundations for the peace of the world, you have got to go in on a basis intelligible to the people you are conferring with.

· · · · ·

. . . Now, we have undertaken very much more than the safety of the United States. We have undertaken to keep what we regard as demoralizing and hurtful European influences out of this hemisphere. And that means that, if the world undertakes, as we all hope it will undertake, a joint effort to keep the peace, it will expect us to play our proportional part in manifesting the force which is going to rest back of that. Now, in the last analysis, the peace of society is obtained by force. And when action comes, it comes by opinion. But back of that opinion is the ultimate application of force, when the greater body of opinion says to the lesser body of opinion, "We may be wrong, but you have to live under our direction for the time being, until you are more numerous than we are." That is what I understand it amounts to.

Now, let us suppose that we have formed a family of nations, and that family of nations says, "The world is not going to have any more wars of this sort without at least the duty at first . . . to go through certain processes to show whether there is anything in the case or not." And if you say we shall not have any war, you have got to have the force to make that "shall" bite. The rest of the world, if America takes part in this thing, will have the right to expect from her that she contributes her element of force to the general understanding. Surely that is not a militaristic ideal. That is a very practical, possible ideal. [Miss Wald] Would that not, Mr. President, logically lead to a limitless expansion of our contribution?

[Wilson] Well, logically, Miss Wald, but I haven't the least regard for logic. What I mean to say is, I think in such affairs as we are now discussing, the circumstances are the logic. I remember a sentence of Burke [Edmund Burke, one of the leading political theorists of eighteenth-century Britain] which runs something to this effect: "If you ask me wherein the wisdom of a certain policy consists, I will say that it consists of the circumstances of that policy."

[Miss Wald] Agreeable philosophy.

[Wilson] I don't think it's merely agreeable. I mean just this, just as you can't suggest any absolute standard by which you should determine the number of men you should have in the army of the United States any more than I can. Logically, to defend an enormous territory such as ours, you should have an almost limitless armament, but practically, you don't have to have, because you have a moral force that takes its place. And so I say that is the reason I meant I didn't have any regard for logic in questions of this sort. It is not a matter which you reason out. It is a matter which you deduce from the circumstances. Now, quite opposite to anything you fear, I believe that, if the world ever comes to combine its force for the purpose of maintaining peace, the individual contributions of each nation will be much less, necessarily, naturally less, than they would be in other circumstances, and that all they will have to do will be to contribute moderately not indefinitely.

. . . . .

DOCUMENT 21

President Wilson's First Endorsement of
a Postwar League of Nations (1916)

Editor's Note: The League to Enforce Peace (LEP) was an association of Americans organized in the summer of 1915 to mobilize public sentiment in the United States in favor of a postwar international organization of sovereign nations. That organization would preserve peace through the threat of united economic or military action against aggressors who refused to accept the peaceful settlement of disputes. Headed by former president William Howard Taft and A. Lawrence Lowell, president of Harvard University, and endorsed by many liberal internationalists such as Hamilton Holt, the LEP was the most active pro-league pressure group during the war. Its aim was to enable the United States to act in concert with other great powers when Washington decided independently that its interests were affected.

Determined to maintain his political flexibility and suspicious of Republican domination in the LEP, Wilson kept his distance from the pro-league group. But with the spreading popularity of the league idea, the president decided to address the organization at its May 27, 1916 meeting. Although he declined to endorse the LEP's program or any specific formula for the league in his address, given below, Wilson made his first public declaration in favor of a postwar association of nations—the first endorsement by a world leader. He also ennunciated eloquently the principles of a peace settlement being espoused by liberals in Great Britain and the United States.

An Address in Washington to the League to Enforce Peace

. . . . .

We are participants, whether we would or not, in the life of the world. The interests of all nations are our own also. We are partners with the rest. What affects mankind is inevitably our affair as well as the affair of the nations of Europe and Asia.

. . . . .

It is plain that this war could have come only as it did, suddenly and out of secret counsels, without warning to the world, without discussion, without any of the deliberate movements of counsel with which it would seem natural to approach so stupendous a contest.

And the lesson which the shock of being taken by surprise in a matter so deeply vital to all the nations of the world has made poignantly clear is that the peace of the world must henceforth depend upon a new and more wholesome diplomacy. Only when the great nations of the world have reached some sort of agreement as to what they hold to be fundamental to their common interest, and as to some feasible method of acting in concert when any nation or group of nations seeks to disturb those fundamental things, can we feel that civilization is at last in a way of justifying its existence and claiming to be finally established. It is clear that nations must in the future be governed by the same high code of honor that we demand of individuals.

. . . . .

The nations of the world have become each other's neighbors. It is to their interest that they should understand each other. In order that they may understand each other, it is imperative that they should agree to cooperate in a common cause, and that they should so act that the guiding principle of that common cause shall be evenhanded and impartial justice.

Source: "An Address in Washington to the League to Enforce Peace," May 27, 1916, in Link et al., *The Papers of Woodrow Wilson* 37: 113–16.

This is undoubtedly the thought of America. This is what we ourselves will say when there comes proper occasion to say it. In the
dealings of nations with one another, arbitrary force must be rejected
and we must move forward to the thought of the modern world, the
thought of which peace is the very atmosphere. That thought constitutes a chief part of the passionate conviction of America.

We believe these fundamental things: First, that every people has a
right to choose the sovereignty under which they shall live.... Second,
that the small states of the world have a right to enjoy the same respect
for their sovereignty and for their territorial integrity that great and
powerful nations expect and insist upon. And, third, that the world has
a right to be free from every disturbance of its peace that has its origin
in aggression and disregard of the rights of peoples and nations. So
sincerely do we believe in these things that I am sure that I speak the
mind and wish of the people of America when I say that the United
States is willing to become a partner in any feasible association of
nations formed in order to realize these objects and make them secure
against violation.

If it should ever be our privilege to suggest or initiate a movement for
peace among the nations now at war, I am sure that the people of the
United States would wish their government to move along these lines.
First, such a settlement with regard to their own immediate interests as
the belligerents may agree upon. We have nothing material of any kind
to ask for ourselves, and are quite aware that we are in no sense or
degree parties to the present quarrel. Our interest is only in peace and
its future guarantees. Second, an universal association of the nations to
maintain the inviolate security of the highway of the seas for the common and unhindered use of all the nations of the world, and to prevent
any war begun either contrary to treaty covenants or without warning
and full submission of the causes to the opinion of the world—a virtual
guarantee of territorial integrity and political independence.

DOCUMENT 22

The Carrizal Incident: The Peace Movement Helps
Avert War with Mexico (1916)

*Editor's Note: The American Union Against Militarism scored its great-
est triumph when it helped avert war with Mexico over a fatal skirmish*

between U.S. and Mexican troops at Carrizal, Chihuahua, Mexico. The clash occurred on June 21, 1916, nearly seventy miles south of the border between units of the Mexican army and a detachment of U.S. cavalry from General John J. Pershing's Punitive Expedition, which was pursuing the irregulars of Francisco ("Pancho") Villa. Nine Americans and thirty Mexican soldiers were killed, twelve Americans and forty-three Mexicans wounded, and twenty-five Americans captured (although they were soon released on orders from Mexican president Venustiano Carranza). To counter pressure for war from U.S. oil interests, the press, and Republican jingoes led by Theodore Roosevelt, the AUAM quickly publicized the Americans' role in provoking the incident. The pacifists also helped to establish binational commissions to investigate problems between the two nations and to allow time for tensions to be eased.

The War Scare: Accounts from Two New York Newspapers

The New York Times
June 22, 1916

AMERICAN CAVALRY AMBUSHED BY CARRANZA TROOPS
OUR PATROL IS MOWED DOWN BUT ACCOUNTS FOR MANY MEXICANS

EL PASO, TEXAS, June 21—American and Carranza troops fought a bloody battle today only a few hours after President Wilson's 6,000-word rebuke yesterday to General Carranza had gone forward to Mexico City [a State Department rejection of Carranza's insistence on the removal of the Pershing Punitive Expedition from Mexico]. With which side victory rested is not known.

The engagement took place on the Santo Domingo ranch near the Mexican town of Carrizal, which is nine miles southwest of Villa Ahumada, the Mexican field headquarters in Northern Chihuahua. The number of dead, American or Mexican, was not definitely known here tonight, but nearly a score of General Pershing's men are said to have been killed and the Mexicans are said to have lost more than two score. Seventeen Americans are declared by Mexican officials to have been captured and to have been hurried to Chihuahua City under adequate guard. A machine gun used by the Mexicans is reported to have done heavy execution. . . .

. . . . .

Source: News Stories, *New York Times,* June 22, 1916, 1.

CLASH STIRS WASHINGTON

WASHINGTON, D.C. June 21—The clash at Carrizal between American and Carranizta troops brings this country to the threshold of actual hostilities with Mexico. The attack by Mexicans on a detachment of the Tenth Cavalry [the Tenth Cavalry Regiment of the U.S. Army] is nothing less than officials have been fearing almost momentarily since Sunday [June 18, 1916], in view of General [Jacinto] Trevino's warning to General Pershing that if American troops were moved south, east, or west, it would be construed as a hostile act, and they would be fired upon.

· · · · ·

...The belief here is that the American regulars of the Tenth were sent eastward by General Pershing....and that while on this mission the American detachment was ambushed by a surprise attack with machine guns....

The New York Herald
June 24, 1916

THE TRUTH ABOUT CARRIZAL

Although at this writing official reports are lacking, definite and apparently reliable information is coming out of Mexico regarding the conflict at Carrizal between our cavalry and the forces of the Carranza government.

These facts bear out the first impression given by the HERALD—that in consequence of this engagement a state of war actually exists between the United States and Mexico. There seems to be no way of evading this. It might be ignored, but with great loss of prestige.

The facts are that two troops of United States cavalry were pursuing bandits and approached the town. They were met by a Mexican commander, who asked them to divert their course and withdraw to the north. After a brief halt a parley took place, during which the parties to the conversation dismounted, leaving their horses to be held by orderlies. Suddenly it was discovered that the United States detachment was being flanked on either side by a large and numerically superior Mexican force, composed of cavalry, infantry and machine gun companies.

Source: Editorial, New York *Herald,* June 24, 1916.

The conflict was quickly precipitated by the Mexicans themselves. The remarkable part of this affair is that while the United States authorities have appeared eager to have the affray regarded as committed by irresponsible persons, the Mexican government has made no concealment that the attack was made in obedience to orders from the Minister of War. Therefore the conclusion is irresistible that a state of war has actually existed between this government and Mexico since the affair at Carrizal on Wednesday morning [June 21, 1916].

Efforts of the American Union Against Militarism

Shall We Have War with Mexico?

To the President and the American People:
June 26, 1916
We are on the point of war. If war comes the American people and the other nations of the world will sit in judgment and render a verdict as to the right and justice of the cause. Every American who is patriotic in the highest sense feels that to go to war without a just cause which will bear the critical judgment of future generations would be an irreparable injury to the nation.
IS THERE A JUST CAUSE FOR WAR?
It is conceded by the State Department that up to the Carrizal engagement between American and Mexican troops nothing has happened that amounts to a substantial cause for war. As we understand it, there is little conflict of opinion in regard to this. If we go to war now it will be understood at home and abroad that it is because of the shooting of Captain [Charles T.] Boyd's troopers by Mexican soldiers under General [Felix] Gomez, outside of the town of Carrizal at about 4:30 A.M., on June 20th [actually, June 21].
Captain [Lewis] Morey, wounded and under the belief that he would not reach the border alive, has given a clear, cool and detailed account of this engagement. His statement follows:

"Carrizal, Mexico,

"June 21, 1916,

9:15 A.M.
"To Commanding Officer, Ojo Frederico: My troop reached Ojo Santo Domingo at 5.30 P.M., June 20. Met C Troop under Captain

Source: *Shall We Have War with Mexico?*, leaflet, June 26, 1916, American Union Against Militarism Papers, Swarthmore College Peace Collection.

Boyd. I came under Captain Boyd's command and marched my troop in rear for Carrizal at 4.15 A.M., reaching open field to southeast of town at 6.30 A.M.

"Captain Boyd sent in a note requesting permission to pass through the town. This was refused. Stated we could go to the north, but not east. Captain Boyd said he was going to Ahumada at this time.

"He was talking with Carranza commander. General Gómez sent a written message that Captain Boyd was bringing force in town and have a conference. Captain Boyd feared an ambush. He was under the impression that the Mexicans would run as soon as we fired.

"We formed for attack, his intention being to move up to the line of about 120 Mexicans on the edge of the town. We formed C Troop on the left in line of skirmishers, one platoon of K Troop on right of line, and another K Troop platoon on extreme right, echeloned a little to the rear.

"When we were within 300 yards the Mexicans opened fire, and a strong one, before we fired a shot; then we opened up. They did not run. To make a long account short, after about an hour's fire both troops had advanced, C Troop to position of Mexican machine gun and K Troop closing in slightly to the left. We were very busy on the right, keeping off a flank attack. A group of Mexicans left town, went around our rear, and led our horses off a-gallop.

"At about 9 o'clock one platoon of K Troop, which was on our right, fell back. Sergeant said he could not stay there. Both platoons fell back about 1,000 yards to the west, and then together with some men of C Troop who were there, these scattered.

"I was slightly wounded. Captain Boyd, a man told me, was killed. Nothing was seen of Lieutenant [Henry R.] Adair after fight started, so man I saw stated.

"I am hiding in a hole 2,000 yards from field and have one other wounded man and three men with me.["]

(Signed) "MOREY, Captain."

This report was evidently written with deliberation. It bears the marks of thoughtful accuracy, and Captain Morey took pains to put it into army code.

You will note that Captain Morey says that Captain Boyd was under the impression that the Mexicans would run if fired on, and that the Americans then "formed for attack" and advanced upon the Mexicans, and that thereupon the Mexican troops opened fire. If this is true—and it seems impossible to doubt it—we submit that THE CARRIZAL EPISODE DOES NOT CONSTITUTE A JUST CAUSE OF WAR.

It has been announced by the Associated Press that the Government will not give weight to Captain Morey's statement as printed above, but will await an "official account" from him as a basis of judgment. The American people will surely not be deceived by any attempt to alter the facts presented in Captain Morey's original report.

It has been stated that the Carrizal engagement was a mere incident; and that Carranza's refusal to allow American troops to proceed further into Mexico, was in itself a cause of war. HISTORY WILL NOT JUSTIFY THIS NATION in going to war because a neighboring republic, having allowed our troops to enter its territory in pursuit of a band of outlaws, demanded that these troops should not march further into its territory after the band of outlaws had been scattered and many of them killed.

The fact that Mexico is a small nation, torn by recent revolutions and now undergoing a period of reconstruction, make[s] it a matter of national honor that we should scrupulously respect its rights. We believe that if this nation should choose to go to war rather than accept the offer of mediation made by the Latin-American Republics and accepted by Mexico, it will be a blot upon American history.

AMERICAN UNION AGAINST MILITARISM
70 Fifth Avenue, New York City
Write or Wire Your Congressman TO-DAY

Woodrow Wilson:
From Fatalism to Determination
to Prevent War with Mexico

Woodrow Wilson to "Colonel" Edward M. House, June 22, 1916

The White House, 22 June 1916

Dearest Friend,
. . . The break seems to have come in Mexico; and all my patience seems to have gone for nothing. I am infinitely sad about it. I fear I should have drawn Pershing and his command northward just after it became evident that Villa had slipped through his fingers but except for that error of judgment (if it was an error) [These and the following are

Source: Link et al., *The Papers of Woodrow Wilson* 37: 281, 308, 333–34.

Wilson's parentheses] I cannot, in looking back, see where I could have done differently, holding sacred the convictions I hold in this matter.

Right or wrong, however, the extremest consequences seem upon us. But INTERVENTION (that is rearrangement and control of Mexico's domestic affairs by the U.S.) there shall not be either now or at any other time if I can prevent it!

· · · · ·

Affectionately Yours,
Woodrow Wilson

Jane Addams Telegram to Woodrow Wilson, June 27, 1916

The Executive Board of the Woman's Peace Party urges the administration by means of direct conference or by mediation through other American nations to avoid hostile conflict with the people of Mexico within their own borders, so that there may not be sown seeds of distrust and enmity which will prevent us—strong enlightened and free— from aiding in the near future, our weak neighbor, uneducated and poor, to secure education, economic independence and political stability.

Woodrow Wilson, Remarks to the New York Press Club,
June 30, 1916

· · · · ·

... Of course it is our duty to prepare this nation to take care of its honor and of its institutions.

· · · · ·

The easiest thing is to strike. The brutal thing is the impulsive thing. No man has to think before he takes aggressive action. But before a man really conserves the honor by realizing the ideals of the nation, he has to think exactly what he will do and how he will do it. Do you think the glory of America would be enhanced by a war of conquest in Mexico? Do you think that any act of violence by a powerful nation like this against a weak and distracted neighbor would reflect distinction upon the annals of the United States? Do you think that it is our duty to carry self-defense to the point of dictation in the affairs of another people? The ideals of America are written plain upon every page of American history.

And I want you to know how fully I realize whose servant I am. . . . I have constantly to remind myself that I am not the servant of those who wish to enhance the value of their Mexican investments, but that I am the servant of the rank and file of the people of the United States. I get a great many letters, my fellow citizens, from important and influential men in this country, but I get a great many other letters. I get letters from unknown men, from humble women, from people whose names have never been heard and will never be recorded, and there is but one prayer in all of these letters. "Mr. President, do not allow anybody to persuade you that the people of this country want war with anybody." I got off a train yesterday and, as I was bidding goodby to the engineer, he said in an undertone, "Mr. President, keep us out of Mexico." And if one man has said that to me, a thousand have said it to me as I have moved about the country. If I have opportunity to engage them further in conversation, they say, "Of course, we know that you cannot govern the circumstances of the case altogether, and it may be necessary, but for God's sake do not do it unless it is necessary."

I am for the time being the spokesman of such people, gentlemen. . . .

. . . . .

"The Mexican Crisis: Some Inside Information" from the Washington Representative of the American Union Against Militarism (AUAM), July 15, 1916

THE MEXICAN CRISIS: SOME INSIDE INFORMATION

Although the pacifists of the country have been unable to make great headway against the combination of hysteria, reaction and big business which has made up the so-called "preparedness" movement, they have certainly scored a dramatic victory—and an eleventh hour one at that— in the Mexican crisis.

That crisis [which began in March 1916 with Villa's raid across the border and Wilson's decision to use the National Guard to patrol the border and to send the regular army under Pershing to pursue Villa deep into Mexico] it seems pretty clear in retrospect, grew out of the

Source: Mimeographed, confidential ("not for publication") report from Charles T. Hallinan, Washington, D.C., to AUAM members. AUAM Bulletin no. 53, July 15, 1916. American Union Against Militarism Papers, Swarthmore College Peace Collection.

politics of the presidential campaign [of 1916]. At any rate the Washington correspondent [David Lawrence] of the New York *Evening Post,* who is known to be a sincere and pronounced admirer of Mr. Wilson, attributes the president's saber rattling [in response to the Villa raids] almost entirely to "presidential politics" and distributes the blame, with an impartial hand, between the Republicans for what he considers their rank abuse of the Mexican situation, and the Democrats for showing "too much regard for Republican criticism." The drastic note [of protest] to Carranza and the rapid and extravagant mobilization of the National Guard certainly had political effect to the extent, at least, of depriving the Republicans of a campaign issue they were obviously planning to use.

But the effects were more than political. The whole country seemed suddenly inflamed against Mexico. The press was fairly violent on the subject. Some of them, like the Philadelphia *Evening Ledger,* went back through their files and re-told the day-by-day developments which preceded the outbreak of the Spanish-American War, pointedly suggesting that the two situations were closely parallel. The "pacifists" in the House—leaderless and none too courageous—fairly tumbled over each other to vote huge appropriations to "back up" the government. In the cloakrooms the members [of the House] told each other stories of men who had vainly attempted to resist the war spirit which swept the country before the Spanish-American War, and what became of them,— how they went down and out. As one congressman said to us: "The mob spirit has got the country and these fellows are playing safe."

The biggest single difficulty in the way was the sharp note to General Carranza [the long State Department note of June 20, 1916, to Venustiano Carranza, head of the Mexican government, asserting the right of the United States to send its army into Mexico to bring stability to the border region] which was couched in language and laid down terms which apparently left him little to do but fight. Certainly it was entirely innocent of the loopholes commonly left in diplomatic exchanges. Perhaps the secret of that note may lie in the fact that it was not written by President Wilson but by Secretary of State [Robert] Lansing who is reported in Washington to have little sympathy with Mr. Wilson's attitude toward the Mexican revolution. Secretary Lansing is the son-in-law of John W. Foster who was Minister to Mexico from 1873 to 1880 and, later on, for a good many years, the "scientific" attorney in Washington for Diaz [Porfirio Díaz, dictator in Mexico from 1877 to 1911]. It has been frequently asserted that Mr. Lansing himself was attorney for the reactionary Huerta [General Victoriano Huerta who seized power from 1913 to 1914] up to the day he entered the State Department as Solicitor [in 1914, actually as counsellor]. Mr. Lansing denies this, claiming that he merely handled some of Huerta's business for his father-in-law. At all events his associations—so far as the Mexican situation is concerned—have all been with the "scientifico" or reactionary element and against the revolutionists. His [Lansing's] drastic note to Carranza sounds fearfully like an evening up of old State Department scores. It staggered the country, silenced the pacifists and apparently headed the administration straight for war.

This was the situation when the executive committee of the American Union Against Militarism called a hurried conference in New York city on June 21. This conference, which included a group of Philadephia members and several men and women who were not members but whose advice and judgment were desired, went over the whole situation at great length and, late at night, voted unanimously to wire a strong protest against war to President Wilson, to wire urgent pleas to the representatives of the "A B C" powers [Argentina, Brazil, and Chile] in Washington to use their influence with Carranza to stave off hostilities while they pressed for mediation and, finally, to launch an "unofficial" peace conference, to be held at our expense in El Paso, to be made up of three representative American citizens and three representative Mexicans. The three Americans tentatively selected, pending their acceptance, were William Jennings Bryan [former secretary of state], Dr. David Starr Jordan [noted zoologist, pacifist, and president of Stanford University], and Frank P. Walsh [former head of the pro-labor U.S Commision on Industrial Relations].

Miss Crystal Eastman [executive secretary of the AUAM] deserves credit, not only for originating the idea but for convincing the members of the conference that it was feasible and that nothing short of some such scheme could save the situation. It sounded wildly quixotic when it was proposed and apparently it had lost none of its quixoticism when it reached Mr. Bryan for his reaction to it was quite conventional. He couldn't accept until he was satisfied that it would not embarrass the administration. We do not know that the administration leaders told Mr. Bryan when he reached them on the long distance telephone but they were evidently opposed to his accepting our invitation. Mr. Frank P. Walsh likewise withdrew and for the same reason. But Dr. David Starr Jordan, who was traveling and only got our invitation through the newspapers, rose to the occasion with a simplicity and courage which mark him as a great man. Waiving all ceremonies, he wired his acceptance, left the train, turned his back on a string of engagements, and started straight for El Paso, straight for unconcealed local hostility and the cheap jibes of the press of the entire country. At that crisis it was David Starr Jordan who forced pacifism into existence as one of the factors of the situation. The newspapers had to reckon with him day by day, and every day they recounted his movements, they increased the tide of telegrams and letters pouring in upon the White House protesting against war with Mexico.

He "held the fort" at El Paso long enough for the committee to secure Mr. Moorfield Storey of Boston [a leading anti-imperialist and civil libertarian], in place of Mr. Bryan, Mr. Amos Pinchot (who was later succeeded by Mr. Paul U. Kellogg, editor of "The Survey" [magazine]) in place of Mr. Walsh, and to get in touch with three Mexican delegates. Then the conference adjourned to Washington where the six "unofficial" peace commissioners met.

In the meantime there was the internal situation in Mexico to be reckoned with. If national feeling was running high in the United States, what must it have been like in Mexico where the people were convinced that our soldiers and our artillery were bent on destroying the sovereignty of the republic. All the "news" out of the United States was in one key,—preparation for war. The newspapers were urging "on to Mexico". On the night of June 21 [after the Carrizal incident] it looked as though Mexico might easily, within twenty-four hours, draw the sword and make peace impossible. It seemed necessary to reach Mexican public opnion and convince it that public opinion in the United States was not wholly in favor of intervention. That night we cabled an 800 word story—at our own expense—to three papers in Mexico City and to two influential papers in Havanna, Cuba,—papers which we were told had a good deal of influence in Latin-American affairs. We also gave the news of our proposed conference to the Latin-American News association and to the correspondent in New York of La Prensa, the leading newspaper of South America which acts as a news association for more than 300 newspapers in Central and South America. How we fared in South America we do not know, but we have seen copies of Mexican [sic] city papers in which the news of the proposed conference was played up with headlines running clear across the front page,—one of the few times, probably, when peace news was screamed in the streets!

The Mexican representatives whom we invited were Mr. Modesto C. Rolland, an engineer from Yucatan with offices in the Equitable Building, New York City; Senor Luis Manuel Rojas, director of the National Library, Mexico City; and Dr. Atl, the editor of "Accion Mondial", a weekly newspaper published in Mexico city. All three men accepted and started for El Paso but before they reached it, the conference was switched to Washington.

When it opened in the New Willard hotel in Washington, the immediate crisis was past.

After several days of discussion of the entire Mexican situation, the six members of the conference voted to form themselves into a permanent body, with headquarters in Mexico City and Washington, to be known as the Inter American Peace Committee, for the purpose of promoting in all possible ways a better understanding between the two peoples. The mere fact that one crisis had passed was rightly regarded as no guarantee that another, equally serious, might not be upon us at any moment, especially in view of the powerful forces which were bent upon intervention. It was decided that some one must undertake the work of checking those forces. Oddly enough, this recognition of hostile factors in the situation seems to have been mutual, for the new committee had scarcely adjourned last week when there arrived in Washington a special representative of the Pierson oil interests of London to investigate the personnel of the American Union Against Militarism and of the new peace committee. He avoided our headquarters but he asked numerous questions around town. Apparently those interests intend to keep an eye on the new committee!

As we have said the crisis was past when the full conference assembled. We have speculated somewhat on how much the mere existence of the committee and the publicity attending it had to do with the marked improvement in the situation both in Washington and in Mexico City. It is hard to measure that influence but it seems probable that it had a very great deal to do with it. Certainly it stimulated pacifist protest against war and it certainly gave General Carranza a chance to argue down the hot-heads who wanted him to draw the sword at once and have done with "shilly-shallying."

The situation now is vastly improved. In all probability, a joint commission will be appointed by Mexico and the United States [It was; a Joint High Commission met from September 1916 through January 1917] to consider, not only the problem of border patrol but the larger question of American intervention,—the character and methods of the forces which seem bound to foment trouble between the two countries. This will ventilate a lot of facts which have been skilfully concealed and it ought to improve the tone of public opinion, especially in this country a good deal.

. . . . .

C.T.H. [Charles T. Hallinan]

DOCUMENT 23

President Wilson Speaks Privately about Mediation
to the American Neutral Conference Committee (1916)

Editor's Note: The American Neutral Conference Committee was orga-
nized in 1916 by Hamilton Holt; David Starr Jordan; Mary Emma
Woolley, president of Mount Holyoke College; Oswald Garrison Villard,
grandson of the abolitionist William Lloyd Garrison and liberal pacifist
publisher of The Nation *magazine and the New York Evening Post; and*
Emily Greene Balch, social worker, cofounder of Boston's settlement
house, economics professor at Wellesley College, and delegate to the
International Congress of Women at The Hague (later she shared the
Nobel Peace Prize for 1946 for leadership of the Women's International
League for Peace and Freedom). Their goal, like that of the Woman's
Peace party, was to have the United States lead in creating a Neutral
Conference for Continuous Mediation. On August 30, 1916, several
members of the committee met with the president, who spoke of the
difficulties he saw in their plan, as the following transcript by the
president's personal stenographer makes clear.

A Colloquy with Members of the American Neutral Conference Committee, August 30, 1916

Mr. Holt: Mr. President. . . . We suggest, and earnestly urge today,
that you call a conference of neutral nations with the object of bringing
the war to an earlier close than otherwise, even if it be by a single
month or a single day.

. . . . .

Now, if we are to win a durable peace, if we are to win a shortening
of the war, it will not be by waiting until those who are in the thick of
the conflict, and cannot pass an unbiased judgment, call upon us to
help. It will be by the assertion strongly on the indivisibility, the rights
and the interests of the public opinion of the neutral nations. And we
believe that the calling of a neutral conference would not only express

Source: "A Colloquy with Members of the American Neutral Conference Committee,"
Aug. 30, 1916, transcript by Wilson's stenographer, Charles L. Swem, Link et al., *The
Papers of Woodrow Wilson* 38: 108–17.

but crystallize and stimulate the public opinion among the neutral nations.

And we also believe that it would release the pent up public opinion among the people of the belligerents. We think it is dangerous to take the point of view of officialdom only and not go to the people themselves.

. . . . .

[W Wilson], Well, in order to say what you are entitled to hear—my real thoughts—of course, it is necessary that I should ask you to regard them as confidential. . . . The United States has nothing to gain and nothing to lose in one sense in respect of this war. . . . In that respect, she differs from all the other nations that could be called into this conference. . . .

. . . But when I have thought of the United States voting one vote out of a large number in the settlement of an essential question and being on an entirely different footing of interest from all the other voters in the conference, I haven't been able to see a satisfactory result brought out of that. Because I have had this distressing experience. . . . [O]utside of America, disinterodness in public matters isn't believed to exist. . . .

If I could hold a conference of neutrals consisting only of representatives who represented the people of the neutral nations, I would hold it in a minute. But inasmuch as I can't hold a conference that represents more than one people, so far as I can see, I am afraid to hold it. . . .

That is the difficulty, frankly stated. You see why I couldn't state that in a voice that would reach beyond this room. It isn't because I distrust the European statesman. I do not. I honor those that I have had a chance to know and to test, but their point of view is utterly different from ours, and their object is utterly different from ours. . . .

Now, in one sense we don't care for what the quarrel is about, because we don't know, partly because nobody knows what the quarrel is about. It is just a fight, as Professor Fisher [Irving Fisher, Yale economist] says, to see who is strong enough to prevent the other from fighting better. I don't see anything else that is involved, so that, when I imagine a conference of neutrals, I imagine Sweden and Denmark and Holland—think of how those countries are shot through with the passions and the dangers of this thing—and Spain, that has been shut out in recent years from influence in European affairs, and I dare say would like to see those influences magnified; and little Switzerland inside of a circle of fire.

The whole problem on this side of the water is this. Dr. Jordan [David Starr Jordan, president of Stanford University, one of Wilson's visitors] said that he didn't think there would be any objection to the including of the three great governments of South America, but one of the difficulties in South America is that the other countries don't admit that those are the great countries of South America and are very jealous of the ABC [Argentina, Brazil, Chile] group, and you can't do much with them if you magnify the ABC group. If we want to have any influence with them, we can't invite the ABC group and exclude the rest.... And if we include all the [Latin] American states in the call, the European states probably won't respond to the call. It is a circle of difficulties and perplexities that you open up in this.

That doesn't mean that I despair at all of the influences that are making for peace. I believe they are growing every day, and I believe that some of the instrumentalities are represented by groups like this that are influential enough to get what they say heard, who have friends enough to get what they say spread, who have channels by which sentiment can be released in the countries which are most interested. The volume is growing, steadily growing, and the voice that is calling for peace will presently be heard. It will be heard by the governments themselves sooner than it will be heard by us. Those governments hear the voices which they suppress, or else they wouldn't suppress them....

... My hope is that we can get them [the belligerent governments] to talk to each other, and the minute that happens, the war is over. They will never go back to it. They will never revive the forces that will sustain them in it.

· · · · ·

DOCUMENT 24

Social Work Leaders Endorse Wilson for President (1916)

Editor's Note: Because the majority of voters continued to be registered Republicans, Woodrow Wilson as a Democrat welcomed endorsements for his reelection in 1916 from individuals who were also known to be Republicans. Among the most important collective endorsement he re-

ceived was from the nearly one hundred progressive leaders of the social work and social reform movement who signed the following full-page advertisement that appeared on the back cover of The Survey *magazine in October 1916.*

Why Wilson?
A Statement by Social Workers

As social workers we believe that Woodrow Wilson should be re-elected president of the United States. The rapid changes which are taking place in economic and social conditions in this country and the many new and unforeseen developments which the war is causing in our industrial and political life, as well as in our international relations, make it imperative that during the next four years there shall be in the White House a man of broad social vision, a man who stands ready, in whatever situations may arise, to initiate and direct policies with regard for the rights, the interests, and the social welfare of the whole people rather than those of any group.

We believe that Woodrow Wilson is such a man. He has shown himself to be truly democratic in his handling of the perplexing problems, both international and domestic, that have arisen during his administration.

In Mexico, his stand against aggrandizement by the United States has made possible the growth of popular government and is bringing about an era of sympathetic understanding between the American Republics.

In foreign affairs, he has stood for a diplomacy of reason and negotiation, with good will toward all peoples, rather than one of bluster and the parade of force.

In domestic affairs, the present administration comes before the country with a social program that carries assurance because of a record of pledges fulfilled and a series of legislative achievements not equaled by any other administration. . . .

. . . . .

[Signed by ninety-five prominent leaders of the social welfare movement, including Jane Addams, Paul Kellogg, and Lillian Wald.]

Source: "Why Wilson? A Statement by Social Workers," (advertisement) *Survey* 37 (Oct. 21, 1916), back cover.

DOCUMENT 25

Crystal Eastman: Suggestions for the American Union
Against Militarism for 1916–1917 (1916)

Editor's Note: Crystal Eastman, 1881–1928, was an attorney, social investigator, authority on industrial accidents, and committed feminist, suffragist, socialist, and pacifist. Eastman ranked with Jane Addams, Lillian Wald, and Emily Greene Balch as one of the founders of the kind of social activist peace groups that succeeded the more staid, conservative, male-led peace organizations of the first decade and a half of the twentieth century. She and her brother, Max, were two of the founders of the American Union Against Militarism, and she served as its executive director from 1915 to 1917. She was also chair of the New York branch of the Woman's Peace party from 1915 to 1919, a chapter that was consistently more radical than the national WPP. Eastman was a creative organizational activist, as indicated by the following plan written for the AUAM membership in October 1916 in which she proposed an expanded program for the AUAM for the winter and spring of 1916–1917.

A Review

We should face the new year, not so much in the mood of defeated reformers doggedly pressing on, as in the mood of fighters who have held their ground and even made a little headway against tremendous odds. It is true that the army was increased (on paper) from 100,000 to 180,000 and that the National Guard has been put on a Federal subsidy, but the demand for a standing army of 250,000 was decisively beaten and the Administration's plan for a Continental Army [a large, purely national reserve force] was dropped overboard early in the fight.

· · · · ·

It is true that Congress passed the largest naval appropriation bill in the history of the United States—yes, in the peace history of any coun-

Source: Crystal Eastman, *A Review*, American Union Against Militarism pamphlet, Oct. 1916, in *Crystal Eastman on Women and Revolution*, ed. Blanche Wiesen Cook (New York: Oxford Univ. Press, 1978), 247–52.

try [$315 million and authorization for 10 battleships and 6 battle cruisers, 50 destroyers, and 67 submarines to be built within three years],—but it was forced to concede the Hensley paragraphs [an amendatory rider added to the bill by Congressman Walter L. Hensley (D., Mo.) at the urging of the AUAM] providing for the abandonment of the program if an adequate international agreement develops after the war. And far more important than anything else in the general progress of our fight, are these so-called Hensley programs, which are safely incorporated in the huge Navy Bill. They read as follows:

"It is hereby declared to be the policy of the United States to adjust and settle its international disputes through mediation or arbitration, to the end that war may be honorably avoided. It looks with apprehension and disfavor upon a general increase of armament throughout the world, but it realizes that no single nation can disarm, and that without a common agreement upon the subject every considerable power must maintain a relative standing in military strength.

"In view of the premises, the President is *authorized and requested to invite, at an appropriate time, not later than the close of the war in Europe, all the great Governments of the world* to send representatives to a *conference* which shall be charged with the duty of formulating *a plan for a court of arbitration* or other tribunal, to which disputed questions between nations shall be referred for adjudication and peaceful settlement, and *to consider the question of disarmament* and submit their recommendation to their respective Governments for approval. The President is hereby *authorized to appoint nine citizens* of the United States, who, in his judgment, shall be qualified for the mission by eminence in the law and by devotion to the cause of peace, to be representatives of the United States in such a conference.

. . . . .

"If at any time *before the construction* authorized by this Act *shall have been contracted* for there shall have been established, with the cooperation of the United States of America, *an international tribunal* or tribunals competent to secure peaceful determinations of all international disputes, and *which shall render unnecessary the maintenance of competitive armaments,* then and in that case *such naval expenditures* as may be inconsistent with the engagements made in the establishment of such tribunal or tribunals *may be suspended,* when so ordered by the President of the United States."

Here, if we can get a strong enough public opinion back of it, is our congressional authority for ditching part, at least, of that preposterous naval program, for sinking the dreadnaughts [superbattleships] before they are built. Here indeed is a new precedent in naval bills,—"We authorize you to build these ships, but we authorize you also to try to get the other nations to stop building theirs: if you succeed, then *don't build ours*." If the next to the last page of the Navy Bill works, many previous pages of it may become so much waste paper.

We propose then the following plan for the next year's work of the American Union Against Militarism.

(1) By bringing popular pressure to bear on Congress, by deputations, public hearing, and the widest possible publicity, we must... increase rather than relax our vigilance in forestalling all other attempts at militarist legislation in Congress, such as the Chamberlain bill [Senator George Chamberlain, D., Ore.] for universal military training, and the [U.S. Army] War College bill which would give military authorities power of censorship over the press in time of war.

(2) We must cooperate with local peace organizations in their efforts to *keep military training out of the public schools* and in their fight against *conscription* and compulsory training in the state laws, by providing effective literature and promoting publicity.

Simultaneously with the opposition campaigns outlined above, we propose to commence these two affirmative programs:

(3) *Create nation-wide publicity about the Hensley paragraphs* in the Navy Bill, and encourage delay on the ship-building program until the international agreement plans can be tried. Let every despairing pacifist in the country, every exhausted anti-militarist, every lover of democracy, every radical, every man who objects to having the taxes, wasted, every trade-unionist, every ordinary citizen who dislikes to feed the war trust,— let them all know that there is an "if" in the Naval Program, that a good share of the $315,000,000 can be saved to the people, if we can hold up the new building contracts until an international understanding is under way.

. . . . .

Then we can begin to suggest nine citizens for the international conference—we should secure an audience with the President to propose our candidates, and cable that story to the world. We should ask him what he can do at once to convince the people of all nations that he takes those paragraphs as seriously as any other legislation in 1916. He's bound to make an earnest statement. This story alone and the story of the big "if" in the contracts will do something to take the challenge and threat out of our new Navy Law.

There's no limit to the enthusiasm we can arouse over such a prospect. We'll have all the munition makers openly against us. It will be a glorious fight.

(4) Finally, *we must make the most of our Mexican experience*. We must make it known to everybody that the *people* acting directly—not through their governments or diplomats or armies—stopped that war, and can stop all wars if enough of them will act together and act quickly. We must celebrate this fact in some great and dignified way. The militarists will be quick to take the credit for peace. Let us too take time to claim our victories. We can contrast vividly the Civil Joint Commission [on the crisis, which met] at Atlantic City with a modern battlefield, and make it our rallying call for new support, new members, and new glory.

Then let us seriously and patiently construct the machinery for instant mobilization of the people for the prevention of any future war that might threaten this country. A war of simple wanton aggression against the United States is unthinkable. There would always be misunderstanding, false national pride, secret diplomacy, financial interests, something crooked at the bottom of it. And our plan for getting the people of the two countries into instant actual contact with and understanding of each other would always prevent it.

This would seem to be the way to begin: first, build up our own organization so that it is a real power in the land and known among liberals *all over the world*. Then educate our membership in what is expected of them if war threatens—so that we can have almost instant mobilization for service. Then get in touch with organizations like ours in other countries—especially those countries expected to be our enemies. Get them to select likely "joint Commissioners" who would start to meet ours on an hour's notice. (Our Mexican-American Commissioners have all pledged to start for the border on an hour's notice if war threatens again and their services are needed.) *Have the names and addresses ready.* (We waited twenty-four hours in the Mexican crisis because we didn't know the name of a single Mexican who would act with us. There's provincialism for you. Let our plan be the beginning of a *practical* internationalism.) Also get these leaders in foreign countries to send us their membership lists. We could then distribute the names among our active members and pledge them to cable at least one "enemy" a message of good-will to stave off war, if we send out the word. Imagine it! a thousand cables from "enemy" to "enemy" stating the firm friendliness of the people and their determination not to fight—all in 48 hours; and meanwhile the heads and subheads of organizations busy cabling stories to foreign papers, and a joint conference on its way to meet and *hold the peace*. There never could be a war if our peace forces could mobilize like that in 48 hours.

. . . . .

For such a program (1-2-3-4) [a reference to her numbered paragraphs above] we need a big membership,—10,000 before the year is out. We have on hand, 1,000 contributing members, 5,000 non-contributing members, and 60,000 likely names. We can build such an organization if we have the money to reach these people.

. . . . .

DOCUMENT 26

President Wilson's "Peace Without Victory" Speech (1917)

Editor's Note: After his reelection, Wilson began plans for his own truly independent mediation. Quite apart from this, on December 12, 1916, Berlin publicly indicated its willingness to discuss peace terms. On December 18, 1916, Wilson initiated his plan by sending notes to all belligerents urging them to state their war aims clearly as a way to begin negotiations. But almost at once Wilson's mediation plan fell apart, partly owing to the active resistance of the British and French to any compromise peace and partly as a result of the subversion of Wilson's proposal by his own secretary of state. The pro-Ally Robert Lansing privately assured the skeptical British and French that the U.S. government was not coordinating its effort with Berlin, and indeed Lansing recommended that the Allies state harsh war aims against Germany. Furthermore, on December 21, Lansing issued to the press a false explanation of Wilson's notes, stating that they were issued because the United States was "drawing nearer the verge of war" and needed to ascertain the belligerents' war aims in order to determine its own policies. Wilson was furious at Lansing's public distortion, but he settled for a half-hearted public correction.   In reality, there was little chance for acceptance of a compromise peace by the German government in the winter of 1916/1917 and none by the British and French. The Allies demanded German evacuation of occupied territory; a return of Alsace-Lorraine to France; sizable indemnities to Belgium, France, and Serbia; and the settlement of the Balkan questions by an international commission (privately, Paris wanted Germany disarmed and the Rhineland made a French protectorate. Also by secret treaties the Allies planned to divide up Germany's colonies and parts of the Austro-Hungarian and Ottoman empires). In return for an armistice, Germany apparently was merely ready to evacuate Belgium and France (but not its territorial gains on the Eastern Front). Indeed, when the diplomatic effort failed, Berlin was poised to take drastic military action—resumption and escalation of unrestricted submarine warfare—to starve the British Isles into accepting Germany's position.

When it became clear that the belligerents would not offer or accept reasonable peace terms, Wilson proceeded on a different tack, proposing independently the general priniciples of a proper peace settlement that would be capped by a mechanism for preventing such wars in the future. On January 22, 1917, Wilson laid out his peace proposals to the U.S. Senate in what quickly came to be known as his "Peace Without Victory" speech. In it, Wilson incorporated, in his own eloquent language, most of the key elements of the proposals of American and British pacifists and liberal internationalists. Wilson offered these to the Senate and to the world. In doing so, he secured his place at the head of the international movement for a liberal peace.

Address of the President of the United States to the Senate
January 22, 1917

．　．　．　．　．

I have sought this opportunity to address you because I thought that I owed it to you, as the council associated with me in the final determination of our international obligations, to disclose to you without reserve the thought and purpose that have been taking form in my mind in regard to the duty of our Government in the days to come when it will be necessary to lay afresh and upon a new plan the foundations of peace among the nations.

．　．　．　．　．

Source: "Address of the President of the United States to the Senate, January 22, 1917," in U.S. Department of State, Foreign Relations of the United States, 1917, Supplement I, The World War (Washington, D.C.: GPO, 1931), 24–29.

It is right that before it [a postwar settlement which would guarantee peace and justice] comes this Government should frankly formulate the conditions upon which it would feel justified in asking our people to approve its formal and solemn adherence to a league for peace. I am here to attempt to state those conditions.

The present war must first be ended; but we owe it to candour and to a just regard for the opinion of mankind to say that, so far as our participation in guarantees of future peace is concerned, it makes a great deal of difference in what way and upon what terms it is ended. The treaties and agreements which bring it to an end must embody terms which will create a peace that is worth guaranteeing and preserving, a peace that will win the approval of mankind, not merely a peace that will serve the several interests and immediate aims of the nations engaged. . . .

No covenant of cooperative peace that does not include the peoples of the New World can suffice to keep the future safe against war; and yet there is only one sort of peace that the peoples of America could join in guaranteeing. The elements of that peace must be elements that engage the confidence and satisfy the principles of the American governments, elements consistent with their political faith and with the practical convictions which the peoples of America have once for all embraced and undertaken to defend.

. . . Mere agreements may not make peace secure. It will be absolutely necessary that a force be created as a guarantor of the permanency of the settlement so much greater than the force of any nation now engaged or any alliance hitherto formed or projected that no nation, no probable combination of nations, could face or withstand it. If the peace presently to be made is to endure, it must be a peace made secure by the organized major force of mankind.

The terms of the immediate peace agreed upon will determine whether it is a peace for which such a guarantee can be secured. The question upon which the whole future peace and policy of the world depends is this: Is the present war a struggle for a just and secure peace, or only for a new balance of power. . . . There must be, not a balance of power, but a community of power; not organized rivalries, but an organized common peace.

Fortunately we have received very explicit assurances on this point. The statesmen of both of the groups of nations now arrayed against one another have said, in terms that could not be misinterpreted, that it was no part of the purpose they had in mind to crush their antagonists. [In reality, the Allies intended to dismember the Ottoman and Austro-

Hungarian empires, and the French in particular wanted to carve off Germany east of the Rhine to serve as a protective buffer zone. Wilson was aware of the belligerents' vehemence, but not all of their war aims. What he sought to do here was to deny that animosity and to increase public pressure on governmental leaders to accept a "peace without victory."] But the implications of these assurances may not be equally clear to all—may not be the same on both sides of the water. I think it will be serviceable if I attempt to set forth what we understand them to be.

They imply, first of all, that it must be a peace without victory. . . . Victory would mean peace forced upon the loser, a victor's terms imposed upon the vanquished. It would be accepted in humiliation, under duress, at an intolerable sacrifice, and would leave a sting, a resentment, a bitter memory upon which terms of peace would rest, not permanently, but only as upon quicksand. Only a peace between equals can last, only a peace the very principle of which is equality and a common participation in a common benefit. The right state of mind, the right feeling between nations, is as necessary for a lasting peace as is the just settlement of vexed questions of territory or of racial and national allegiance.

The equality of nations upon which peace must be founded if it is to last must be an equality of rights; the guarantees exchanged must neither recognize nor imply a difference between big nations and small, between those that are powerful and those that are weak. . . .

And there is a deeper thing involved than even equality of right among organized nations. No peace can last, or ought to last, which does not recognize and accept the principle that governments derive all their just powers from the consent of the governed, and that no right anywhere exists to hand peoples about from sovereignty to sovereignty as if they were property. . . .

. . . . .

And the paths of the sea must alike in law and in fact be free. The freedom of the seas is the *sine qua non* of peace, equality, and cooperation. . . . The free, constant, unthreatened intercourse of nations is an essential part of the process of peace and of development. . . .

It is a problem closely connected with the limitation of naval armaments and the cooperation of the navies of the world in keeping the seas at once free and safe, and the question of limiting naval armaments opens the wider and perhaps more difficult question of the limitation of armies and of all programmes of military preparation. Difficult and delicate as these questions are, they must be faced with the utmost candour and decided in a spirit of real accommodation if peace is to come with healing in its wings, and come to stay. . . .

I have spoken upon these great matters without reserve and with the utmost explicitness because it has seemed to me to be necessary if the world's yearning desire for peace was anywhere to find free voice and utterance. Perhaps I am the only person in high authority amongst all the peoples of the world who is at liberty to speak and hold nothing back. . . . May I not add that I hope and believe that I am in effect speaking for liberals and friends of humanity in every nation and of every programme of liberty? I would fain believe that I am speaking for the silent mass of mankind everywhere who have as yet had no place or opportunity to speak their real hearts out concerning the death and ruin they see to have come already upon the persons and the homes they hold most dear.

And in holding out the expectation that the people and Government of the United States will join the other civilized nations of the world in guaranteeing the permanence of peace upon such terms as I have named I speak with the greater boldness and confidence because it is clear to every man who can think that there is in this promise no breach in either our traditions or our policy as a nation, but a fulfillment, rather, of all that we have professed or striven for. . . .

. . . . .

DOCUMENT 27

Jane Addams Recalls Wilson and Peace Efforts, 1915 to 1917 (1922)

Editor's Note: Nearly four years after the end of the war, Jane Addams, then international president of the Women's International League for Peace and Freedom, wrote an account of the peace movement during the tumultous era of World War I. Her 1922 memoir, an excerpt of which is reprinted below, was based upon her published writings, pri-

vate papers, and recollections. It was also influenced, of course, by
perceptions from the immediate postwar period about the consequences
of earlier attitudes, actions, and events.

President Wilson's Policies

. . . Up to the moment of his nomination for a second term our hopes
[those of the Woman's Peace party and the American Union Against
Militarism] had gradually shifted to the belief that the President would
finally act, not so much from his own preferences or convictions, but
from the impact upon him of public opinion, from the momentum of
the pressure for Peace, which we were sure the campaign itself would
make clear to him.

. . . . .

We were, to be sure, at moments a little uneasy in regard to his
theory of self-government, a theory which had reappeared in his campaign speeches and was so similar to that found in his earlier books. It
seemed at those times as if he were not so eager for a mandate to carry
out the will of the people as for an opportunity to lead the people
whither in his judgment their best interest lay. Did he place too much
stress on leadership?

But moments of uneasiness were forgotten and the pacifists in every
part of the world were not only enormously reassured but were sent up
into the very heaven of internationalism, as it were when President
Wilson delivered his famous speech to the Senate in January, 1917, [the
"Peace Without Victory" speech; see document 26] which forecast his
fourteen points [in which Wilson spelled out his vision of a peace settlement in more detail in a speech of January 8, 1918; see document 39].
Some of these points had, of course, become common property among
Liberals since the first year of the war when they had been formulated
by The league for Democratic Control in England and later became
known as a "union" program [the league was also known as the Union
of Democratic Control]. Our Woman's International Congress held at
The Hague in May, 1915, had incorporated most of the English formula
and had added others. *The President himself had been kind enough to*
say when I presented our Hague program to him in August, 1915, that

Source: Jane Addams, *Peace and Bread in Time of War* (New York: Macmillan 1922),
57–60.

they were the best formulation he had seen up to that time. [Emphasis added.]

President Wilson, however, later not only gathered together the best liberal statements yet made, formulated them in his incomparable English and added others of his own, but he was the first responsible statesmen to enunciate them as an actual program for guidance in a troubled world. . . . We considered that the United States was committed not only to using its vast neutral power to extend democracy throughout the world, but also to the conviction that democratic ends could not be attained through the technique of war. In short, we believed that rational thinking and reasonable human relationships were once more publicly recognized as valid in international affairs.

· · · · ·

DOCUMENT 28

Theodore Roosevelt's Critique in Favor of Increased Military Forces and Complete Victory Against Germany (1917)

Editor's Note: Former President Theodore Roosevelt had long viewed Woodrow Wilson as his personal nemesis as the two men vied with each other for the leadership of American opinion and public policy. Roosevelt had run against Wilson (and Taft) in 1912 as an insurgent Republican candidate; in 1916 he had campaigned against Wilson on behalf of the regular Republican candidate, Charles Evans Hughes. Both Roosevelt and Wilson were moralistic as well as pragmatic political leaders; both also saw that the United States had an expanded role to play in the world. They differed greatly, however, over specific military and foreign policy. Unlike Wilson, Roosevelt loathed pacifists and personally relished combat. Between 1915 and 1917, the former president believed in greatly increasing American military and naval forces and in taking the United States into the war on the side of the Allies. In the following statement to the press on January 28, 1917, Roosevelt used an inflammatory style to repudiate Wilson's foreign policy and instead to mobi-

lize support for U.S. military preparation and aid to the Allies in their quest for victory against Germany.

Roosevelt Renews Attack on Wilson

. . . . .

President Wilson has announced himself in favor of peace without victory, and now he has declared himself against universal [military] service—that is, against all efficient preparedness by the United States.

Peace without victory is the natural ideal of the man who is too proud to fight. In the event of war it is the only kind of peace open to the nation whose governors and leaders are too proud to fight and too foolish to prepare. It is spurned by all men of lofty soul, by all men fit to call themselves fellow-citizens of Washington and Lincoln, or of the war-worn fighters who followed Grant and Lee.

The Tories of 1776 [Loyalists who opposed the break with England] demanded peace without victory. The Copperheads of 1864 [pro-Southern, peace Democrats in the North during the Civil War] demanded peace without victory. These men were Mr. Wilson's spiritual forbears. But neither Washington nor Lincoln was among the men who draw the sword lightly, or who, when once it has been drawn, sheath it without victory. If a righteous war is concluded by a peace without victory, such a peace means the triumph of wrong over right, and neutrality between right and wrong means the support of wrong against right.

Mr. Wilson asks the world to accept a Copperhead peace of dishonor, a peace without victory for the right, a peace designed to let wrong triumph, a peace championed in neutral countries by the apostles of timidity and greed. In Mexico he has accepted and is accepting such a peace, and by his Mexican policy he has brought disaster to Mexico and dishonor to the United States. His policies throughout his four years have brought woe to humanity and shame and bitterness of heart to all Americans proud of the honor of their flag.

President Wilson talks of the "freedom of the seas." The basic form of freedom is to be free from murder. Yet, President Wilson has not dared to secure even this elementary freedom for our men, women and children on the seas. Let him first act in the present to secure this

Source: Theodore Roosevelt, Statement to the press, Jan. 28, 1917, *New York Times,* Jan. 29, 1917.

elementary freedom from Germany before, in the interest of Germany, he asks the abolition of naval power. Let him remember that to work for disarmament on the seas until after there has been disarmament on land by the great military powers of Europe and Asia, is to put this non-military country at the mercy of every military monarchy; for inasmuch as we are now defenseless on land, our navy is our only safeguard against invasion.

. . . . .

DOCUMENT 29

Peace Movement Leaders Meet with President Wilson
During the War Crisis (1917)

Editor's Note: In January 1917, the military and civilian leaders of the Imperial German government concluded that the Allies would not agree to serious negotiations. With discontent mounting in Germany, the military-dominated government decided on a desperate strategic gamble— to renew and expand unrestricted submarine warfare, this time even against American shipping. The goal was to blockade the British Isles effectively and to force concessions from the western Allies within six months, long before there could be any major U.S. reinforcement on the Western Front. Following the German announcement on January 31 of unrestricted submarine warfare, Wilson severed diplomatic relations with Berlin on February 3. On February 26, in hope of deterring U-boats from attack, the president asked Congress for authority to arm American merchant ships. Two days earlier, the British had given the U.S. government an intercepted message from the German foreign minister (the Zimmermann telegram) proposing an alliance with Mexico against the United States. (Wilson would release it to the press on March 1, 1917, in an attempt to get his armed ship resolution through Congress.)

As the crisis mounted, pacifists sought to coordinate their efforts. On February 22 and 23, 1917, about 150 delegates from twenty-two leading peace societies met in New York City and formed the Emergency Peace Federation. One of the results was a visit to the White House by a delegation that included Jane Addams; Emily Greene Balch; Joseph D. Cannon, an organizer for the Western Federation of Miners and Socialist party candidate for U.S. senator from New York in 1916; Frederick H. Lynch, secretary of the Church Peace Union and director of the New York Peace Society; and William I. Hull, prominent Quaker, pacifist, and professor of history and international relations at Swarthmore College. Hull was probably the author of the following account, which appeared in March 1917 in a leading Quaker magazine, of the meeting with the president on February 28, 1917.

A Visit to the President

. . . . .

It was a time of very grave national tension, and the President talked most feelingly with the delegation, but as he pledged its members to hold in entire confidence whatever he might say, no statement of his side of the conversation can be given. It might be of interest, however, to give in outline the message which the delegation presented to him.

Dr. [William I.] Hull emphasized a number of historical precedents for the peaceful solution of exceedingly difficult international problems. Among these were precedents set by Washington, John Adams, Lincoln, and President Wilson himself. . . .

. . . . .

In view of these and other notable precedents, Doctor Hull ventured to urge that two joint commissions of inquiry and conciliation should be appointed to negotiate with Germany and Great Britain, respectively, a *modus vivendi* [a temporary arrangement pending a final settlement] relating to neutral rights and duties—possibly in line with an Declaration of London—until the end of the war. [The declaration of an international conference in London in 1909 represented liberal thought on maritime warfare, including definitions of the kind of commerce that could be prohibited in wartime. It had been approved by a number of countries, including Germany, but not by Great Britain.] This attempt might seem especially helpful for the reason that both Great Britain and Germany have endorsed in principle the offer of the United States to investigate and settle by conciliatory means disputes which might arise

Source: "A Visit to the President," *Friends' Intelligencer* 74 (Mar. 10, 1917): 147–48; reprinted in Link et al., *The Papers of Woodrow Wilson* 41: 302–4.

between them; and also because such an offer would seem so reasonable to the *people* of the two belligerent governments that those governments could not well decline it.

Miss [Jane] Addams emphasized especially the anxiety and distress of the German and Austrian immigrant families domiciled within our country, and mentioned several moving illustrations which had come to her personally in connection with her work at Hull House in Chicago. She quoted some of her immigrant friends as declaring that "Your President will not go to war, because he is a man of peace." She also expressed her conviction that our country cannot be precipitated into war by the "hyper-nationalism" which has forced the European belligerents into war, because of the cosmopolitan character of our American population; and she made a fervent appeal to the President that the great program of social legislation upon which his administration has made so splendid a beginning should not be sidetracked or destroyed by leading the country into a military means of settling international disputes.

Mr. [Joseph] Cannon, a representative of the miners, especially of those in the far West, reminded the President that all of the political parties in the recent Presidential campaign had endorsed the President's policy of keeping the country out of war, and he emphasized especially the overwhelming advocacy of the peace policy in the Democratic Convention, platform, and campaign; and finally he assured the President that only a small minority of the people were in favor of the war, and that the great majority of the American people would support unwaveringly whatever peaceful method the President decided upon for a solution of the outstanding questions with Germany and Great Britain.

Miss [Emily Greene] Balch expressed her conviction, on the basis of personal experience [including trips to Europe in 1915 and 1916] since the war began, that the German people were wholly adverse to war with the United States, and that if the President could decide upon some peaceful means of settling the dispute with their government, they would force their government to consider it.

After these preliminary statements were presented to the President, he entered into a very frank and earnest conversation with the delegation, in which he gave further convincing evidence of his earnest desire to find some peaceful means of settling our present international difficulties.

· · · · ·

DOCUMENT 30

Jane Addams's Recollection of the February 28, 1917,
Meeting with Wilson (1922)

*Editor's Note: In her postwar memoir, Addams no longer felt obligated
to maintain the confidentiality of the February 28, 1917, meeting (see
document 29). In her 1922 memoir, she offered the following recollection of Wilson's remarks to the pacifists.*

President Wilson's Policies

... Professor Hull of Swarthmore College, a former student of the
President's, presented a brief résumé of what other American presidents
had done through adjudication when the interests of American shipping
had become involved during European war; notably, George Washington during the French Revolution and John Adams in the Napoleonic
War, so that international adjudication instituted by Chief Justice Jay
became known in Europe as "the American plan." The President was,
of course, familiar with that history, as he reminded his old pupil, but
he brushed it aside as he did the suggestion that if the attack on American shipping were submitted to The Hague tribunal, it might result in
adjudication of the issues of the great war itself. The Labor man on the
committee [Joseph D. Cannon] still expressed the hope for a popular
referendum before war should be declared, and we once more pressed
for a conference of neutrals. . . . The President's mood was stern and far
from the scholar's detachment as he told us of recent disclosures of
German machinations in Mexico [the Zimmermann telegram; see editor's
note to document 29] and announced the impossibility of any form of
adjudication. He still spoke to us, however, as to fellow pacifists to
whom he was forced to confess that war had become inevitable. He
used one phrase which I had heard Colonel House [Edward M. House,
a Texas "colonel," the president's intimate if unofficial foreign policy
adviser] use so recently that it still stuck firmly in my memory. The
phrase was to the effect that, as head of a nation participating in the
war, the President of the United States would have a seat at the Peace
Table, but that if he remained the representative of a neutral country he
could at best only "call through a crack in the door." The appeal he
made was, in substance, that the foreign policy which we so extrava-

Source: Addams, Peace and Bread in Time of War, 63–65.

gantly admired could have a chance if he were there to push and to defend them [*sic*], but not otherwise. It was as if his heart's desire spoke through his words and dictated his view of the situation. But I found my mind challenging his whole theory of leadership. Was it a result of my bitter disappointment that I hotly and no doubt unfairly asked myself whether any man had the right to rate his moral leadership so high that he could consider the sacrifice of the lives of thousands of his young countrymen a necessity? I also reminded myself that all the study of modern social science is but a revelation of the fallacy of such a point of view, a discrediting of the Carlyle contention [Thomas Carlyle, 1795–1881, English author and social critic] that the people must be led into the ways of righteousness by the experience, acumen and virtues of the great man.

. . . . .

PART THREE

The Challenge of American Belligerency:
Mobilization, War Aims, and Wartime Dissent,
1917 to 1918

DOCUMENT 31

President Wilson's War Message (1917)

Editor's Note: On March 5, 1917, Wilson began his second term as president. On March 12, at the outset of the Russian Revolution, Tsar Nicholas II was replaced by a provisional constitutional government under Prince Lvov. Wilson considered this event part of the liberal tide toward democratic government that might also affect the German and Austro-Hungarian empires. However, on March 18, Washington learned that three American merchant ships had been sunk by U-boats without warning with the loss of fifteen American lives. Two days later, after a unanimous cabinet vote for war, Wilson called a special session of Congress for April 2. For nearly two weeks he worked on his speech.

Wilson's war message of April 2, 1917, reprinted below, emphasized that the war had been thrust upon the United States. In its most inspiring passages, the speech appealed to American idealism, portraying intervention as a means of achieving a just and lasting peace and creating a liberal world order. In Wilson's memorable words, "the world must be made safe for democracy."

Address of the President of the United States, April 2, 1917

．．．．．

On the 3d of February last I officially laid before you the extraordinary announcement of the Imperial German Government that on and after the 1st day of February it was its purpose to put aside all restraints of law or of humanity and use its submarines to sink every vessel that sought to approach either the ports of Great Britain and Ireland or the western coasts of Europe. . . . Vessels of every kind, whatever their flag, their character, their cargo, their destination, their errand, have been ruthlessly sent to the bottom without warning and without thought of help or mercy for those on board, the vessels of friendly neutrals along with those of belligerents. Even hospital ships and ships carrying relief to the sorely bereaved and stricken people of Belguim, though the latter were provided with safe-conduct through the proscribed areas by the

Source: "Address of the President of the United States Delivered at a Joint Session of the Two Houses of Congress, April 2, 1917," U.S. Department of State, *Foreign Relations of the United States, 1917, Supplement I, The World War,* 194–203.

German Government itself and were distinguished by unmistakable marks of identity, have been sunk with the same reckless lack of compassion or of principle.

I was for a little while unable to believe that such things would in fact be done by any government that had hitherto subscribed to the humane practices of civilized nations. International law had its origin in the attempt to set up some law which would be respected and observed upon the seas, where no nation had right of dominion and where lay the free highways of the world. . . . This minimum of right the German Government has swept aside . . . throwing to the winds all scruples of humanity of respect for the understandings that were supposed to underlie the intercourse of the world. . . . The present German submarine warfare against commerce is a warfare against mankind.

It is a war against all nations. American ships have been sunk, American lives taken, in ways which it has stirred us very deeply to learn of . . . . We must put excited feeling away. Our motive will not be revenge or the victorious assertion of the physical might of the nation, but only the vindication of right, of human right, of which we are only a single champion.

When I addressed the Congress on the 26th of February last, I thought that it would suffice to assert our neutral rights with arms, our right to use the seas against unlawful interference, our right to keep our people safe against unlawful violence. But armed neutrality, it now appears, is impracticable. . . . It is practically certain to draw us into the war without either the rights or the effectiveness of belligerents. . . .

With a profound sense of the solemn and even tragical character of the step I am taking and of the grave responsibilities which it involves, but in unhesitating obedience to what I deem my constitutional duty, I advise that the Congress declare the recent course of the Imperial German Government to be in fact nothing less than war against the Government and people of the United States; that it formally accept the status of belligerent which has thus been thrust upon it; and that it take immediate steps not only to put the country in a more thorough state of defense but also to exert all its power and employ all its resources to bring the Government of the German Empire to terms and end the war.

. . . . .

. . . [L]et us be very clear, and make very clear to all the world what our motives and our objects are. . . . Our object now, as then, is to vindicate the principles of peace and justice in the life of the world as against selfish and autocratic power and to set up amongst the really free and self-governed peoples of the world such a concert of purpose and of action as will henceforth ensure the observance of those principles. . . . We have seen the last of neutrality in such circumstances. We are at the beginning of an age in which it will be insisted that the same standards of conduct and of responsibility for wrong done shall be observed among nations and their governments that are observed among the individual citizens of civilized states.

We have no quarrel with the German people. We have no feeling towards them but one of sympathy and friendship. It was not upon their impulse that their Government acted in entering this war. It was not with their previous knowledge or approval. It was a war determined upon as wars used to be determined upon in the old, unhappy days when peoples were nowhere consulted by their rulers and wars were provoked and waged in the interest of dynasties or of little groups of ambitious men who were accustomed to use their fellow men as pawns and tools. . . .

A steadfast concert for peace can never be maintained except by a partnership of democratic nations. No autocratic government could be trusted to keep faith within it or observe its covenants. It must be a league of honour, a partnership of opinion. . . .

. . . . .

We are glad, now that we see the facts with no veil of false pretence about them, to fight thus for the ultimate peace of the world and for the liberation of its peoples, the German peoples included; for the rights of nations great and small and the privilege of men everywhere to choose their way of life and of obedience. The world must be made safe for democracy. Its peace must be planted upon the tested foundations of political liberty. We have no selfish ends to serve. We desire no conquest, no dominion. We seek no indemnities for ourselves, no material compensation for the sacrifices we shall freely make. We are but one of the champions of the rights of mankind. We shall be satisfied when those rights have been made as secure as the faith and the freedom of nations can make them.

. . . . .

. . . It is a fearful thing to lead this great peaceful people into war, into the most terrible and disastrous of all wars, civilization itself seeming to be in the balance. But the right is more precious than peace, and we shall fight for the things which we have always carried nearest our hearts—for democracy, for the right of those who submit to authority to have a voice in their own governments, for the rights and liberties of small nations, for a universal dominion of right by such a concert of free peoples as shall bring peace and safety to all nations and make the world itself at last free. . . .

DOCUMENT 32

Socialist Party Position on American Belligerency (1917)

Editor's Note: Immediately following the congressional declaration of war on April 6, the Socialist party of America held an emergency convention in St. Louis, April 7 to 14, 1917, to determine its position on U.S. intervention. The party's Committee on War and Militarism produced the antiwar "majority" report, reprinted below, which was endorsed by eleven members of the committee and which received 140 votes at the convention. (An unofficial pro-intervention "minority" report was written by one member of the committee and received five votes at the convention.) Although it opposed war and the draft, the "majority" report alienated some of the more radical Socialists because it failed to call for a general strike. Its primary author was Morris Hillquit, 1869–1933, a New York labor lawyer and a leader of the Socialist party's centrist faction.

The "Majority" Report of the St. Louis Convention

The Socialist Party of the United States in the present grave crisis, solemnly reaffirms its allegiance to the principle of internationalism and working class solidarity the world over, and proclaims its unalterable opposition to the war just declared by the government of the United States.

Modern wars as a rule have been caused by the commercial and financial rivalry and intrigues of the capitalist interests in the different countries. Whether they have been frankly waged as wars of aggression

Source: "The 'Majority' . . . Report of the St. Louis Convention," [April 1917], in Alexander Trachtenberg, ed., *The American Socialists and the War* (N.Y.: Rand School of Social Science, 1917), 38–45.

or have been hypocritically represented as wars of "defense", they have always been made by the classes and fought by the masses. Wars bring wealth and power to the ruling classes, and suffering, death and demoralization to the workers.

The forces of capitalism which have led to the war in Europe are even more hideously transparent in the war recently provoked by the ruling class of this country.

When Belgium was invaded [by Germany in 1914], the government enjoined upon the people of this country the duty of remaining neutral, thus clearly demonstrating that the "dictates of humanity," and the fate of small nations and of democratic institutions were matters that did not concern it. But when our enormous war traffic was seriously threatened, our government calls upon us to rally to the "defense of democracy and civilizations."

Our entrance into the European war was instigated by the predatory capitalists in the United States who boast of the enormous profit of seven billion dollars from the manufacture and sale of munitions and war supplies and from the exportation of American food stuffs and other necessaries. They are also deeply interested in the continuance of war and the success of the allied arms through their huge loans to the governments of the allied powers and through other commercial ties. It is the same interests which strive for imperialistic domination of the Western Hemisphere.

The war of the United States against Germany cannot be justified even on the plea that it is a war in defense of American rights or American "honor." Ruthless as the unrestricted submarine war policy of the German government was and is, it is not an invasion of the rights of the American people, as such, but only an interference with the opportunity of certain groups of American capitalists to coin cold profits out of the blood and sufferings of our fellow men in the warring countries of Europe.

It is cant and hypocrisy to say that the war is not directed against the German people, but against the Imperial Government of Germany. If we send an armed force to the battlefields of Europe, its cannon will mow down the masses of the German people and not the Imperial German Government.

Our entrance into the European conflict at this time will serve only to multiply the horrors of the war, to increase the toll of death and destruction and to prolong the fiendish slaughter. It will bring death, suffering and destitution to the people of the United States and particularly to the working class. It will give the powers of reaction in this country, the pretext for an attempt to throttle our rights and to crush our democratic institutions, and to fasten upon this country a permanent militarism. . . .

We brand the declaration of war by our government as crime against the people of the United States and against the nations of the world.

. . . . .

In harmony with these principles, the Socialist Party emphatically rejects the proposal that in time of war the workers should suspend their struggle for better conditions. On the contrary, the acute situation created by war calls for an even more vigorous prosecution of the class struggle, and we recommend to the workers and pledge ourselves to the following course of action:

1. Continuous, active, and public opposition to the war through demonstrations, mass petitions, and all other means within our power.

2. Unyielding opposition to all proposed legislation for military or industrial conscription. Should such conscription be forced upon the people, we pledge ourselves to continuous efforts for the repeal of such laws and to the support of all mass movements in opposition to conscription. We pledge ourselves to oppose with all our strength any attempt to raise money for payment of war expense by taxing the necessaries of life or issuing bonds which will put the burden upon future generations. We demand that the capitalist class, which is responsible for the war, pay its cost. . . .

3. Vigorous resistance to all reactionary measures, such as censorship of press and mails, restriction of the rights of free speech, assemblage, and organization, or compulsory arbitration and limitation of the right to strike.

4. Consistent propaganda against military training and militaristic teaching in the public schools.

5. Extension of the campaign of education among the workers to organize them into strong, class-conscious, and closely unified political and industrial organizations. . . .

. . . . .

. . . The end of wars will come with the establishment of socialized industry and industrial democracy the world over. The Socialist Party calls upon all the workers to join it in its struggle to reach this goal, and thus bring into the world a new society in which peace, fraternity, and human brotherhood will be the dominant ideals.

DOCUMENT 33

Resolutions of the People's Council (1917)

Editor's Note: The People's Council of America for Peace and Democracy was organized by pacifists and socialists in the spring of 1917 to sustain civil liberties and democratic peace terms against wartime chauvinism. At a giant rally in New York's Madison Square Garden on May 30 and 31, 1917, the new organization adopted the following program.

Resolutions of the . . . People's Council of America

1. PEACE

The Conference favors an early, general and democratic peace, to be secured through negotiation in harmony with the principles outlined by the President of the United State[s] and by revolutionary Russia, and accepted substantially by the progressive and democratic forces of France, England, Italy, Germany, Austria and other countries, namely:

(a) No forcible annexation of territory.

(b) No punitive indemnities.

(c) Free development of all nationalities.

We favor international reorganization for the maintenance of peace. As steps leading thereto, we suggest: The adjudication of disputes among nations; simultaneous disarmament; freedom of the seas and international waterways; protection of small nations; and other similar measures.

2. STATEMENT OF TERMS

We urge the Government of the United States immediately to announce its war aims in definite and concrete terms upon the above principles and to make efforts to induce the Allied countries to make similar declarations, thus informing our public for what concrete objects they are called upon to fight, and thereby forcing a definite expression of war aims on the part of the Central Powers.

Source: Resolutions of the First American Conference for Democracy and Terms of Peace, Organized by the People's Council of America for Democracy and Peace, New York City, May 30–31, 1917, undated [ca. June 1917] pamphlet in the Swarthmore College Peace Collection.

We demand that this country shall make peace the moment its announced aims shall have been achieved, and that it shall not carry on
war for the territorial and imperialistic ambitions of other countries.
Further, we demand that it shall make no agreement with other governments limiting its freedom of action nor any agreement or understanding looking toward an economic war after the war.

3. American Liberties

The first victims of war are the people's liberties. . . .
We hereby protest to the President and Congress against the abridgement of these rights, and call upon the American people to defend them.
We shall oppose with all legal means at our disposal the censorship of
newspapers and of other printed matter or interference with their distribution by the postal department.

. . . . .

Secret diplomacy must be abolished. We demand democratic control
of our foreign policy. We call for a referendum on questions of war and
conscription. We insist on discussion in Congress, in the press and in
public meetings of the terms of all alliances, agreements and treaties. It
seems to be the intention of the government now to forbid even the
discussion of the terms of peace in the press and in public meetings.

4. Conscription

We pledge ourselves to work for the repeal of all laws for compulsory military training and compulsory service and to oppose the enactment of all such laws in the future.

. . . . .

5. Industrial Standards

The standard of living of American workers prior to the war was low
enough, as revealed by the report of the industrial relations commission
and other impartial investigators.
The long struggle that has been waged to reduce hours, to raise
wages, to abolish child labor, to protect the life, limbs and health of the
wage-earners, has created definite minimum labor standards. A nation-
wide assault on these standards is now in progress. Labor laws are

being suspended or repealed; cheap alien labor is to be imported; women are replacing the men who leave for the front. We call upon the working people to resist this assault by insisting that the labor laws be preserved and enforced; by maintaining the rights gained through the labor movements; by opposing the importation of cheap alien labor and prisoners of war, and by insisting that where women take the place of men they receive men's wages.

. . . . .

DOCUMENT 34

Jane Addams on Patriotism and Pacifists in Wartime (1917)

Editor's Note: With the declaration of war, many reformers joined the crusade to make the world "safe for democracy," leaving former colleagues who remained pacifists isolated and often scorned. Among the pacifists, Jane Addams continued to oppose war, and as a member of the newly formed National Civil Liberties Bureau of the American Union Against Militarism, she protested the passage of the conscription act and the censorship provisions of the Espionage Act. She also helped to monitor the treatment of conscientious objectors who were conscripted into the army. On May 15, 1917, Addams spoke to the City Club of Chicago in rebuttal against accusations, following the declaration of war, that pacifists were unrealistic, unpatriotic, and cowardly. Her address was reprinted in the June 1917 issue of the City Club's Bulletin from which the following excerpt is taken.

Patriotism and Pacifists in War Time

. . . . .

In the stir of the heroic moment when a nation enters war, men's minds are driven back to the earliest obligations of patriotism, and

Source: Jane Addams, "Patriotism and Pacifists in War Time," [Chicago] City Club Bulletin 10, no. 9 (June 16, 1917).

almost without volition the emotions move along the worn grooves of blind admiration for the soldier and of unspeakable contempt for him who, in the hour of danger, declares that fighting is unnecessary. We pacifists are not surprised, therefore, when apparently striking across and reversing this popular conception of patriotism, that we should not only be considered incapable of facing reality, but that we should be called traitors and cowards. It makes it all the more incumbent upon us, however, to demonstrate, if we can, that in our former advocacy we urged a reasonable and vital alternative to war, and that our position now does not necessarily imply lack of patriotism or cowardice.

. . . . .

First: The similarity of sound between the words "passive" and "pacifism" is often misleading. . . . [W]e pacifists, so far from passively wishing nothing to be done, contend on the contrary that this world crisis should be utilized for the creation of an international government able to make the necessary political and economic changes when they are due; we feel that it is unspeakably stupid that the nations should have failed to create an international organization through which each one, without danger to itself, might recognize and even encourage the impulse toward growth in other nations.

Pacifists believe that in the Europe of 1914, certain tendencies were steadily pushing towards large changes which in the end made war, because the system of peace had no way of effecting those changes without war, no adequate international organization which could cope with the situation. The conception of peace founded upon the balance of power or the undisturbed *status quo,* was so negative that frustrated national impulses and suppressed vital forces led to war, because no method of orderly expression had been devised.

We are not advocating the mid-Victorian idea that good men from every country meet together at The Hague or elsewhere, where they shall pass a resolution, that "wars hereby cease" and that "the world hereby be federated." What we insist upon is that the world can be organized politically by its statesmen as it has been already organized into an international fiscal system by its bankers or into an international scientific association by its scientists. . . .

The very breakdown exhibited by the present war reinforces the pacifists' contention that there is need of an international charter—a Magna Charta indeed—of international rights, to be issued by the nations great and small, with large provisions for economic freedom.

In reply to the old charge of lack of patriotism, we claim that we are patriotic from the historic viewpoint as well as by other standards. American pacifists believe—if I may go back to those days before the war, which already seem so far away—that the United States was especially qualified by her own particular experience to take the leadership in a peaceful organization of the world. . . .

. . . . .

With such a national history back of us, as pacifists we are thrown into despair over our inability to make our position clear when we are accused of wishing to isolate the United States and to keep our country out of world politics. We are, of course, urging a policy exactly the reverse. . . .

We had also hoped much from the varied population of the United States, for whether we will or not, our very composition would make it easier for us than for any other nation to establish an international organization founded upon understanding and good will, did we but possess the requisite courage and intelligence to utilize it.

. . . . .

Some of us once dreamed that the cosmopolitan inhabitants of this great nation might at last become united in a vast common endeavor for social ends. We hoped that this fusing might be accomplished without the sense of opposition to a common enemy which is an old method of welding people together, better fitted for military than for social use. If this for the moment is impossible, let us at least place the spirit of cooperation above that of bitterness and remember the wide distinction between social control and military coercion.

. . . . .

When as pacifists we urge a courageous venture into international ethics, which will require a fine valor as well as a high intelligence, we experience a sense of anti-climax when we are told that because we do not want war, we are so cowardly as to care for "safety first," that we place human life, physical life, above the great ideals of national righteousness.

But surely that man is not without courage who, seeing that which is invisible to the majority of his fellow countrymen, still asserts his conviction and is ready to vindicate its spiritual value over against the world. Each advance in the zigzag line of human progress has traditionally been embodied in small groups of individuals, who have ceased to be in harmony with the *status quo* and have demanded modifications. . . .

. . . . . .

With visions of international justice filling our minds, pacifists are always a little startled when those who insist that justice can only be established by war, accuse us of caring for peace irrespective of justice. Many of the pacifists in their individual and corporate capacity have long striven for social and political justice with a fervor perhaps equal to that employed by the advocates of force, and we realize that a sense of justice has become the keynote to the best political and social activity in this generation.

We believe that the ardor and self sacrifice so characteristic of youth could be enlisted for the vitally energetic role which we hope our beloved country will inaugurate in the international life of the world.

With such a creed, can the pacifists of today be accused of selfishness when they urge upon the United States not isolation, not indifference to moral issues and to the fate of liberty and democracy, but a strenuous endeavor to lead all nations of the earth into an organized international life worthy of civilized men?

DOCUMENT 35

Government Censorship and *The Masses* Magazine (1917)

Editor's Note: Through social criticism and scathing satire, The Masses became the leading magazine for political and literary radicalism in America during its short existence from 1911 to 1918. Although not formally connected to the Socialist party, the monthly magazine was generally socialistic in its viewpoint. It was edited by Max Eastman, with regular articles by Upton Sinclair, John Reed, Mary Heaton Vorse, and Floyd Dell, as well as drawings by John Sloan and Art Young. Highly critical of the war and conscription, the August 1917 issue of The Masses was denied mailing privileges by the U.S. Post Office, as attested by the following statement in the September issue. After a stinging rebuff by Judge Learned Hand, a leading jurist and defender of civil liberties, the Post Office Department found a sympathetic circuit court judge to rule against the August issue, a judgment upheld unanimously in November by the U.S. Court of Appeals, Second Circuit.

Eventually, Postmaster General Albert S. Burleson suppressed The Masses *completely, taking away its mailing privileges on the grounds that it was no longer a regularly issued periodical. In 1918, the government went further and indicted Eastman, Reed, Dell, and Young under the Espionage Act of June 15, 1917, which prohibited not only aid to the enemy but also words or deeds which obstructed recruiting or caused insubordination, disloyalty, or refusal of duty in the armed forces. The government failed to convict, however, when two lengthy trials in New York City ended in hung juries. The following account appeared in the September 1917 issue of* The Masses.

What Happened to the August *Masses?*

1. August issue presented for mailing at the New York post office, July 3d [1917].

2. Copies of August issue forwarded to Washington for "examination." The Solicitor of the Post Office Department [William H. Lamar], the Attorney General [Thomas W. Gregory], and Judge Advocate General [Enoch] Crowder, of the United States Army, conferred about excluding it from the mails and decided that this should be done.

3. Letter received July 5th from T[homas]. G. Patten, postmaster of New York City, informing us that:

"according to advices received from the Solicitor of the Postoffice [sic] Department, the August issue of *The Masses* is unmailable under the Act of June 15th, 1917" [Espionage Act].

4. The business manager of *The Masses* interviewed in Washington Solicitor Lamar, who refused to state what provisions of the Espionage Act the August *Masses* violated, or what particular parts of the magazine violated the law. (July 6th.)

5. *The Masses* retained as counsel Gilbert E. Roe [a well known civil liberties lawyer]. Bill in equity to federal court, to enjoin postmaster from excluding the magazine from the mails, filed July 12th. Motion made returnable before Judge Learned Hand on July 16.

6. Hearing postponed till July 21st, the Post Office Department being unprepared.

Source: "What Happened to the August *Masses?*" *The Masses* 9 (Sept. 1917): 3.

7. Argument lasting all day, July 21st, on motion for injunction.

The Post Office Department was represented by Asst. U. S. District Attorney [Earl B.] Barnes. He explained that the Department construed the Espionage Act as giving it power to exclude from the mails anything which might interfere with the successful conduct of the war.

Four cartoons and four pieces of text in the August issue were specified as violations of the law. . . .

Gilbert E. Roe, on behalf of *The Masses,* urged that the Espionage Act was not intended to prohibit political criticism or discussion, and that to permit the Post Office Department to use it as cover for arbitrary acts of suppression, would be to recognize a censorship set up without warrant of law.

8. Preliminary injunction against postmaster granted by Judge Hand.

Judge Hand, in an extended decision, sustained *The Masses* contention at all points. The construction placed by the postal authorities on the Espionage Act was shown to be invalid. The specific provisions of the law, he points out, are not violated by the magazine. Its cartoons and editorials "fall within the scope of that right to criticise, either by temperate reasoning or by immoderate and indecent invective, which is normally the privilege of the individual in countries dependent upon the free expression of opinion as the ultimate source of authority. . . . "

9. Formal order, requiring postmaster to transmit the August *Masses* through the mails, served on District Attorney, July 25th, with notice that it would be presented to Judge Hand for signature, under the rule, the following day.

10. *United States Circuit Judge C. M. Hough signed at Windsor, Vt. an order staying execution of Judge Hand's order and requiring parties to appear before him at Windsor, Vt., Aug. 2, to show cause why stay should not be made permanent pending an appeal which had been taken the same day by Postmaster Patten and which cannot be heard for several months* [Emphasis in original]. . . .

That is the history of the case—so far. Our attorney will oppose the staying of Judge Hand's order. . . .

We will do our best to reach you. We publish *The Masses* because you want it. *The Masses* is your property. This is your fight as much as it is ours. We are not going to quit. We do not believe you are, either. . . . You know the facts. The way in which you will help us is up to you.

DOCUMENT 36

Woodrow Wilson on the Limits of Wartime Dissent (1917)

Editor's Note: During World War I some liberals, radicals, and civil libertarians protested about excessive wartime suppression of freedom of speech, assembly, and the press by federal, state, and local authorities. Max Eastman, editor of The Masses, *appealed to Wilson on July 12 and September 8, 1917, complaining particularly about suppression of radical journals such as his own by the Post Office Department. In reply, the president wrote of the need for some control of criticism in wartime and the difficulty of determining specific limits.*

Woodrow Wilson to Max Eastman, September 18, 1917

[The White House] 18 September 1917

My dear Mr. Eastman:

. . . I wish that I could agree with those parts of your letter which concerned the other matters we were discussing when you were down here. [There is no record of this meeting, but presumably it involved the criticism of government censorship in Eastman's letter of September 8, 1917.] I think that a time of war must be regarded as wholly exceptional and that it is legitimate to regard things which would in ordinary circumstances be innocent as very dangerous to the public welfare, but the line is manifestly exceedingly hard to draw and I cannot say that I have any confidence that I know how to draw it. I can only say that a line must be drawn and that we are trying, it may be clumsily but genuinely, to draw it without fear or favor or prejudice.

Cordially and sincerely yours,
Woodrow Wilson

Source: Woodrow Wilson to Max Eastman, Sept. 18, 1917, in Link et al., *The Papers of Woodrow Wilson* 44: 210–11.

DOCUMENT 37

Theodore Roosevelt Attacks Pacifism and Disloyalty in Wartime America (1917 and 1918)

Editor's Note: During American involvement in the war, former president Theodore Roosevelt, a leading ultra-nationalist, urged that the strongest possible action be taken against dissenters, including political and economic radicals, on the grounds of disloyalty and treason. In fact, Roosevelt sought to use wartime attitudes and emergency powers to forge a "100 per cent Americanism." Concluding by early 1918 that civilian legal procedure was too slow in wartime, he called for the use of martial law in America. As the following speeches indicate, Roosevelt employed his oratorical skills to inflame public opinion against those he considered internal enemies—pacifists, conscientious objectors, political and economic radicals, and many ethnic Americans—as well as liberal internationalists such as President Wilson who sought a "peace without victory."

Speech at Oyster Bay, Long Island, New York, April 1917.

THE DUTY OF EVERY AMERICAN

. . . . .

... Germany has become a menace to the whole world. She is the most dangerous enemy of liberty now existing. She has shown herself utterly ruthless, treacherous and brutal. . . . The American who is not now heart and soul against her and heart and soul in favor of fighting this war through to a victorious conclusion, to the peace of overwhelming victory, is a traitor to this country and a traitor to mankind. He is unfit to live in America. He is unfit to be a free man, for his soul is the soul of a slave. . . .

No man can serve two masters in this country at this time. There can be no such thing as a fifty-fifty allegiance here. If the man is not an American, and nothing else, he should be sent out of this country. If he plays the part of sedition in this country, he should be shot. But if he is just neutral, then let him get out to some other neutral country. Don't

Source: Theodore Roosevelt, speech of Apr. 1917, in Griffith, ed., *Theodore Roosevelt: His Life, Meaning, and Messages* 3: 866–67.

let him be neutral here any longer. And, incidentally, I wish to say that is my view of the conscientious objector, too.

. . . . .

Speech at Springfield, Illinois, August 26, 1918.

YANKEE BLOOD VERSUS GERMAN BLOOD

. . . . .

. . . We can tolerate no half-way attitude, no fifty-fifty loyalty. The man must be an American and nothing else, or he is not an American at all.

If a man is loyal to any other flag, whether a foreign flag or the red flag of anarchy, or the black flag of Germanized socialism, he is disloyal to the American flag. . . .

We are not internationalists. We are American nationalists. . . . Professional internationalism stands towards patriotism exactly as free love stands toward a clean and honorable and duty-performing family life. And American pacifism has been the tool and ally of German militarism, and has represented, and always will represent, deep disloyalty to our beloved country.

. . . . .

For the moment the pacifists and internationalists and pro-Germans dare not be noisy. But let our people beware of them as soon as the peace negotiations begin and from that time onward. They have worked together in the past and they will work together in the future, the pro-Germans furnishing the most powerful and most sinister element of the combination while the pacifists and the internationalists prance in the foreground and furnish the rhetoric. . . .

Let us remember this when the peace comes. Don't trust the pacifists; they are the enemies of righteousness. Don't trust the internationalists; they are the enemies of nationalism and Americanism. Both of these groups appeal to all weaklings, illusionists, materialists, lukewarm Americans and faddists of all the types that vitiate nationalism. . . .

. . . . .

Source: Theodore Roosevelt, speech of Aug. 26, 1918, in Griffith, 3: 958–64.

DOCUMENT 38

Woman's Peace Party of New York City,
"Our War Record: A Plea for Tolerance" (1918)

Editor's Note: U.S. entry into the war virtually paralyzed the Woman's Peace party. Many branches suspended activities, some disbanded. However, the militant New York City branch, with Crystal Eastman as its head, continued to challenge the government's war policies (on Crystal Eastman, see editor's note to document 25). The New York branch often took more radical confrontational positions than were acceptable to the national leaders of the coalition organization. In the following signed pamphlet of January 1, 1918, Eastman sought to protect the branch against public rejection and governmental repression by emphasizing the legality and legitimacy of its wartime position.

Our War Record: A Plea for Tolerance

It is true that we opposed the entrance of this country into the war and used every honorable means at our command to prevent it. We believed that cooperation with other neutrals would have furnished a method of maintaining our joint rights without recourse to war, and at the same time a means with which to hasten peace negotiations in Europe. We especially urged that if a democracy is to go to war it should go by direct mandate of the people through a referendum. After war had become a fact, we further urged that conscription was no fit weapon for a democracy to fight its wars with, that forcing men to kill and to be killed against their will does violence to the vital spirit and essence of democracy.

However, once the war and conscription became the law of this land, our agitation against them ceased. . . .

What then has been our position, what have we asked of our government during these critical months? Briefly this:

To begin with, we have insisted not merely upon the right, but upon the need for a full, free and continuous discussion in the press and on the platform of America's war aims and peace terms. We have urged

Source: Woman's Peace Party of New York City, *Our War Record: A Plea for Tolerance*, pamphlet, Jan. 1, 1918, in the WPP Papers, Swarthmore College Peace Collection; and reprinted in Cook, ed., *Crystal Eastman on Women and Revolution*, 263–65.

this that the militarists and imperialists might be exposed, that ignorance might be destroyed, that we might be faithful to the declared ideals for which our armed forces are fighting. . . .

We have at no time demanded an immediate peace or a separate peace. But, when revolutionary Russia first pronounced its simple, generous, practical peace formula—no forcible annexations, no punitive indemnities, free development for all nations,—we urged that our government should respond, stating its willingness to make peace on this formula. When the German Reichstag passed a resolution substantially endorsing this formula, we asked our government to welcome the resolution officially, and thus strengthen the hands of the German liberals who were struggling to make it the avowed policy of their government. . . .

. . . [W]e also look ahead to the inevitable cessation of hostilities, to the peace conference which must come. We are urging that the ultimate agreement to be reached by the nations at that conference shall include Free Markets and Free Seas, Universal Disarmament, and A League of Nations, the obvious essentials of an enduring peace. And since we are wise enough to know that these ends cannot be achieved at a gathering of military personages and appointed diplomats, we are demanding direct democratic representation of the people of all countries at the peace conference.

This is our complete war record. We hold that there is nothing treasonable or unpatriotic or even emotional about it. On the basis of that record we ask protection from the government for our propaganda no matter how unpopular it may become. . . .

DOCUMENT 39

President Wilson's "Fourteen Points" Speech (1918)

Editor's Note: In his wartime efforts on behalf of the movement for a liberal peace, Wilson battled chauvinists like Roosevelt and the British and French imperialists on the Right and Socialists and the Russian Bolsheviks on the Left. In May 1917, the president was given copies of the secret treaties by which the European Allies planned to divide up many of the territorial holdings of the Central Powers. These treaties confirmed that the Allied leaders held much different views of the peace than Wilson did. By late 1917, Wilson learned of the extensive war weariness among the Allies and Central Powers and the growing criti-cism there among liberals and the Left of their governments' commit-ment to complete victory.

After Lenin and the Bolsheviks took power in Russia in the Novem-ber 1917 Revolution, Wilson feared that the growing international move-ment for peace would be captured by these and other Communists committed to world revolution. On November 22, Trotsky published the secret treaties from the Russian archives in an attempt to discredit the Allies (although publication was largely suppressed in the Allied countries and in the United States). In December 1917, the Bolshevik government signed an armistice with the Central Powers and urged the calling of a general peace conference.

Wilson wanted to show that the United States was fighting for ideals, not for private gain; he also sought to seize the peace initiative from the Bolsheviks on the Left and diplomatic leadership of the war from the Allied leaders on the Right. To do so, he made one of the most impor-tant public speeches of the twentieth century—the "Fourteen Points" address of January 8, 1918.

Filled with grand principles, most of them derived from liberal inter-national thought, the president's speech appealed to liberals and the Left everywhere to put pressure on their governments to curtail war aims. In addition, Wilson sought to encourage immediate dissent in the Central Powers. For example, he recommended that the map of Europe be redrawn along nationality lines in part to encourage factionalism within the Austro-Hungarian Empire. Yet, Wilson also gave the Ger-mans and Austrians hope by recommending a peace which, in seeking freedom of the seas, removal of international economic barriers, reduc-tion of armaments, impartial adjustment of colonial claims, and a gen-eral association of nations, suggested that they would not be crushed. Rather, as Wilson indirectly indicated, they might as democratic and peaceful nations obtain access to world markets and be assured of reasonable security.

Address of the President of the United States, January 8, 1918

· · · · ·

We entered this war because violations of right had occurred which touched us to the quick and made the life of our own people impossible

Source: "Address of the President of the United States Delivered at a Joint Session of the Two Houses of Congress, January 8, 1918," in U.S. Department of State, *Foreign Rela-tions of the United States, 1918, Supplement I* (Washington, D.C.: GPO, 1933), 12–17.

unless they were corrected and the world secured once for all against their recurrence. What we demand in this war, therefore, is nothing peculiar to ourselves. It is that the world be made fit and safe to live in; and particularly that it be made safe for every peace-loving nation which, like our own, wishes to live its own life, determine its own institutions, be assured of justice and fair dealing by the other peoples of the world as against force and selfish aggression. All the peoples of the world are in effect partners in this interest, and for our own part we see very clearly that unless justice be done to others it will not be done to us. The programme of the world's peace, therefore, is our programme; and that programme, the only possible programme, as we see it, is this:

I. Open covenants of peace, openly arrived at, after which there shall be no private international understandings of any kind but diplomacy shall proceed always frankly and in the public view.

II. Absolute freedom of navigation upon the seas, outside territorial waters, alike in peace and in war. . . .

III. The removal, so far as possible, of all economic barriers and the establishment of an equality of trade conditions among all the nations. . . .

IV. Adequate guarantees given and taken that national armaments will be reduced to the lowest point consistent with domestic safety.

V. A free, open-minded, and absolutely impartial adjustment of all colonial claims, based upon a strict observance of the principle that in determining all such questions of sovereignty the interests of the populations concerned must have equal weight with the equitable claims of the government whose title is to be determined.

VI. The evacuation of all Russian territory [by Germany and Austria] and such a settlement of all questions affecting Russia as will secure the best and freest cooperation of the other nations of the world in obtaining for her an unhampered and unembarrassed opportunity for the independent determination of her own political development and national policy and assure her of a sincere welcome into the society of free nations under institutions of her own choosing. . . .

VII. Belgium, the whole world will agree, must be evacuated [by the German Army] and restored. . . .

VIII. All French territory should be freed and the invaded portions restored, and the wrong done to France by Prussia in 1871 in the matter of Alsace-Lorraine, which has unsettled the peace of the world for nearly fifty years, should be righted [it should be returned to France]. . . .

IX. A readjustment of the frontiers of Italy [with the Austro-Hungarian Empire] should be effected along clearly recognizable lines of nationality.

X. The peoples of Austria-Hungary, whose place among the nations we wish to see safeguarded and assured, should be accorded the freest opportunity of autonomous development.

XI. Rumania, Serbia, and Montenegro should be evacuated [by the Austro-Hungarian army]; occupied territories restored . . . and international guarantees of the political and economic independence and territorial integrity of the several Balkan states should be entered into.

XII. The Turkish portions of the present Ottoman Empire should be assured a secure sovereignty, but the other nationalities which are now under Turkish rule should be assured an undoubted security of life and an absolutely unmolested opportunity of autonomous development, and the Dardanelles should be permanently opened as a free passage to the ships and commerce of all nations under international guarantees.

XIII. An independent Polish state should be erected which should include the territories inhabited by indisputably Polish populations, which should be assured a free and secure access to the sea, and whose political and economic independence and territorial integrity should be guaranteed by international covenant.

XIV. A general association of nations must be formed under specific covenants for the purpose of affording mutual guarantees of political independence and territorial integrity to great and small states alike.

. . . . .

. . . An evident principle runs through the whole programme I have outlined. It is the principle of justice to all peoples and nationalities, and their right to live on equal terms of liberty and safety with one another, whether they be strong or weak. Unless this principle be made its foundation no part of the structure of international justice can stand. . . .

DOCUMENT 40

"Absolutist "Conscientious Objectors in Prison:
Statement to the Court by Roger N. Baldwin (1918)

Editor's Note: Roger N. Baldwin, Harvard educated social worker, executive director of the National Civil Liberties Bureau (an agency of the American Union Against Militarism), was an "absolutist" conscientious objector who refused on libertarian and religious grounds to cooperate in any manner with the conscription law or the military. In September 1918, the thirty-four-year-old civil libertarian notified his draft board that he would refuse induction and turned himself over to civil authorities for prosecution.

Convicted in federal court in New Jersey for violation of the draft law, Baldwin made the following widely publicized statement to the court on October 30, 1918. He was subsequently sentenced to one year in jail. After the war, in 1920, Baldwin, John Dewey, and others founded the American Civil Liberties Bureau (see document 51), of which Baldwin served as director until 1950.

Baldwin's Statement to the Court, October 30, 1918

. . . . .

The compelling motive for refusing to comply with the draft act is my uncompromising opposition to the principle of conscription of life by the State for any purpose whatever, in time of war or peace. I not only refuse to obey the present conscription law, but I would in future refuse to obey any similar statute which attempts to direct my choice of service and ideals. I regard the principle of conscription of life as a flat contradiction of all our cherished ideals of individual freedom, democratic liberty and Christian teaching.

I am the more opposed to the present act, because it is for the purpose of conducting war. I am opposed to this and all other wars. I do not believe in the use of physical force as a method of achieving any end, however good.

The District Attorney calls your attention your Honor, to the inconsistency in my statement to him that I would, under extreme emergencies, as a matter of protecting the life of any person, use physical force. I don't think that is an argument that can be used in support of the wholesale organization of men to achieve political purposes in nationalistic or domestic wars. I see no relationship between the two.

My opposition is not only to direct military service but to any service whatever designed to help prosecute the war. I could accept no service, therefore, under the present [conscription] act, regardless of its character.

. . . . .

Source: The Individual and the State, The Problem as Presented by the Sentencing of Roger N. Baldwin, pamphlet (New York: National Civil Liberties Bureau, 1918).

I realize that your Honor may virtually commit me at once to the military authorities, and that I may have merely taken a quicker and more inconvenient method of arriving at a military camp. I am prepared for that—for the inevitable pressure to take an easy way out by noncombatant service—with guard-house confinement—perhaps brutalities, which hundreds of other objectors have already suffered and are suffering today in camps. I am prepared for court martial and sentence to military prison, to follow the 200–300 [absolutist] objectors already sentenced to terms of 10–30 years for their loyalty to their ideals....

· · · · ·

But I believe most of us [absolutist objectors who refused any cooperation with the military or the war effort] are prepared even to die for our faith, just as our brothers in France are dying for theirs. To them we are comrades in spirit—we understand one another's motives, though our methods are wide apart. We both share deeply the common experience of living up to the truth as we see it, whatever the price.

Though at the moment I am of a tiny minority, I feel myself just one protest in a great revolt surging up from among the people—the struggle of the masses against the rule of the world by the few—profoundly intensified by the war. It is a struggle against the political state itself, against exploitation, militarism, imperialism, authority in all forms.

· · · · ·

PART FOUR

Plans for the Postwar Order:
The Peace Movement Reborn,
1919 to 1922

DOCUMENT 41

Wilson and "Colonel" Edward M. House Discuss Wilson's
First Draft of the League of Nations Covenant (1918)

*Editor's Note: Wilson had publicly supported the principle of a postwar
international organization several times since his first endorsement in
May 1916, but he did not turn to the details of the international body
until late summer 1918. Then as a result of a plan by a British governmental committee sent to him on July 3, 1918, and an exchange with
his intimate if unofficial foreign policy adviser Edward M. ("Colonel")
House, Wilson drew up a first and rather sketchy draft of the Covenant
for a League of Nations.*

*Wilson's initial plan was to have ambassadors to The Hague desig-
nated representatives of a League of Nations. The League would guarantee territorial and political integrity, supervise arms reduction, and
provide for the arbitration of disputes. It could also use economic sanctions against member states that violated the covenant, and economic
and military sanctions against nonmember states that went to war with
a member state.*

*Edward M. House, 1858–1938, a Texas landowner, banker, and ad-
viser to the state's Democratic governors, had worked for Woodrow
Wilson's presidential candidacy in 1912 and had become Wilson's close
friend and adviser. During World War I, the president used the pro-
British Texan as an emissary and a conduit for discussions with the
Allied governments as well as a confidant to discuss many of his ideas.
Wilson consulted with House over the Fourteen Points speech and
the initial draft of the League of Nations' Covenant. In House's extensive diary, however, the egotistical adviser frequently overstated his influence on Wilson, which was in fact greatest when he agreed with the
president.*

*Contrary to the assertions in the following entry in House's diary, the
ideas for the specific nature of the League came from Wilson and the
British committee, not from House, who had written up the proposal
only after discussing the idea with the president. Wilson rewrote House's
draft and sent him a copy on September 7, 1918. In edited and revised
form, that version, the so-called Washington Draft of the League Covenant, is what Wilson took to the Paris Peace Conference in January
1919, after which it went through a number of changes during the
negotiations.*

Edward M. House, Diary Entry, August 15, 1918

[Manchester, Mass.]
August 15, 1918

The President and his party arrived this morning on schedule time around nine o'clock. . . .

Instead of going to his room to refresh himself, the President went with me to the beautiful loggia overlooking the sea and we at once plunged into a discussion of the League of Nations. I knew intuitively that this was the purpose of his visit, although I had no intimation from him. He started off by saying that he had written the Platform for the Indiana Democratic Convention of the other day; that he had given it to Secretary Baker [Newton D. Baker, secretary of war, 1916 to 1921, and former Democratic mayor of Cleveland] to take out and put through. Baker returned and reported "we put it through just as you wrote it except we cut your six pages down to three." "This," the President said, "is what I have done with your constitution of a league of nations.["] He then proceeded to read it as he had rewritten it. As a matter of fact, he has cut but little except he has tried to reduce the number of articles to thirteen, his lucky number. To bring this about he has been compelled to have an addenda.

He takes two or three of the first clauses and incorporates them into the "preamble." He has cut out the Court [the proposal for a World Court]. We were in absolute disagreement about this and I finally contented myself by the feeling of assurance that the Peace Conference would maintain my position. The balance of the document is about as I wrote it. The only change of note is that I provided only for two belligerent nations and he makes the machinery include two or more, which is as it should be.

We discussed the advisability of making a [public] statement in regard to it, and we agreed that it would be best not to do so. . . . He thought if it were published in advance of the Peace Conference it would cause so much criticism in this country, particularly by Senators of the Lodge type [Henry Cabot Lodge of Massachusetts, an ardently nationalistic Republican], that it would make it difficult to do what we both have in mind at the Peace Conference. He also thought that some of the American group favorable to a league would feel that we had not

Source: The Diary of "Colonel" House, entry for Aug. 15, 1918, Edward M. House Papers, Yale University Library, reprinted in Link et al., The Papers of Woodrow Wilson 49: 265–66.

gone far enough and other[s] would feel that we had gone too far. We concluded that if a governmental report was made by any of the Allied Nations at this time it would inevitably cause more or less friction and would increase the difficulties of getting a proper measure through at the Peace Conference. I am sure this is true just now. However, if the President had taken the lead earlier and had pushed the matter vigorously, he might have given out his own conception of what a league of nations should be, and have rallied the world around it.

The President thinks, and I agree with him, that a league of nations might be incorporated in the Peace Treaty. In our discussion I stated that, in my opinion, it seemed impracticable to think of the smaller nations as members of the league on equal terms with the larger ones. He dissented quite warmly and said to exclude them would be to go contrary to all our protestations concerning them. . . .

. . . . .

DOCUMENT 42

The Treaty of Versailles, Covenant of the League of Nations (1919)

Editor's Note: The Treaty of Versailles, ending the war with Germany and including the following Covenant of the League of Nations, was negotiated in Paris by Wilson and the other leaders of the victorious powers between January and April 1919. It was presented to the new German government on May 7; the German representatives signed it on June 28, 1919. It was a victor's peace.

Wilson hoped that the problems in the peace settlement would be eased over time through the operation of the new League of Nations, and he insisted on including the League Covenant in the peace treaty. With its headquarters to be located in Geneva, Switzerland, the League was to consist of an assembly, composed of all member nations, each with one vote, and a council, composed of the Great Powers (originally England, France, Italy, Japan, and, it was expected, the United States) and several nonpermanent members, with key decisions requiring unanimity. There would also be a secretariat and several allied and sub-

ordinate bodies, including a World Court and an International Labor Organization.

The original signatories of the treaty were the victors in World War I, including the United States, and most of the neutral nations. Between 1920 and 1932 the former Central Powers were individually admitted to the League (including the German Republic in 1926), and in 1934 the USSR became a member. Because of objections by the Senate, the United States never joined the League or the World Court attached to it.

The Covenant of the League of Nations

THE HIGH CONTRACTING PARTIES,
In order to promote international co-operation and to achieve international peace and security

by the acceptance of obligations not to resort to war,

by the prescription of open, just and honourable relations between nations,

by the firm establishment of the understandings of international law as the actual rule of conduct among Governments, and

by the maintenance of justice and a scrupulous respect for all treaty obligations in the dealings of organised peoples with one another,

Agree to this Covenant of the League of Nations.

ARTICLE 1.

The original Members of the League of Nations shall be those of the Signatories. . . .

· · · · ·

Any Member of the League may, after two years' notice of its intention to do so, withdraw from the League, provided that all of its international obligations and all its obligations under this Covenant shall have been fulfilled at the time of its withdrawal.

[Articles 2 to 7 concerned organizational details.]

Source: "The Treaty of Versailles, the Covenant of the League of Nations," in U.S., Congress, Senate, *Treaties*, 67th Cong., 4th sess., 1923, S. Doc. 348, 3336–45.

ARTICLE 8.

The Members of the League recognise that the maintenance of peace requires the reduction of national armaments to the lowest point consistent with national safety and the enforcement by common action of international obligations.

The Council, taking account of the geographical situation and circumstances of each State, shall formulate plans for such reduction for the consideration and action of the several Governments.

. . . . .

ARTICLE 10.

The Members of the League undertake to respect and preserve as against external aggression the territorial integrity and existing political independence of all Members of the League. In case of any such aggression or in case of any threat or danger of such aggression the Council shall advise upon the means by which this obligation shall be fulfilled.

ARTICLE 11.

Any war or threat of war, whether immediately affecting any of the Members of the League or not, is hereby declared a matter of concern to the whole League, and the League shall take any action that may be deemed wise and effectual to safeguard the peace of nations. . . .

. . . . .

ARTICLE 12.

The Members of the League agree that if there should arise between them any dispute likely to lead to a rupture, they will submit the matter either to arbitration or to inquiry by the Council, and they agree in no case to resort to war until three months after the award by the arbitrators or the report by the Council.

. . . . .

ARTICLE 14.

The Council shall formulate and submit to the Members of the League for adoption plans for the establishment of a permanent Court of International Justice [the World Court]. The Court shall be competent to hear and determine any dispute of an international character which the parties thereto submit to it. . . .

. . . . .

ARTICLE 16.

Should any Member of the League resort to war in disregard of its covenants . . . , it shall *ipso facto* be deemed to have committed an act of war against all other Members of the League, which hereby undertake immediately to subject it to the severance of all trade or financial relations, the prohibition of all intercourse between their nationals and the nationals of the covenant-breaking State, and the prevention of all financial, commercial or personal intercourse between the nationals of the covenant-breaking State and the nationals of any other State, whether a Member of the League or not.

It shall be the duty of the Council in such case to recommend to the several Governments concerned what effective military, naval or air force the Members of the League shall severally contribute to the armed forces to be used to protect the covenants of the League.

. . . . .

ARTICLE 21.

Nothing in this Covenant shall be deemed to affect the validity of international engagements, such as treaties of arbitration or regional understandings like the Monroe doctrine, for securing the maintenance of peace.

ARTICLE 22.

To those colonies and territories which as a consequence of the late war have ceased to be under the sovereignty of the States which formerly governed them and which are inhabited by peoples not yet able to stand by themselves under the strenuous conditions of the modern world, there should be applied the principle that the wellbeing and development of such peoples form a sacred trust of civilisation and that securities for the performance of this trust should be embodied in this Covenant.

The best method of giving practical effect to this principle is that the tutelage of such peoples should be entrusted to advanced nations who by reason of their resources, their experience or their geographical position can best undertake this responsibility, and who are willing to accept it, and that this tutelage should be exercised by them as Mandatories on behalf of the League.

. . . . .

. . . The Mandatory must be responsible for the administration of the territory under conditions which will guarantee freedom of conscience and religion, subject only to the maintenance of public order and morals, the prohibition of abuses such as the slave trade, the arms traffic and the liquor traffic, and the prevention of the establishment of fortifications . . . , and will also secure equal opportunities for the trade and commerce of other Members of the League.

. . . . .

In every case of mandate, the Mandatory shall render to the Council an annual report in reference to the territory committed to its charge.

. . . . .

ARTICLE 23.

Subject to and in accordance with the provisions of international conventions existing or hereafter to be agreed upon, the Members of the League:

(a) will endeavour to secure and maintain fair and humane conditions of labour for men, women, and children . . . and for that purpose will establish and maintain the necessary international organisations;

(b) undertake to secure just treatment of the native inhabitants of territories under their control;

(c) will entrust the League with the general supervision over the execution of agreements with regard to the traffic in women and children, and the traffic in opium and other dangerous drugs;

(d) will entrust the League with the general supervision ofthe trade in arms and ammunition with the countries in which the control of this traffic is necessary in the common interest;

(e) will make provision to secure and maintain freedom of communications and of transit and equitable treatment for the commerce of all Members of the League. . . .

(f) will endeavour to take steps in matters of international concern for the prevention and control of disease.

. . . . .

ANNEX

The original members of the League of Nations signatories of the Treaty of Peace [Versailles]:

United States of America.	Haiti.
Belgium.	Hedjaz [Saudia Arabia].
Bolivia.	Honduras.
Brazil.	Italy.
British Empire.	Japan.
Canada.	Liberia.
Australia.	Nicaragua.
South Africa.	Panama.
New Zealand.	Peru.
India.	Poland.
China.	Portugal.
Cuba.	Roumania.
Ecuador.	Serb-Croat-Slovene State [Yugoslovia].
France.	Siam [Thailand].
Greece.	Czecho-Slovakia.
Guatemala.	Uruguay.

States [immediately] invited to accede to the Covenant:

Argentine Republic.	Persia [Iran].
Chili [Chile].	Salvador.
Colombia.	Spain.
Denmark.	Sweden.
Netherlands.	Switzerland.
Norway.	Venezuela.
Paraguay.	

DOCUMENT 43

Scott Nearing, Socialist Economist,
Criticizes the League of Nations (1919)

Editor's Note: Scott Nearing, 1883–1983, a radical economist with a doctorate from the University of Pennsylvania, taught at the university's

Wharton School of Finance from 1909 to 1915, during which time he gained widespread attention for his attacks against the use of child labor and his criticism of capitalism. His dismissal in 1915 because of his views also drew national attention. Shortly after the U.S. entry into the war, Nearing joined the Socialist Party of America and helped to establish the People's Council. As a result of Nearing's antiwar activities, the University of Toledo dismissed him from his deanship and from the faculty, and the federal government indicted him under the Espionage Act. He was tried and acquitted in 1919 but was blacklisted by universities and many publishers. Nearing remained a leading radical economist as seen in the following critique of the League of Nations. It was first published in the March 1919 issue of The World Tomorrow *magazine, edited by Norman Thomas, of the Fellowship of Reconciliation, a nondenominational, religious antiwar and social-reform organization founded in the United States in November 1915.*

The League of Nations as Seen by an Economist

Peace on earth will not be established through the World League plan, read by President Wilson to the Peace Conference. The document is a weak compromise that ignores the vital factors underlying international relations.

The draft of the League Constitution is a purely political document. It ignores economic factors entirely. The great capitalist nations of the world that are asked to endorse the plan are interested primarily in market, shipping and investments. The document contains no reference to any of these subjects, and is, therefore, fundamentally incomplete. *Commercial and financial rivalries will breed wars in the future as they have bred them in the past.* This fact has been acknowledged by President Wilson; it has been insisted upon by the Navy League, and preached for years by leading economists all over the world yet the League Constitution does not cover economic questions. A political document of this character might have had some reason for existence in 1915. Today, it is archaism.

The plan is faulty in other important respects. First, it is undemocratic. Treaties are not to be published till after they are made—the processes of diplomacy are still secret. There is no provision for the

Source: Scott Nearing, *The League of Nations as Seen by an Economist* undated [ca. Mar./Apr. 1919], leaflet, Swarthmore College Peace Collection.

democratic selection of the members of the delegate body. Under the Constitution as drawn, all of them may be appointed by the Governments. The people may have no voice in choosing them. Again, out of the nine votes of the Executive Council, five are to belong permanently to the United States, France, Italy, Great Britain and Japan. In short, the decisions of the League may all be reached by hand-picked diplomats of the old school from the "big five" allied nations.

The plan is arbitrary. It contains no provision for and no suggestion of self-determination. Ireland, India, the Philippines and China will be no freer after the plan is adopted than before.

The plan is imperialistic. The "big five" are to take the German Colonies in addition to their present possessions. The allied empires will still be empires. [In the final version of the treaty, the powers that obtained mandated territories included Britain, France, Belgium, South Africa, Australia, New Zealand, and Japan. In fairness to Wilson, it should be noted that he refused to accept any mandated territories for the United States.]

The plan is weak. It takes no stand on the question of armaments, other than to state that they must be "fair" and "reasonable." Evidently, the members of the "big five" are not yet ready to "bury the hatchet."

The plan is ineffective. No adequate means are provided for the enforcement of the League's decisions. The organization contemplated is weaker than that of the Thirteen Colonies under the Articles of Confederation.

The League plan is political treaty of the old variety, providing for a continuation of the alliance among the victorious Allies. This alliance will inevitably force a defensive alliance of Russia, Germany and the other socialist countries of Europe, so that the world will be arrayed in two camps—capitalist nations against socialist nations. It is this class conflict alone that will hold the League together. Lacking such a compelling motive, the plan will hold until commercial and financial rivalries among the members of the League grow bitter and sharp. Then, like thousands of similar treaties, this one will go into the discard *while the world busies itself with the next great war.*

DOCUMENT 44

Senator Henry Cabot Lodge Attacks the League Covenant (1919)

Editor's Note: Henry Cabot Lodge, 1850–1924, Harvard graduate and Boston Brahmin, served in the U.S. Senate from 1893 until his death. A conservative member of the Republican Old Guard, Lodge was actively partisan toward the Democratic party and bitterly hostile toward Woodrow Wilson. In foreign policy, Lodge endorsed high-tariff protectionism, immigration restriction, the Spanish-American War, acquisition of a colonial empire, and U.S. entry into World War I. A dedicated nationalist who believed in relying particularly upon a strong and modern navy, Lodge opposed compulsory international arbitration as well as Wilson's concept of a League of Nations.

From 1918 to 1924, Lodge chaired the Foreign Relations Committee, and between 1919 and 1920 he led the fight in the Senate against the Treaty of Versailles and the League of Nations. As an adroit politician, Lodge did not recommend outright rejection, but instead emphasized problems with the treaty and the League. Eventually, he added his own amendments or "reservations" to the document, stimulating opposition to the amended treaty by the president and loyal Democrats, and thus helping to ensure its defeat. The excerpt printed below indicates some of Lodge's criticism of the League before a Boston audience on March 19, 1919, in a debate with A. Lawrence Lowell, president of Harvard University, who was a co-founder of the Association for a League to Enforce Peace, and a vigorous advocate of U.S. membership in the League of Nations.

Remarks by Senator Lodge in Boston, Mass., March 19, 1919

... Now, ladies and gentlemen, we are all agreed in desiring the security of the peace of the world. ...

The question before us, the only question of a practical nature, is whether the League that has been drafted by the Commission of the Peace Conference and laid before it will tend to secure the peace of the world as it stands, and whether it is just and fair to the United States of America. ...

Source: "Joint Debate on the Covenant of Paris," reprinted in World Peace Foundation, *League of Nations* (Boston: World Peace Foundation, 1919), 2: 52–56, 90–97.

I now come to what seems to me a very vital point indeed, and that is the Monroe doctrine. . . . The Monroe doctrine was the invisible line that we drew around the American hemisphere. It was the fence that we put around it to exclude other nations from meddling in American affairs, and I have never been able to get it through my head how you can preserve a fence by taking it down. . . .

They [the European powers] say that if we demand the exclusion of the Monroe doctrine from the operation of the League, they will demand compensation. Very well. Let them exclude us from meddling in Europe. That is not a burden that we are seeking to bear. We are ready to go there at any time to save the world from barbarism and tyranny, but we are not thirsting to interfere in every obscure quarrel that may spring up in the Balkans. . . .

Then comes Art[icle]. X. That is the most important article in the whole treaty. That is the one that I want the American people to consider . . . . This article pledges us to guarantee the political independence and the territorial integrity against external aggression of every nation a member of the League. That is, every nation of the earth. We ask no guaranties, we have no endangered frontiers; but we are asked to guarantee the territorial integrity of every nation, practically, in the world—it will be when the League is complete. As it is to-day, we guarantee the territorial integrity and political independence of every part of the far-flung British Empire.

Now mark! A guaranty is never invoked except when force is needed. If we guaranteed one country in South America alone, if we were the only guarantor, and we guaranteed but one country, we should be bound to go to the relief of the country with army and navy. We under that clause of this treaty—it is one of the few that is perfectly clear—under that clause of the treaty we have got to take our army and our navy and go to war with any country which attempts aggression upon the territorial integrity of another member of the League.

Now, guaranties must be fulfilled. They are sacred promises,—it has been said only morally binding. Why, that is all there is to a treaty between great nations. If they are not morally binding they are nothing but "scraps of paper." If the United States agrees to Art. X, we must carry it out in letter and in spirit; and if it is agreed to I should insist that we did so, because the honor and good faith of our country would be at stake. . . .

I repeat again, I want a League of Nations that will advance the cause of peace on earth, that will make war as nearly impossible as it can be made. I want to bring about a general disarmament. I know arbitration can do much. I do not wish to put into any league articles which I believe impossible of fulfillment and which I believe nations will readily abrogate. But I am so firm a believer in the strength of the great peace movement that I am not ready to back it by the argument of fear. The United States has not come to where she is through fear. We have known[:]

> That in ourselves our safety must be sought;
> That by our own right hands it must be wrought;
> That we must stand unpropped or be laid low.

We are a great moral asset of Christian civilization. . . . How did we get there? By our own efforts. Nobody led us, nobody guided us, nobody controlled us. . . .

I would keep America as she has been—not isolated, not prevent her from joining other nations for these great purposes—but I wish her to be master of her fate. . . .

DOCUMENT 45

Hamilton Holt, "The League or Bolshevism?" (1919)

Editor's Note: Hamilton Holt, editor and publisher of The Independent *magazine and longtime champion of a league of nations (see documents 6, 12, 21) sought actively in 1919 and 1920 to mobilize support for Wilson's league. Although he initially favored a league without the Lodge "reservations," Holt came in the winter of 1919 to 1920 to support a compromise position in order to achieve Senate ratification. In the following editorial in April 1919, Holt had sought to frighten and shame opponents, particularly in the Senate, into supporting the league.*

The League or Bolshevism?

Are American people aware that Europe is on the verge of a volcano? No one, I think, can have visited England, France and Germany, as I have during the past three months, without realizing that this is the

Source: Hamilton Holt, "The League or Bolshevism?" *Independent* 98 (Apr. 5, 1919): 3–4.

case. The Allies have won the war, but while the delegates at Paris are engaged in winning the peace, the Bolshevik cloud grows blacker and blacker on the horizon, till today it overshadows all Europe. As the hope of Europe turned to America in those dark days of April, May and June last year when the fate of cilivization trembled in the balance, so again today the world looks to America to save her from perhaps a greater menace.

. . . Without a League Europe knows she must return to the old system of alliances, with its colossal armaments, secret diplomacy and mutual hates and suspicions. Once such a reversion to pre-war conditions is seen inevitable or even likely the people will revolt. The issue before the world therefore is a League of Nations or Bolshevism.

Everywhere I went men asked me if it were possible that America would refuse to join the League of Nations. . . .

I did not meet a single man in Europe who thought a League could succeed for a moment if the United States was not a member. I met many who assured me that if America refused to join revolutions would follow everywhere. . . .

It has been intimated by Senator Lodge and others that the Covenant is a British document. Nonsense. I read in advance the original English "secret" draft bought by Lord Robert Cecil to Paris, and while I must say that it was the most admirably worked out proposal presented by any delegation, the Covenant as it stands today is more American than English. . . .

.   .   .   .   .

On my return home I find a far greater amount of discussion going on in respect to the minutiae of the Covenant than was the case in Europe. There the disposition was to insist passionately on the establishment of a League of Nations, provided that it was a real League with "teeth in it," but to leave the technical details to be settled by the experts. . . .

But what we object to is not the criticism that will help the delegates to perfect and strengthen the Covenant, but the criticism that would weaken and destroy it. Most of the senatorial criticism seems to be of the latter kind. . . .

.   .   .   .   .

The fact is that all the trouble at the Peace Conference, like trouble everywhere else in the world, is owing to human selfishness. The Peace Conference has been accused of "unconscionable" delays. The truth is that all the delays have been made by those blind reactionaries of Europe who are trying to avoid the obligations they assumed when they agreed to accept our President's fourteen points. Wilson and Lloyd George would have been measurably nearer the goal of peace today had it not been for the machinations of those selfish individuals, groups, classes and nations who have been trying to play at the peace table the old diplomatic game of getting something at the expense of the other fellow. And these reactionaries, I am ashamed to say, have of late dared to show their heads the more openly owing to the attitude of some of our Senators and public men who have left no stone unturned to divide our country on this greatest of all issues and to discredit the President.

. . . . .

I hope to discuss the Covenant later in some detail, but here I wish to say that even without a single amendment it is unquestionably the greatest document since the Declaration of American Independence. It should be amended without doubt, but better not a syllable changed than that it should be emasculated at the behest of timidity, selfishness or partizan advantage. . . . If now we take no counsel of cowardice from our senatorial reactionaries, but pledge "our lives, our fortunes and our sacred honor" to the Declaration of Interdependence so nobly championed by Presidents Wilson and Taft, and the host of the great men in Europe and Asia, then the United Nations of the World will result.

DOCUMENT 46

Official Report on the Women's International Congress
for Permanent Peace at Zurich, Switzerland (1919)

Editor's Note: From May 12 to 16, 1919, nearly 150 women pacifists from fifteen countries attended the Women's International Congress for Permanent Peace held in Zurich, Switzerland. (The largest of the delegations came from the United States, England, Germany, and Switzerland). The women kept in touch with the concurrent peace conference in Paris, criticized the vindictive elements of the Treaty of Versailles, divided over the Covenant of the League of Nations, and condemned the food blockade of Germany, which the Allies continued until the new

German Republic agreed to the treaty.

Jane Addams presided over this second international congress of women (the first had been at The Hague in 1915—see document 15), and she was also chosen as international president of the newly formed Women's International League for Peace and Freedom (WILPF). Addams personally delivered to the U.S. government delegation in Paris the conference's resolutions condemning the terms of the Treaty of Versailles and the food blockade and criticizing much of the Covenant of the League. The following is the American section's official report on the conference:

The [Women's] Congress in Session

The Congress which met at Zurich on May 12th, 1919, was the first international meeting of organized women which has ever come together to discuss a treaty or to make representations to a Conference of the Powers on the subject of peace. They met to carry out a resolution passed by the Women's International Congress at The Hague in April, 1915, [actually, the title had been the International Congress of Women; see document 15] by which it was decided that an international meeting of women for the purpose of presenting practical proposals should be held at the same place and at the same time as the Conference which framed the terms of the Peace settlement after the war.

· · · · ·

. . . [In 1919] the whole atmosphere surrounding the idea of a Women's Congress had changed. This was due partly to the growth of pacifist ideals, partly to the changed outlook with regard to women which the war had brought, and partly, no doubt, to the fact of their political emancipation. The Jingo press was silent, after hysterical outbursts for over four years, and ridicule gave way to genuine interest as to the tone and policy which women were likely to adopt.

· · · · ·

Source: Women's International League for Peace and Freedom, *Towards Peace and Freedom,* pamphlet (New York: Women's International League for Peace and Freedom, Aug. 1919): 6–19, in the WILPF Papers, Swarthmore College Peace Collection.

"THE BEST FORMULATIONS"

The resolutions passed at The Hague [by the International Congress of Women in 1915], though regarded in many quarters as unrealizable at the time, had been received with interest and appreciation by the statesmen of the belligerent and neutral countries and were strikingly similar to the Fourteen Points subsequently enumerated by President Wilson.

"The best formulations I have so far seen," was President Wilson's comment, as reported by Miss Addams at one of the opening meetings of the [1919] Congress. It was the elaboration of these "formulations," their application to feminist and educational programmes, and, above all, to the immediate question of the Peace Settlement, the Blockade, and the League of Nations, that occupied the more important sessions of the Congress.

On the resolution on the Peace Terms there was little difference of opinion and criticism was unrelenting. This was a foregone conclusion for the gloom of the settlement in the act of being announced from Paris hung like a shadow over the whole Congress.

The breach of faith by the Allies in tearing up President Wilson's Fourteen Points; the proposals for one-sided disarmament; for bartering about millions of Germans "like chattels and pawns in a game"; the tacit sanction of the secret treaties, the crushing financial and economic proposals; with such terms linked to the Covenant[,] Mrs. Snowden [Mrs. Philip Snowden of Britain, feminist and pacifist, wife of the anti-war chairperson of the Independent Labour party] declared that the League of Nations would be "like a boat with a hole in it." . . .

Next to the Peace Terms the question of the blockade dominated the whole Congress. In moving the resolution on this subject Mrs. Pethick Lawrence described the state of Europe—maddened by hunger and misery—worse than anything which had ever occurred in the world's history since the Plague, and maintained that the raising of the blockade was insufficient, that the Nations must pool their resources and jointly carry out the provisioning of the peoples, developing international organization for the saving of life, instead of destroying it. Both these resolutions were forwarded to the representatives of the Powers at Paris.

In reply to the resolution on the blockade, President Wilson wired to Miss Addams, "Your message appeals both to my head and to my heart, and I hope most sincerely that means may be found, though the present outlook is extremely unpromising because of infinite difficulties." During the discussion on both these subjects great restraint was shown by the delegates from the Central Empires [Germany and Austria-Hungary]. They refrained from voting on the Peace Terms, they spoke very little of their sufferings from hunger; but at the non-official gatherings, speech after speech, through mere statement of fact, emphasized the state of starvation and misery into which the blockade had plunged large tracts of Europe.

THE LEAGUE OF NATIONS

The discussions on the League of Nations continued throughout the week's Session, the proposals on this subject falling mainly under two headings: amendments for incorporation in the treaty of peace, and recommendations which might form a programme for future propaganda. The warmest supporters of the Covenant were found amongst the American delegation: though conscious of its imperfections, they maintained that the Covenant "was a vehicle of Life" and that it represented a real effort of statesmanship . . . .

The opponents of the Paris Covenant, including delegates from the U.S.A. and some from Great Britain, while welcoming the fact that the idea of a League of Nations was so generally accepted, declared that in its present form it was a league of conquerors against the conquered, that it maintained the old discredited system of the Balance of Power, excluded some nations from membership, and would not save the world from future wars.

Between these two sections was another which took the medium line expressed in French by one of the delegates, "L'Enfant est né, la grande chose c'est de ne pa le tuer" [The baby is born; the great challenge now is not to kill it]. . . .

. . . . .

PACIFISTS AND REVOLUTION

While accepting special responsibility to counsel against violence the Congress declared its belief that there was a fundamentally just demand underlying most of the revolutionary movements and its sympathy with the workers who were everywhere seeking to make an end of exploitation and to claim their world. The attitude of the women from the revolutionary countries, in face of the huge changes impending in the world, was remarkable. Many of them had been through terrible experiences unknown to the rest of Europe. Loathing militarism, they welcomed the promise of the coming democracy, and appeared in some cases to have unbounded faith in the dawn of the new era. In the

Central Empires progress has been sudden and complete; at one bound they had gained equal opportunity for men and women alike, and some of the highest posts in the Government had been thrown open and actually occupied by women.

Other delegates took a less optimistic view, and their sufferings were expressed in the words of an Austrian woman—"it is not only our countries which are desolated, but our souls." ... One and all agreed that progress and freedom must be achieved without violence and the reports from the Germans delegates of their efforts to avoid bloodshed were amongst the most interesting records of the Congress.

Further resolutions dealt with the right of Ireland to self-determination, with protection for Jews and national minorities, with political amnesty, with the right of asylum, and with Conscientious Objectors. [The congress also urged that the Treaty of Versailles include a Woman's Charter recognizing the importance of equal political, economic, and social rights for women and urging that the League of Nations and all nations recognize and guarantee those rights. The Women's Congress also adopted a resolution urging the creation of an International Council of Education to help establish "a basis for a new human civilization" by educating people about the value of human life and individuality and international understanding, through the promotion of the teaching of foreign cultures and foreign languages, supplemented by the development of an auxiliary universal world language and extensive exchange programs.]

. . . . .

The most moving incident during the whole Congress occurred when Mlle[.] Mélin, one of the French delegates, arrived at the last moment from Carignan. Standing on the platform while business was suspended, she told with marvellous power of her own experience in the Ardennes, how her home had been devastated, how she had seen youths driven under the machine-guns and slaughtered. With passionate emotion she denounced war as the common enemy of women and, calling on all to use every effort to annihilate it and to renounce all desire for vengeance and a peace of conquest, she appealed to "Les forces de demain" [the forces of the future]. "I greet you, forces of the future, not men nor women anywhere, not nationalities. War alone is our enemy." In a moment Gustava Heymann [Lida Gustava Heymann, 1868–1943, a leading German left-wing feminist, suffragist, and pacifist, who had been a delegate to the International Congress of Women at The Hague in 1915] rose, and with clasped hands the two women stood together pledging themselves, with every delegate in the Congress, to live and work for international fellowship.

. . . . .

EVENING [PUBLIC] MEETINGS

. . . . .

[Women and Peace]

MISS JANE ADDAMS, in her opening speech, sketched the evolution of ideas of law and order in social life through the conditions imposed on men's predatory instincts by the mere necessity of providing food for their children. Through women and the care of children had come the curbing of the instinct which in primitive races caused men to rove and destroy. Just as the family had tended to concentrate his energies on one spot and on the more human responsibilities of fatherhood, so perhaps now out of the horrors of war and destruction would emerge again, through women and the primitive cry for food, a restraining influence which might again seek to create a home and rebuild the suffering nations on the lines of a higher social and moral evolution. The world had been brought to its needs by hunger and in this women must see their opportunity for developing their powers of co-operation in international life.

The child was the symbol of that need and the world would be led through the child to realize at last that one human life was as sacred as another. Apparently, they had not yet learned to come together on that higher plane. They had not yet learned that the human and spiritual needs of the race were so blended that they could not be separated.

Some had feared that the spiritual bonds themselves might break under the strain, but if this was not to be they must turn the material needs of the world to the highest purpose; they must remember that the distribution of food itself was a holy thing and that when women, as sisters, pleaded for the raising of the blockade they were pleading for the restoration of the normal balance of the world. Women had still to be taught that the conditions of the world were not altogether creditable to men and especially must they remember this at a time when the humanitarian needs appealed to them so overwhelmingly, lest they might be tempted to leave the field of politics in order to attend to material needs only.

. . . . .

MRS. TERRELL (America) [Mary Church Terrell, peace delegate and activist in the woman suffrage and civil rights movements, who was one of the founders of the Colored Woman's League of Washington, D.C., the first and long-time president of the National Association of Colored Women] spoke for the coloured races, for the black women whose husbands, she said, were fighting in the war for liberty—a liberty they themselves did not possess, for in the State to which she belonged [the United States] 400,000 black men had been conscripted. She appealed especially to mothers to interest their children in the fate of the black children abroad.

Miss Ashton described the difficulties which women had laboured under in Great Britain. . . . If women could make a chain round the world it would be impossible to separate them. . . .

. . . . .

Mrs. Swanwick (President of the British Section of the Women's International League) [Helena Maria Sickert Swanwick, 1864–1939, Cambridge graduate, journalist, pacifist, feminist author, member of the executive committee of the Union of Democratic Control] reviewed the work since its inauguration at The Hague in 1915. In Great Britain the same groups of women had been attracted as in many other countries—suffragists, peace workers and social workers. . . . The League of Nations was also to be urged to set up a Commission of an equal number of men and women to investigate the question of marriages between persons of different nationality [because the brides often lost their original citizenship].

The Feminist programme also emphasized the importance of giving due weight to the value of women's work in the home in connexion with questions of land laws, taxes, and tariffs. The Congress further recommended to the consideration of its national sections the whole question of population [i.e., birth control], considering it was not yet ripe for decision, but laying it down that full information scientific and other, should be made available on the subject.

DOCUMENT 47

An Exchange of Telegrams Between Jane Addams and
Woodrow Wilson on Ending the Food Blockade (1919)

Editor's Note: With the adoption by the Women's International Congress for Permanent Peace (see document 46) of a resolution protesting the continuation of the Allied food blockade of Germany and much of central and eastern Europe, Jane Addams wired this information to President Wilson at the Paris Peace Conference. The president responded quickly and sympathetically but without much hope of influencing the British and French blockade.

An Exchange of Telegrams

Jane Addams to Woodrow Wilson, ca. May 13, 1919

Zurich, [ca. May 13, 1919]
Following resolution moved by Mrs. [Emmeline] Pethick Lawrence England seconded by Madame [Gustava Elisabeth] Waern-Bugge of Sweden and supported by Signora [Rosa] Genoni Italy was unanimously adopted today by women representing fifteen countries majority from Entente [the Allied nations] QUOTE This international congress of women regards the unemployment famine and pestilence extending throughout great tracts of central and eastern Europe and through parts of Asia as a profound disgrace to civilization. This congress urges the governments of all the powers assembled at the Peace Congress to develop the interallied organization formed for purposes of war into an international organization for purposes of peace and urges that the following immediate steps be taken: one that the blockade be immediately lifted, two that all resources of the world food, raw materials, finance, transport be organized immediately for the relief of the peoples from famine and pestilence; three that if there is an insufficiency either of food or of transport to supply all the demands luxuries shall not be given transport from one country to another until the necessaries of life are supplied to all and that the people of every country be rationed in order that all the starving shall be fed. We believe that only immediate

Source: Jane Addams to Woodrow Wilson, ca. May 13, 1919; Wilson to Addams, May 16, 1919, in Link, et al., *The Papers of Woodrow Wilson* 59: 117, 189.

international action of this kind can save humanity and bring about the permanent reconciliation and union of the peoples.

JANE ADDAMS, President

Woodrow Wilson to Jane Addams, May 16, 1919.

Paris, 16 May 1919

Your message appeals both to my head and to my heart and I hope most sincerely that means may be found, though the present outlook is extremely unpromising because of infinite practical difficulties.

Woodrow Wilson

DOCUMENT 48

Alice Hamilton Reports on the Women's International
Congress at Zurich (1919)

Editor's Note: Alice Hamilton again accompanied Jane Addams to a women's international peace congress (see document 15 for her account of the 1915 women's congress at The Hague). In the following letter, she described the 1919 Women's International Congress at Zurich to a friend at Hull House. The account in this private letter can be compared with the official account of the Women's International Congress (document 46) and with the actual exchange of telegrams between Jane Addams and Woodrow Wilson (document 47).

After the 1919 conference, Addams and Hamilton traveled through Germany under the auspices of the American Friends Service Committee (a newly founded Quaker relief organization) in order to assess and publicize the plight of the European populations suffering under the impact of the Allied blockade.

Alice Hamilton to Mary Rozet Smith, May 19, 1919

Zurich
May 19th [1919]

Dearest Mary,

. . . . .

. . . I suppose you are wondering what it has all amounted to. I think it has been tremendously worth while. None of us from the Allied Countries can help now doing all we can to get the food blockade raised and have the troops withdrawn from Russia and Hungary. And it has done us good to be able to show the other women that we didn't feel toward them as enemies, to really speak out our detestation of the hatred and intolerance the war has brought. Of course I don't know that anything practical will come of it directly but then what comes from these great medical, or educational, or feminist congresses, yet they are very worth while. We did send two telegrams to Paris, one to Wilson signed by J.A. [Jane Addams], the other to the Big Four. The first protested against the food blockade and that one Wilson answered to J.A., sympathetically though not very hopefully, saying that the practical difficulties were great. The other, protesting against the peace terms as a source of future wars, hasn't been answered. Of course Wilson's reply was a nice addition to J.A.'s prestige here.

It is really amazing how little nonsense and even how little undigested radicalism was talked, when one considered all the newly enfranchised and revolutionary women there were here. Really the most foolish ones were the Australians who talked a good deal of half-baked nonsense, but luckily they arrived very late. There were some intensely interesting times, one when the women from Bavaria, Austria, Wurtemberg, Prussia, Hungary, described the revolutions that they had themselves lived through. Another was when one of the German women told of the protests they had sent to the Government against the invasion of Belgium, the annexation of Belgium, the deportations, the Brest Litovsk treaty and the offensive of 1918. Naturally they were silenced, no paper could publish the protest, their mail was held up, telephone service denied them and they could hold no meetings even in private, and had domiciliary visits of the police over and over again. But we were all so thankful that they did protest. Of course their tales of the hunger blockade have been heart-rending.

Source: Alice Hamilton to Mary Rozet Smith, May 19, 1919, in Sicherman, *Alice Hamilton: A Life in Letters,* 228–32.

Nevertheless, to be quite honest, I must admit that they are a bit difficult, these German women. They may be excellent but the best of them are dense. All the first days we Americans and the British were almost over-doing it in our eagerness to make them feel we were against the treatment being meted out to them since the armistice. We sympathized and we pitied and we passionately declared that our governments were cruel (this the British said) or culpably yielding (this we said). And then little by little the atmosphere changed. We grew a bit tired of having all the repentance on our side. The Germans lapped it up eagerly and begged for more, but never a word came from them of any "mea culpa" on their side. I don't think that in the nicest of them it was more than denseness but that is just it, the nicest are dense. The last day of the Congress a Frenchwoman arrived, a lovely, sad-faced woman from the devastated regions. We gave her a great welcome, of course, and one of the Munich women stepped forward and gave her her hand and said, "A German woman gives her hand to a French woman and hopes that together they may heal the wounds the men have made." The French woman received her with much gentle dignity and went on to make a really beautiful speech and we were all greatly moved, but if only the German woman could have put in a little of the other thing, if she could have said "Help you heal to [sic] wounds our men have given you," people would have welcomed it. [In fairness, the philosophy of Lida Gustava Heymann of Munich (see document 46) was that violence and war were less a human instinct than a specifically masculine problem, embodied in the male dominated state and economic system. In her writings and speeches, Heymann had long put her hopes in feminist impulses and women's suffrage, and she had urged pacifists to oppose not only war but also the general male tendency to resort to force as a solution to problems.] Then at dinner today a very sweet German woman from Wiesbaden said that they were now under French occupation and could realize at last how Belgium felt. Well, really, you know Wiesbaden is not Louvain [the historic Belgian city burned by the German army]. And one would have thought nice German women could realize it without a personal experience. Of course this isn't enough to give the least sense of friction, it is only that the Germans just are different and one wishes they weren't.

· · · · ·

Goodbye and much love,
AH [Alice Hamilton]

DOCUMENT 49

President Wilson's Statement to the Senate Foreign Relations
Committee on the League of Nations Covenant (1919)

*Editor's Note: The U.S. Senate began formal consideration of the Treaty
of Versailles, including the Covenant of the League of Nations, on July
10, 1919. It soon became clear, however, that the Senate Foreign Relations Committee, like the Senate itself, was divided into four factions on
the issue: loyal Democrats, who favored immediate ratification; mild
"reservationists," who favored some limited amendments to the treaty;
strong "reservationists," led by Henry Cabot Lodge, Republican chairperson of the committee, who insisted on numerous important amendments; and isolationist "irreconcilables," including a dozen Republicans
and two Democrats, who advocated complete rejection of the League
in any form. Because six of the ten members of the Senate Foreign Relations Committee were "irreconcilables," the treaty could not
be recommended to the full Senate and remained bottled up in
committee.*

*On August 19, 1919, the president held a luncheon conference at the
White House with the Senate Foreign Relations Committee. In the following prepared statement (which began the three-and-a-half-hour discussion), Wilson sought to persuade the recalcitrant members of the
committee to report the treaty favorably to the entire Senate. He agreed
to accept interpretive reservations that were not embodied in the resolution of ratification and that, therefore, would not require consent by
other nations that had already ratified the treaty. This concession failed
to satisfy the Republican majority on the committee, which on September 10 proposed a resolution that would include four reservations and
forty-five amendments. It was then that Wilson took the issue to the
·voters, eventually collapsing at Pueblo, Colorado, on September 25 and
suffering a paralytic stroke on October 2. On November 6, Senator
Lodge reported out a resolution of ratification accompanied by fourteen
reservations. The Senate voted down the treaty on November 19, 1919,
and again on March 19, 1920 (see document 53).*

Statement of the President, August 19, 1919

．．．．．

Nothing, I am led to believe, stands in the way of the ratification of the treaty except certain doubts with regard to the meaning and implication of certain articles of the covenant of the league of nations; and I must frankly say that I am unable to understand why such doubts should be entertained. You will recall that when I had the pleasure of a conference with your committee and with the Committee of the House of Representatives on Foreign Affairs at the White House in March last [Wilson misremembered; that full and frank meeting took place on February 26, 1919] the questions now most frequently asked about the league of nations were all canvassed with a view to their immediate clarification. The covenant of the league was then in its first draft and subject to revision. It was pointed out that no express recognition was given to the Monroe doctrine; that it was not expressly provided that the league should have no authority to act or to express a judgment on matters of domestic policy; that the right to withdraw from the league was not expressly recognized; and that the constitutional right of the Congress to determine all questions of peace and war was not sufficiently safeguarded. On my return to Paris all these matters were taken up again by the commission on the league of nations and every suggestion of the United States was accepted.

．．．．．

Article 10 is in no respect of doubtful meaning when read in the light of the covenant as a whole. The council of the league can only "advise upon" the means by which the obligations of that great article are to be given effect to. Unless the United States is a party to the policy or action in question, her own affirmative vote in the council is necessary before any advice can be given, for a unanimous vote of the council is required. If she is a party, the trouble is hers anyhow. And the unanimous vote of the council is only advice in any case. Each Government is free to reject it if it pleases. Nothing could have been made more clear to the conference than the right of our Congress under our Constitution to exercise its independent judgment in all matters of peace and war. No

Source: "A Conversation with Members of the Senate Foreign Relations Committee; Conference at the White House, Tuesday, August 19, 1919," in Link et al., *The Papers of Woodrow Wilson* 62: 340–44.

attempt was made to question or limit that right. The United States will, indeed, undertake under article 10 to "respect and preserve as against external aggression the territorial integrity and existing political independence of all members of the league," and that engagement constitutes a very grave and solemn moral obligation. But it is a moral, not a legal, obligation, and leaves our Congress absolutely free to put its own interpretation upon it in all cases that call for action. It is binding in conscience only, not in law.

Article 10 seems to me to constitute the very backbone of the whole covenant. Without it the league would be hardly more than an influential debating society.

It has several times been suggested, in public debate and in private conference, that interpretations of the sense in which the United States accepts the engagements of the covenant should be embodied in the instrument of ratification. There can be no reasonable objection to such interpretations accompanying the act of ratification provided they do not form a part of the formal ratification itself. Most of the interpretations which have been suggested to me embody what seems to me the plain meaning of the instrument itself. But if such interpretations should constitute a part of the formal resolution of ratification, long delays would be the inevitable consequence, inasmuch as all the many governments concerned would have to accept, in effect, the language of the Senate as the language of the treaty before ratification would be complete [Arthur S. Link, Wilson biographer and editor of his papers, has concluded that this last statement "was, to say the least, a dubious and debatable assertion, but it was a point that Wilson had made and would continue to make during the treaty fight, in spite of advice to the contrary"]. . . . If the United States were to qualify the document in any way, moreover, I am confident from what I know of the many conferences and debates which accompanied the formulation of the treaty that our example would immediately be followed in many quarters, in some instances with very serious reservations, and that the meaning and operative force of the treaty would presently be clouded from one end of its clauses to the other.

. . . . .

DOCUMENT 50

The Reverend Anna Garlin Spencer Urges Women to Support
the Peace Treaty and the League (1919)

Editor's Note: The Reverend Anna Garlin Spencer, educator, minister, pacifist, and member of the American Peace Society and the National Council of Women (NCW) of the United States, spoke to the annual meeting of the NCW about the Versailles treaty at its annual meeting in St. Louis, November 11 to 14, 1919. In doing so, Spencer, one of the founders of the Woman's Peace party (see document 14), sought diplomatically to move the divided membership of the NCW, which consisted of thirty women's organizations with some ten million members, toward support for the treaty and the League of Nations. Her speech was reprinted in the magazine of the American Peace Society.

Woman and the Peace Treaty

. . . . .

During this war, especially since the signing of the armistice, a great movement, said to represent in petitions hundreds of thousands of women, has been established in this country to protest against the horrible violations and outrages of women in the recent war, and asking that measures be taken to personally punish personal offenders. These women thought they were doing a new thing, but the International Council of Women was more than a decade in advance of them. This Council [in 1903] sent to all the governments of the countries represented in its constituent membership a demand that the special cruelties and outrages which women have always suffered in all wars should in some way be provided against, and that personal responsibility for such wrongs should be insisted upon. The present war has proved that the spirit that inflames men's passions in one direction renders it extremely difficult for any law to prevent these special outrages upon women.

. . . . .

This meeting [in November 1919] has not been asked to put itself on record by any resolution concerning the proposed League of Nations

Source: The Reverend Anna Garlin Spencer, "Woman and the Peace Treaty," *Advocate of Peace* 81 (Dec. 1919): 359–60.

which could be a divisive element in our membership; but I venture the hope that every woman will go from here and study the Covenant and the Treaty. . . . We have all wondered how any newborn League could carry some of the heavy burdens which would be placed upon it by the provisions of the Treaty.

I wish to say here I hope that every woman in this Council will disassociate herself from the type of opposition which the League is meeting in many quarters in our country. It is all right, if you believe so, to say that the Covenant is not good enough; but I beg you not to believe that it is too good, and not to take the ground of those who say that because it binds us in fellowship with all the nations of the world therefore we will not have it.

My complaint of it is that the Treaty that accompanies the Covenant is not good enough; but I see no other way by which to begin to clarify and rectify the mistakes that have been made in the first flush of victory, and the first recoil from the dangers and difficulties of war, except to begin to try to live together. I once knew a man who was very slow. He had a very quick wife, and, of course, it is very difficult for a lightning express to accommodate itself to a freight train, so often there would be a great deal of, I will not say friction, but there would be some excited talk when the wife would try to get him to move faster. Once he said: "Why, don't be impatient; I am beginning to get ready to commence to go." It looks to me as if, at worst, the League of Nations was beginning to get ready to commence to go, and I think that through the proverbial quickness, I would not say impatience, of women we may make it go a little faster. At any rate, we must work with all our might, must we not, for some effective organization—the world [organization—] to substitute law for war and to build good-will into the fabric of the common life.

DOCUMENT 51

Creation of the American Civil Liberties Union (1920)

Editor's Note: The American Civil Liberties Union (ACLU) grew out of a bureau formed by the American Union Against Militarism in the spring of 1917 to aid conscientious objectors and to defend in wartime the rights of free speech and freedom of the press and assembly of Socialists, pacifists, and other dissenters accused of violating the hastily passed Espionage Act of 1917. Roger N. Baldwin (see document 40), social worker and pacifist, was for more than thirty years the dominant figure in the AUAM's temporary National Civil Liberties Bureau and in its permanent successor.

The ACLU was the first permanent national organization dedicated to defending the civil liberties of all citizens and not merely to representing the special interests of one group. In the following account, The Survey magazine reported the founding of the ACLU in January 1920.

A New Civil Liberties Union

The National Civil Liberties Bureau, which was formed during the war not to oppose the war but to preserve the civil liberties of free speech, free press, freedom of thought and peaceable assemblage, has dissolved its organization and in its place a new national organization has been formed to extend the fight for civil liberties to industrial conflicts. The name of the new organization is the American Civil Liberties Union, with headquarters at 41 Union Square, New York City. The National Civil Liberties Bureau states that its work under war statues restricting free speech and free press is practically ended and that a new organization is needed to meet peace time issues. The only work remaining to be done under the war statutes is to secure amnesty for political and industrial prisoners; efforts to this end will be continued by the new organization.

District organizations representing the union in eight different centers, will carry on the work with the national office. The announcement also states that speakers and free speech organizers will be sent into areas of industrial conflict where restrictions are being placed on free speech, free press and the right of assemblage. Local regulations violating constitutional provisions will be fought in the courts. Lawyers and investigators "will be sent into districts where serious trouble arises."

The National Civil Liberties Bureau, in a statement issued telling of the new organization, says:

> The industrial struggle is clearly the essential challenge to the cause of civil liberty today. The whole gamut of activities aimed at

Source: "A New Civil Liberties Union," *Survey* 43 (Jan. 31, 1920): 480.

"reds, radicals, Bolshevists and I. W. W. [the Industrial Workers of the World]" is in substance only the one purpose of suppressing the revolt of labor against intolerable industrial autocracy. The efforts are not by any means confined to radicals. They strike at the vitals of established trades unionism. The issues of free speech, free press, lawful assemblage, and peaceful picketing are everywhere involved. No association is organized to deal broadly and generally with these issues in the struggle of labor. Each labor group makes its own unaided fight, without relation to the common problems they face together.

The new work is in charge of a national committee of fifty members. The chairman is Prof. Harry F. Ward, Union Theological Seminary, New York city. Other members are: Jane Addams, head resident of Hull House, Chicago; James H. Maurer, president of the Pennsylvania State Federation of Labor; Duncan McDonald, president of the Illinois State Federation of Labor; Henry R. Linville, president of the Teachers' Union, New York city; Herbert Bigelow, of Cincinnati; Elizabeth Gurley Flynn, secretary of the Workers' Defence Union; Morris Hillquit; Lincoln Concord; Scott Nearing; James Weldon Johnson, of the National Association for the Advancement of Colored People; Oswald Garrison Villard, editor of the Nation; Rev. John Haynes Holmes and Dr. Judah L. Magnes. The executive staff is composed of two directors, Albert De Silver, who was director of the National Civil Liberties Bureau, and Roger N. Baldwin. Walter Nelles is counsel.

DOCUMENT 52

The Survey Magazine Warns Against Peacetime Conscription (1920)

Editor's Note: The Survey magazine, published by pacifist and social reformer Paul U. Kellogg, was a sympathetic supporter of the American Union Against Militarism's campaigns against a larger peacetime army. In February 1920, William L. Chenery, associate editor of the magazine, took up the AUAM's cause. In the following article, he warned against hidden dangers behind efforts to obtain legislation establishing a permanent system of universal military training (UMT) and a stand-by draft.

Partly as a result of such adverse publicity, and more importantly because of the upcoming 1920 elections, a majority of Republicans and Democrats in the House rejected in March a plan (the Army Reorganization Bill) introduced by Senator James W. Wadsworth that envisioned a regular army of 300,000, augmented by a system of universal military training, which would have prepared 2 million trained reservists within five years. In the National Defense Act of June 4, 1920, Congress eliminated the proposal for UMT and a stand-by draft and provided instead for a regular army of 298,000 with the National Guard as the primary ready reserve.

Conscription in Peace Times

. . . . .

Two arguments have risen to the surface of that discussion of the Army Reorganization bill. The first is that presented by its advocates. In a word it is "Now or Never." If this opportunity is lost, say those who support Senator Wadsworth [James W. Wadsworth (R., N.Y.), chairperson of the military affairs committee, and the originator of the bill], it may never again be possible to write such a measure upon the statute books of the nation. This line of reasoning is not the most persuasive conceivable. If the merits of the Senate proposal are real, the American people can be relied upon to act wisely even though haste is foresworn. . . .

The chief argument so far advanced by those who agree with Representative Mondell [Frank Mondell (R., Wyo.), House majority leader] in opposing the bill is that of economy. These say, not without reason, that taxes are high. They assert that governmental economy is of first importance at this particular moment in our history. Without retrenchment, it is argued, it is futile to hope for any lowering of the burdensome cost of living. The passage of the Wadsworth bill, they say, will call for enormous expenditures. The precise cost is debatable, but the opponents of the measure are convinced that it will be not less than a half a billion dollars [annually] from the very outset and probably more.

Neither the importunate plea of those who say "Now or Never" nor the argument of the opposition who urge the universal desire for public economy goes to the heart of the matter.

Source: William L. Chenery, "Conscription in Peace Times," *Survey* 43 (Feb. 14, 1920): 575–76.

Not without guile, in this suggested reorganization of the army, two far reaching policies are offered. These are:

1. The establishment of a system of universal military training.
2. The enactment of a permanent draft system.

Were the measure to be accepted by Congress, further discussion either of universal military training or of conscription would be vain. The choice would have been made and the consequences would have to be endured even though these rendered the industrial workers of the nation infinitely more servile than any plan for compulsory arbitration or the abolition of trade unionism could possibly effect.

It should be recognized at the outset moreover that the enactment of a draft system in peace times for peace purposes is a very different thing from the approval of such a system for the emergency of war. During the World War no other method of distributing the burden of national service seemed practical. The American people accepted for the purpose of overthrowing the German autocracy the draft act. Defeating Hohenzollernism [Hohenzollern was the family name of Wilhelm II and his ancestors who ruled Prussia for four centuries and then a united Germany from 1871 to 1918], however, is one thing; choking off industrial evolution is quite another. . . .

. . . . . .

In [the] sentence which authorizes the President "in national emergency" to require the registration of male citizens and residents between eighteen and forty-five the secret of the Military Reorganization bill is revealed. A national emergency is a flexible phrase. When in 1910 the French railway men struck Premier [Aristide] Briand called the railway workers to military service. The strike was effectually broken. That is one way of handling industrial questions. . . . It is indisputable that these sections of the Wadsworth measure could be utilized to suppress any expression of the grievances of workers.

In truth the industrial rather than the military aspect of world affairs offers the principal excuse for the consideration of such a measure as the Wadsworth bill at this time. Whatever the arguments for universal military training and for conscription were prior to the World War it is certainly obvious that no foreign enemy has either the resources or the will to invade America at the present time or in the immediate future. . . . Against whom must we mobilize our entire manpower?

. . . The only rational explanation of military policies such as those offered by Senator Wadsworth lies therefore in the domestic rather than in the foreign field.

...The war against war has been won. ... The determination of nations associated with the United States to reduce their military forces has been plainly expressed. Should we cooperate with them in reducing the size of armies or force them to meet a new competition?

DOCUMENT 53

Final Defeat of the Treaty of Versailles; Senate Failure to
Ratify Treaty Even with the Lodge Reservations (1919 and 1920)

Editor's Note: From July to November 1919, the Treaty of Versailles was bottled up in the Senate Foreign Relations Committee by a coalition of irreconcilable isolationists and of reservationists led by Senator Henry Cabot Lodge (see document 44), the committee chairperson, who amended more than a dozen major "reservations" (reprinted below) to the treaty. Public opinion appeared divided, with substantial opposition from isolationists, as well as from some conservatives and a number of liberal internationalists who were disillusioned with the treaty. Industrialists Andrew Mellon and Henry C. Frick helped to finance a nationwide campaign by the "irreconcilables" against ratification. Wilson had met with the Senate Foreign Relations Committee in August (see document 49) but to no avail. In September, the president took the case for ratification to the people in a ten-thousand-mile speaking tour of the West. Exhausted, he collapsed in Pueblo, Colorado, on the night of September 25, 1919.

After the president returned to Washington, he suffered a massive paralytic stroke on October 2 that almost killed him. The White House withheld the seriousness of his condition; virtually no one except doctors and his family saw him for a month. Yet Wilson did not resign or delegate his authority to the vice-president. After a month, he began a gradual, partial recovery. Nevertheless, the stroke permanently paralyzed his left side, impaired his speech, impeded his vision and his power of concentration, and weakened his emotional control. Not until three months later, in late December, was he able to work and then not for more than five or ten minutes at a time; he remained a semi-invalid for the rest of his term, indeed until his death in 1924. Although he retained most of his intellectual ability, Wilson seems to have lost his

*political judgment and his emotional ability to deal with such complex
and difficult issues as the treaty fight.*

*The stroke almost certainly prevented any chance Wilson had in the
treaty fight of gaining at least a partial victory. There was some evidence
that Wilson had been gaining popular support for the treaty. But his
illness prevented him from continuing his campaign for ratification. At
the same time, it seems to have made him dogmatic, unable to distin-
guish detail from principle, and unwilling to accept any compromise.
Instead, he viewed the situation in stark terms of good versus evil.
Crucially, he would not let pro-League Democrats offer limited interpretive reservations that might have attracted Republican "mild
reservationists."*

*Caught between the opposing leadership of Lodge and the ailing
Wilson, with their different views of the kind of international commitments appropriate for the United States, the Senate failed to ratify the
treaty in several votes on November 19, 1919, and in a final reconsideration on March 19, 1920. Consequently, the United States did not
become a member of the League of Nations. In recognition of Woodrow
Wilson's efforts, however, he was awarded the Nobel Peace Prize for
1919.*

The Senate Votes on the Treaty, November 19, 1919.

*Editor's Note: On November 19, 1919, the Versailles treaty failed three
times to obtain even a majority, let alone the two-thirds required for
ratification.*

*The first vote was on the treaty with Lodge's strong reservations
(Wilson had urged a vote against the treaty with the reservations, which
he said nullified rather than amended the treaty). The treaty with the
Lodge reservations was defeated 39 in favor to 55 against. The opposi-
tion included 42 Democrats and 13 "irreconcilable" Republicans and
Democrats. (Had all but the irreconcilable Democrats voted for the
Lodge reservations, the treaty would have carried 81 to 13.)*

*The second vote was virtually the same; the treaty with the reserva-
tions was again defeated, this time by 41 in favor to 51 against.*

*The third vote was on the treaty without any reservations. It failed
with 38 in favor and 53 against. The opposition included virtually all
the Republicans, while all the Democrats except the two irreconcilables
voted in support.*

The Senate Votes again on the Treaty, March 19, 1920.

Editor's Note: Pressure from public opinion and pro-League groups forced the Senate to reconsider the treaty. On March 19, 1920, although Wilson still refused to consider any compromise, 21 Democrats deserted him and joined Republican reservationists in support of the treaty with the Lodge reservations. Nevertheless, 23 Democrats voted with the 13 Republican "irreconcilables," and the treaty fell 7 votes short of the necessary two-thirds majority. The vote for the treaty with the Lodge reservations was 49 in favor to 35 opposed.

The Lodge Reservations

RESOLUTION OF RATIFICATION.

Resolved (two-thirds of the Senators present concurring therein), That the Senate advise and consent to the ratification of the treaty of peace with Germany concluded at Versailles on the 28th day of June, 1919, subject to the following reservations and understandings, which are hereby made a part and condition of this resolution of ratification, which ratification is not to take effect or bind the United States until the said reservations and understandings adopted by the Senate have been accepted as a part and a condition of this resolution of ratification by the allied and associated powers. . . .

1. The United States so understands and construes article 1 that in case of notice of withdrawal from the League of Nations, as provided in said article, the United States shall be the sole judge as to whether all its international obligations and all its obligations under the said covenant have been fulfilled. . . .

2. The United States assumes no obligation to preserve the territorial integrity or political independence of any other country by the employment of its military or naval forces, its resources, or any form of economic discrimination . . . under the provisions of article 10 . . . unless in any particular case the Congress, which, under the Constitution, has the sole power to declare war or authorize the employment of the military or naval forces of the United States, shall, in the exercise of full liberty of action, by act or joint resolution so provide.

Source: U.S. Congressional Record, 66th Cong., 2d sess., Vol. 59, pt. 5 (March 19, 1920), 4599.

3. No mandate shall be accepted by the United States under article 22, part 1, or any other provision of the treaty of peace with Germany, except by action of the Congress of the United States.

4. The United States reserves to itself exclusively the right to decide what questions are within its domestic jurisdiction and declares that all domestic and political questions relating wholly or in part to its internal affairs, including immigration, labor, coastwise traffic, the tariff, commerce, the suppression of traffic in women and children and in opium and other dangerous drugs, and all other domestic questions [such as race relations], are not under this treaty to be submitted in any way either to arbitration or to the consideration of the council or of the assembly of the League of Nations, or any agency, thereof, or to the decision or recommendation of any other power.

5. The United States will not submit to arbitration or to inquiry by the assembly or by the council of the League of Nations provided for in said treaty of peace, any questions which in the judgment of the United States depend upon or relate to its long-established policy, commonly known as the Monroe doctrine. . . .

· · · · ·

9. The United States shall not be obligated to contribute to any expenses of the League of Nations . . . unless and until an appropriation of funds available for such expenses shall have been made by the Congress of the United States. . . .

10. No plan for the limitation of armaments proposed by the council of the League of Nations under the provisions of article 8 shall be held as binding the United States until the same shall have been accepted by Congress, and the United States reserves the right to increase its armament without the consent of the council whenever the United States is threatened with invasion or engaged in war.

· · · · ·

15. In consenting to the ratification of the treaty with Germany the United States adheres to the principle of self-determination and to the resolution of sympathy with the aspirations of the Irish people for a government of their own choice adopted by the Senate June 6, 1919, and declares that when such government is attained by Ireland, a consummation it is hoped is at hand, it should promptly be admitted as a member of the League of Nations. [Lodge inserted this endorsement of Ireland's struggle for independence in part to win support for Republicans from Irish Americans in the Democratic party.]

DOCUMENT 54

Debate over Releasing Wartime Offenders (1920)

Editor's Note: Under federal and state statutes passed during the war, perhaps up to four thousand persons were imprisoned as wartime offenders. These "political prisoners" included "absolutist" conscientious objectors as well as men and women convicted of violating wartime federal laws against statements or activities that would hamper recruiting or the draft—Socialist leader, Eugene V. Debs, 1855–1926, was the most noted wartime prisoner— or state sedition and anarcho-syndicalist laws that in effect prohibited political or economic radicalism.

After the armistice in November 1918, civil libertarians, pacifists, Socialists, labor unions, and some religious groups began a campaign for amnesty for political prisoners. Although sentiment grew by 1920 for the prisoners' release, the issue remained divisive, particularly in an election year. The following account of differences in the press was reported in The Literary Digest *one month before the 1920 election.*

Forgiving War-Offenders

The "CROWD OF MARPLOTS and conspirators" who are confined in State and Federal prisons for opposing the Government during the war should not, in the opinion of a Washington paper, "be dumped upon an already outraged nation." But, argue the friends of these prisoners, the war is really over, the offenders were merely lovers of peace whose souls shrank from the bloodthirstiness of armed conflict, and it is cowardly and tyrannical to keep them in jail now.

Some of our more conservative editors say we should let bygones be bygones and release them, but others hold that they would at once join the "Red" agitators who are trying to stir up Bolshevism here. Of course, the Socialist papers have been calling for their release almost ever since the armistice was signed, but recently such well-known metropolitan dailies as the New York *World,* the New York *Evening Post,* and the Brooklyn *Citizen* aligned themselves in this respect with the New York *Call* (Socialist) and the Milwaukee *Leader,* Victor Berger's Socialist daily.

Source: "Forgiving War-Offenders," *Literary Digest* 67 (Oct. 2, 1920): 18–19.

... Attorney-General [A. Mitchell] Palmer, however, recently refused to consider the proposal of Samuel Gompers, president of the American Federation of Labor, and representatives of the Socialist party that a blanket proclamation freeing the prisoners be issued; each case must be reviewed separately, ruled Mr. Palmer. Including persons imprisoned by the various States, there are said to be four thousand political prisoners serving sentences at the present time. . . .

.   .   .   .   .

"It should not be difficult now to write at a fairer judgment concerning the culpability of these culprits than was possible in the time of war," thinks the New York *World,* which adds that "in nearly all cases where guilt was solely a matter of opinion the penalties inflicted were extremely severe and might properly be modified." . . .

.   .   .   .   .

One of Mr. Gompers's arguments in behalf of political prisoners was that their cases "should be treated with love and reason and a sense of democracy." The Philadelphia *Public Ledger,* however, points out that "there was neither love nor reason nor a sense of democracy in many of the people who systematically tried to hinder the Government and belittle it in the eyes of enemies at a time when we were exerting all our energies to preserve such freedom as remained in a world ridden by militarists on one hand and by anarchists on the other." . . .

.   .   .   .   .

DOCUMENT 55

Jane Addams, "Feed the World and Save the League" (1920)

Editor's Note: As international president of the Women's International League for Peace and Freedom from 1919 to 1929, Jane Addams worked continuously to build up the organization and to encourage humanitarianism, disarmament, and world peace. In the immediate postwar years, she and Emily Greene Balch, international secretary-treasurer of the

WILPF, sought to focus public attention on the widespread hunger and starvation in a disrupted world. (Addams was awarded the Nobel Peace Prize jointly with Nicholas Murray Butler in 1931; Balch shared it in 1946 with John R. Mott of the YMCA and the World Council of Churches.) In the following November 1920 article in The New Republic, *the leading liberal magazine in America at the time, Addams urged both food relief and a transformation of the League of Nations.*

Feed the World and Save the League

. . . . .

. . . The great danger ahead of the League of Nations is implicit in the fact that its first work involves the guaranteeing of a purely political peace and a dependence upon the old political motives. Whereas if from the very first it could perform an act of faith, if it evinced the daring to meet new demands which could be met in no other way, then and then only would it become the necessary instrumentality to carry on the enlarged life of the world and gradually be recognized as indispensable.

Since the cessation of war, there is all over the world a sense of loss in motive power, the consciousness that there is no driving force equal to that furnished by the heroism and self-sacrifice demanded in war time. Yet the great purposes of the League of Nations could be made sufficiently appealing to absorb these to the full. What could afford a more primitive, genuine and abiding motive than feeding the people of the earth on an international scale? It would utilize all the courage and self-sacrifice evolved by warfare and turn into immediate efficiency all that international cooperation which performed such miracles of production in the prosecution of the war. Both are ready to its hand. The British Labor party has pointed out the beginning of international order as follows: "During the period of the war we had great international bodies for the control and distribution of shipping, credit, and raw material in accordance not with capacity to pay, but with vital need. Only so could the common enemy be met. There was in these arrangements the beginnings of an organized economic government of the world, real international society, subjecting to a common control those things essential to the common life. Here was a world-government actually in being."

Source: Jane Addams, "Feed the World and Save the League," *New Republic* 24 (Nov. 24, 1920): 325–27.

If the League of Nations had maintained the system, remedied its defects, enlarged its functions, and democratized its administration, the de facto beginnings of an organized economic government of the world would have been constituted. The eighteenth century phrases in which diplomatic intercourse has been so long conducted would have dropped away as not fitted to discuss the need of an internationally guaranteed loan, the functions of an Economic Council for the control of food stuffs and raw material, the fuel shortage, credits granted to enemy and liberated countries alike for reconstruction purposes, the effect of malnutrition on powers of production, the irreparable results of "hunger oedema [a pathology of extreme malnutrition characterized by effusion of fluids into cells and body cavities accompanied by serious swelling]." . . .

. . . . .

We are told by those familiar with the work carried on at the temporary headquarters of the League of Nations in London that "the economic section has for many months been engaged in a world wide study of such questions as coal, production, markets, food and the movement of raw material. At the first meeting of the Assembly a full report will be ready." But how many people may starve to death before those reports are acted upon. It suggests a committee studying the best method of extinguishing fires while precious granaries are burning down.

It is quite obvious that the League must proceed carefully but there are times when even well considered delay is fatal. While these reports are being prepared, the starving people themselves have ceased to look to the League for help, it has lost all that popular confidence and hope which was its greatest asset. . . .

. . . . .

It is absurd for us, as advocates of the League, to complain that it is difficult to endear it to "the people" when it is precisely the people who are most ready for an act of faith, to whom it seems most natural to feed the hungry. It may take years to popularize the principles of the League, but citizens of civilized nations have already received much religious instruction. "To do the will" on an international scale might result in that world wide religious revival which the war in spite of many predictions, has as yet failed to evoke. It would certainly establish the sort of League of which thousands of people dreamed when they hailed the President of the United States as the Savior of Europe. . . .

DOCUMENT 56

Senator William E. Borah's Resolution for
a Naval Disarmament Conference (1920)

Editor's Note: Senator William E. Borah, 1865–1940, maverick Republican from Idaho, and second ranking member of the Senate Foreign Relations Committee in the immediate postwar era (later, committee chairperson from 1924 to 1933), was a dedicated isolationist. As a leader of the "irreconcilables," he helped defeat the Treaty of Versailles. His isolationism, plus a desire to refurbish his reputation, led Borah again into national prominence, this time as a champion of naval arms reduction. Suddenly and dramatically on December 14, 1920, Borah introduced a joint resolution requesting the president to call a conference of the three leading naval powers—Britain, the United States, and Japan—to discuss cutting their naval programs in half within five years.

Because of a threatened naval arms race among the three powers for maritime and commercial influence in the postwar world and because of a growing public and congressional desire for tax cuts and economy in government, Borah seized on naval disarmament as a highly popular and promising issue. It was, to his way of thinking, also an effective means of heading off renewed pressure for U.S. membership in the League as a way of avoiding the arms competition cycle. Borah believed Britain and Japan were using the lack of U.S. membership in the League as an excuse for modernizing and expanding their navies. There is some evidence that Borah expected the two nations to reject, or at least subvert, an American-sponsored arms limitation conference. Such action would have exposed what Borah considered their fundamental hypocrisy. Their rejection would also have undermined pressures for the United States to join them in the League of Nations. Whatever Borah's motives, his shrewd proposal promised considerable rewards without significant financial costs or added international obligations on the part of the United States. For if the conference did meet and achieved results, Borah could (and did) argue that such arms limitation conferences rendered the League of Nations superfluous.

A precedent for the Borah resolution was the rider introduced by Congressman Walter L. Hensley (D., Mo.), which had been amended to the Naval Appropriations Act of 1916 (see document 25). Borah ignored this precedent and put foward a proposal which was simple, easily understood, and apparently practical. The following account of the introduction of Borah's resolution on December 14, 1920, is from the Congressional Record.

Reduction of Naval Armament—Disarmament

Mr. Borah: I introduce a joint resolution which I ask may be read and referred to the Committee on Foreign Relations.

. . . . .

Resolved by the Senate and House of Representatives of the United States of America in Congress assembled. That the President of the United States is requested, if not incompatible with the public interests, to advise the Governments of Great Britain and Japan, respectively, that this Government will at once take up directly with their Governments and without waiting upon the action of any other nation the question of disarmament, with a view of quickly coming to an understanding by which the building [*sic*] naval programs of each of said Governments, to wit, that of Great Britain, Japan, and the United States, shall be reduced annually during the next five years 50 per cent of the present estimates or figures.

Second, that it is the sense of the Congress, in case such an understanding can be had, that it will conform its appropriation and building plans to such agreement.

Resolved further, That this proposition is suggested by the Congress of the United States, to accomplish immediately a substantial reduction of the naval armaments of the world.

DOCUMENT 57

The Peace Movement Mobilizes for Naval Arms Control (1921)

Editor's Note: Despite its appeal, Senator Borah's joint resolution of December 14, 1920, calling for a naval arms limitation conference, failed to come to a vote in that session of Congress. The Republican

Source: Senate Joint Resolution 225, U.S. *Congressional Record,* 66th Cong., 3d sess., Vol. 60, pt. 1 (Dec. 14, 1920), 310.

majority responded to the opposition of the Navy League and especially of President-elect Warren G. Harding, who opposed congressional encroachment on executive discretion in foreign affairs. Harding was also a traditional "big navy" Republican who supported building a fleet at least equal to Britain's before engaging in any negotiations limiting naval construction.

Growing press and public support for Borah's proposal, however, increased the pressure on the incoming administration to do something about the threatened naval arms race among Britain, Japan, and the United States. In early 1921, Borah attached his resolution to the naval appropriations bill, but it died with that bill at the end of the session. Borah reintroduced it after the Harding administration took office in March 1921.

Rallying around the resolution, pressure groups, led initially by the American Union Against Militarism, flocked to the fight for naval disarmament. Although largely drawn from congressional sources, including Borah, who busily cultivated support for his proposal, the following report to the AUAM membership by Henry R. Mussey, the organization's new lobbyist in Washington, D.C., offered an insider's view of developments in the capital.

Report from the Washington Representative of the American
Union Against Militarism (AUAM) January 11, 1921

The First Step First

Men and brethren, be not deceived. There is little genuine disarmament sentiment in Congress, but members [of Congress] realize that taxes are pressing hard on the pocket nerve.... Mr. [Frank] Mondell [Republican majority leader in the House] says that the most useful service right now is to give Congress all possible support in cutting next year's appropriations....

That means work for you. *Write, write, write,*—to your own Congressmen and Senators ....

Out the war appropriations. That's the first step.

The second, I am confident, is to pass the Borah resolution.... So write again, to Senator William E. Borah and to Henry Cabot Lodge,

Source: Henry R. Mussey, report to the membership, AUAM Bulletin, no. 31, Jan. 11, 1921, American Union Against Militarism Papers, Swarthmore College Peace Collection.

chairman of the Senate Committee on Foreign Relations. . . . Its enemies (and some of its unwary friends) will try to kill it by inviting France and Italy, too. That will bring in the land forces. France won't touch her army, and—poof! The whole thing goes up in smoke.

First, slaughter the appropriations. Second, with that action to show good faith, ask Great Britain and Japan to join us in a naval holiday. These are possible first steps. . . .

． ． ． ． ．

On all these matters stir up your business friends. They are coming our way and the farmers are playing our game. If you can get up a meeting, do it now. Pour in resolutions and petitions—specific ones urging these two steps.

Last week I spent three days at the Capitol with a delegation of Philadephia Friends [Quakers]. We saw all the big leaders. The result, while highly encouraging superficially, chiefly is a summons to vigorous work. Universal [military] training for the present is dead as a coffin-nail. The war crowd are on the defensive. Congress is going to prohibit the Secretary of War from keeping the army above 175,000 men next year. Responsible men like Knox and Penrose [Senator Philander C. Knox and Senator Boies Penrose, both conservative Republicans from Pennsylvania] and [Frank] Mondell, not to speak of the so-called "progressives," today want help in muzzling the military monster, which they see is like to devour us with all the rest of the world. If they look at it chiefly as a financial question, never mind.

Women Mobilize for Disarmament

Editor's Note: In rousing public support for Borah's proposal for a naval arms reduction conference, the AUAM soon found many allies, including pacifists, religious organizations such as the Friends (Quakers) Disarmament Council, and a host of groups seeking economy in government—business, agriculture, and organized labor.

Particularly important were newly enfranchised women (national woman's suffrage was achieved by ratification of the Nineteenth Amendment in 1920), seeking an issue after suffrage upon which to exert their public influence. In the spring of 1921, activists formed the Women's Committee on World Disarmament, staged mass meetings, and worked in cooperation with disarmament groups and existing women's organizations, such as the Women's Christian Temperance Union and the

League of Women Voters as well as the Women's International League for Peace and Freedom. The following is a sympathetic account in The Survey *magazine in mid-April 1921.*

Women of the World

Public meetings on disarmament have, during the last few weeks, been held throughout the country. The encouraging feature has been that these meetings have not in all cases been called by the same organization but represent a spontaneous rise of different groups to the present political opportunities. At most of these meetings resolutions have been passed or speeches made urging the government of the United States to take the lead in this matter. Thus, at a very largely attended meeting held in New York City last Saturday by the United States section of the Women's International League [for Peace and Freedom], a motion was passed with enthusiasm endorsing the resolution introduced in the last Congress by Senator Borah asking the government to call a conference with Great Britain, France, Japan and Italy to advance simultaneously disarmament in these countries. . . .

Another resolution, offered by Jane Addams, requested the league to hold a special international conference of women on the Pacific Coast to prepare recommendations on a naval holiday. . . . Miss Addams pointed out that the present huge naval program of the United States not only fomented the spirit of fear that led to unnecessary and wasteful armament throughout the world, but stood in the way of other national measures which would directly make for a pacification of the world, such as a greatly increased and national program for stimulating foreign trade and feeding Europe, cancellation of the war debts of France to this country, and an effective protest against imperialistic activities on the part of other powers. Dr. [T.] Iyenaga [director of the East and West News Bureau] maintained that the friendly attitude of this country toward Japan and the conciliatory policy on outstanding questions in which both nations are interested was discounted in Japanese public opinion by the constant official and semi-official talk here about the need for a huge navy.

. . . . .

Source: "Women of the World," *Survey* 46 (Apr. 16, 1921): 75.

A Report by the New Washington Representative of the AUAM,
on Progress Towards Disarmament, July 14, 1921

*Editor's Note: Popular support for a naval arms reduction conference
reached such levels in the spring of 1921 that when President Harding
withdrew his opposition, Congress adopted Borah's resolution by the
end of June in nearly unanimous votes.*

*The Harding administration and many others were concerned not
merely with the idea of naval arms reduction but also with problems in
the Far East, most immediately the scheduled automatic renewal in July
1921 of the Anglo-Japanese Defensive Alliance. The treaty of 1902 was
orginally directed against Russian and German expansion in East Asia
and the Pacific, but it had come to serve Tokyo in other ways, particularly by having its British ally as a counterbalance to U.S. expansion in
the Pacific. It served London by helping to prevent Japanese expansion
into areas of British interest in southern China. However, by July 1921,
Britain and the Commonwealth nations, such as Canada and Australia,
had become uncomfortable with the alliance, especially in light of increasing Japanese friction with the United States. In London's view a
rapprochement with the United States linked with avoidance of an ex-
pensive naval arms race was preferable to a defensive alliance with
Japan.*

*When President Harding in July 1921 issued a call for a disarmament
conference in Washington, he virtually ignored Borah's resolution, extending invitations also to France and Italy and enlarging the agenda to
include Far Eastern questions involving the Anglo-Japanese Alliance
and conflicting international goals in Asia. The following report to the
AUAM membership by Belle Rankin, who succeeded Henry R. Mussey
as the organization's Washington representative, largely reflected Borah's
own suspicions of the administration's agenda.*

Disarmament to Date

The formal call for a conference to discuss limitation of armaments
on land and sea is about to be issued by the President, the much her-
alded "feelers" having met with a satisfactory response. This is a victory

Source: Belle Rankin, "Disarmament to Date," report to AUAM members, AUAM Bulletin no. 35, July 14, 1921, American Union Against Militarism Papers, Swarthmore College Peace Collection.

for the advocates of disarmament in the sense that the enormous pressure of public opinion has forced some real action. But we must not be blind to the dangers that beset the road to a limitation of armaments, to say nothing of disarmament. The conference is to be called ostensibly to discuss limitation of armaments but first there is to be a discussion of the problems relating to the Pacific and the Far East. The situation is well stated in the New York World of July 12. "If the discussion is successful in removing Shantung, Yap, Saghalien [Sakhalin] Island, the California anti-Japanese legislation, mandates in the Pacific generally and the Anglo-Japanese alliance [of 1902], from the category of troublesome problems, a measure of naval disarmament will come along naturally, for the causes for the present big naval appropriations will no longer exist. Should the conference fail to settle those differences, there is little chance that the ostensible purpose of the conference will prevail.["]

A conference of the three naval powers only, to discuss a reduction in armament building during the next five years, as proposed by Senator Borah's amendment, might have accomplished something in a short time. The danger is that the proposed conference may drag out indefinitely and even "approximate" disarmament may be buried under a host of complicated issues.

And all the time we are to go on building battleships at full speed, as the jingo papers are careful to point out. We are to talk piously about limitation, but we are to hold the big stick ready for instant use. The naval appropriation bill, after a storm-tossed career, has finally reached port. Of the approximate $414,000,000 it provides, $90,000,000 is for further construction of ships already under way, besides $6,000,000 for additional air-craft building. . . . The enlisted personnel of the Navy was reduced to 106,000 and the Marines to 21,000. . . . The officer personnel is not eaffected as it is fixed at a certain percentage of the *authorized* enlisted personnel which is at this time 137,451.

In the army the situation is different. The enlisted personnel is to be reduced to 150,000 by October 1 but the officer personnel which is fixed by law at 17,717 men, will remain the same. . . . The total of the Army Appropriation bill was $328,000,000. . . . Congress may be said to have the germ of economy but it can't be said to have developed a fever as yet.

So much for the news. Now for the work.

The call for a conference is a step in the right direction. The thing to do now is to insist that the negotiations be open and that the question of a reduction of armaments be not lost sight of.

The situation must not be allowed to die down. Keep up the meetings. . . . The country does not half realize yet the proportion of our wealth that goes into the war budget. The need for educational work is great. . . .

Fears That the Military and other Conservatives Will Sabotage the Disarmament Conference, July 1921

Editor's Note: Oswald Garrison Villard, 1872–1949, pacifist, reformer, a founder of the American Union Against Militarism, and the publisher of the left-liberal Nation *magazine (he sold the New York* Evening Post *in 1918), had been shocked by the compromises Wilson had made to obtain allied acceptance of the Covenant of the League of Nations—"a covenant with death" as Villard bitterly called it. The publisher campaigned vigorously against the League and the Treaty of Versailles. With their defeat, he took up the cause of arms reduction and warned against the forces of reaction in this article in* The Nation *magazine in July 1921.*

The Disarmament Conference and Its Possibilities

With the English [liberals'] protests against the sending of Lloyd George and Lord George Curzon to represent Great Britain at the Washington disarmament conference we heartily sympathize, . . . because we believe . . . that the less the coming conference smacks of Versailles and its personalities the better it will be for the conference and the world.

．　．　．　．　．

Above all we trust that there will be no generals and no admirals assigned or appointed to the conference by any member of it. It was the German admirals and generals, who, as Joseph H. Choate testified, wrecked the Second Hague Conference. [Choate, 1832–1917, a corporation lawyer and diplomat, headed the U.S. delegation to The Hague conference of 1907.] The best of these men in all countries are partisans unable to free themselves from professional prejudices and usually wedded to the idea that nothing can be done to cure the human being of his propensity to fight. . . .

Source: "The Disarmament Conference and Its Possibilities," *Nation* 113 (July 28, 1921): 86.

... [T]here are many practical things that can be done.... [A]s for battleships the rapidly enlarging doubt as to whether they have any value in view of the development of aircraft . . . ought to make it easy for the nations invited to agree upon the barring of all further battleship construction. It is this type of craft that has run up the costs of navies so enormously, the latest types costing between 40 and 50 millions of dollars apiece; moreover, those that are building will be years behind the times in their technical construction the day they are launched.

The danger will be, of course, that the various nations will endeavor to manipulate affairs so that they may be left each of them in the strongest naval position. Hence the only way to reduce them all to absolute equality is to abolish all navies. . . .

. . . . .

... [A]ny one can conjure up obstacles; the encouraging thing is that necessity is the whip that drives. If the European nations do not disarm they can hardly escape bankruptcy. Curiously enough, and happily, too, it is, according to the Washington correspondent of the New York *Globe,* the fortunate situation of disarmed Germany which is also compelling the Allies to act; they see that Germany, freed from her crushing military taxes, will be able to get ahead in her economic reconstruction far more rapidly than the Allies. Indeed, Senator Borah has brought out the astonishing fact, which ought to be printed in large type on the front page of every American newspaper, that if we go on with our present armament burdens the people of the United States will have to disburse exactly as much for them during the next thirty years as will the Germans if they pay the 33 billions of dollars imposed by the Allies! Exactly the same burden placed upon Germany as penalty for her share in the war is, in other words, to be voluntarily assumed by the American taxpayers as their tribute to Mars. Was there ever greater folly? Every sane American ought to make it clear to the President that thoroughgoing and radical disarmament on sea and land is what this country wishes and proposes to obtain from the conference.

Formation of an Umbrella Organization: The National Council on Limitation of Armament (September 1921)

Editor's Note: The National Council on Limitation of Armament, formed in Washington, D.C., in September 1921, was a coordinating body for seventeen organizations committed to arms control. It included repre-

sentatives of the General Federation of Women's Clubs, the League of Women Voters, the International Association of Rotary Clubs, the National Catholic Welfare Council, the Federal Council of Churches, the National Education Association, and a number of peace organizations.

Through the work of its staff and its director, Frederick J. Libby, an ordained Congregational minister from Maine and a committed pacifist, the National Council on Limitation of Armament monitored the meetings of the arms limitation conference. It also maintained pressure on the delegates by keeping the public informed of their proceedings through daily forums; regular news releases; biweekly bulletins; and a series of posters, letters, articles, and speeches. With the adoption of naval arms limitation, the AUAM became defunct and was replaced by the National Council, which in October 1922 became the National Council for the Prevention of War, an influential lobbying group throughout the 1920s and 1930s. The following leaflet from the fall of 1921 is an example of the kind of instructional material for grass-roots lobbying distributed by the National Council on Limitation of Armament, a prototypical modern pressure group.

An Efficient Disarmament Campaign

1. Organize a representative local disarmament committee.
2. Help your church to turn men's minds from might to right.
3. Give prizes for disarmament essays in the local schools.
4. Buy Will Irwin's "The Next War" ($1.50) [which predicted air raids with poison gas bombs on urban centers in the next war], at your book store. Read it! Lend it!
5. Become a well-informed speaker on disarmament.
Free information at the address below.
6. Write a letter to "the Editor" in favor of disarmament.
7. Distribute literature on disarmament.
Free pamphlets and leaflets at the address below.
8. Present books to your public library for a disarmament shelf. You can get a list at the address below.
9. Devise an attractive disarmament window for your store.
10. Show a set of these 20 posters everywhere. Sold for $1.00.
11. Talk disarmament instead of hard times.

Source: National Council on Limitation of Armament, *An Efficient Disarmament Campaign,* undated [ca. Sept./Oct. 1921] leaflet in the Swarthmore College Peace Collection.

12. March with the rest in an "End War" parade.
13. Have a disarmament lecture in your lodge or club.
14. Add your letter to the pile on the President's desk.

What will you do?

THE NATIONAL COUNCIL ON LIMITATION OF ARMAMENT

An Evaluation of the Disarmament Campaign by
Belle Rankin, Washington Representative of the
American Union Against Militarism (October 1921)

Carry On

Demand for an actual reduction of armaments is increasing daily. In the inner circle fear is growing that the conference will be unable to ignore this demand. Repeatedly we are warned that not "disarmament" but limitation of armaments, "a very different thing," is what the conference was called to bring about. Or we are told that the "success of the conference may be endangered by unbridled or unguided enthusiasm of the people for attainment of the objects for which the conference has been called."! Foreign delegates might think the American representatives bound to make concessions in order to bring about results it seems.

No longer are the advocates of reduction in the army and navy to be sneered at and ignored; their power is acknowledged and they must be reckoned with. Our old friend, the Army and Navy Journal, admits the great indifference to the army on the part of both the general public and the ex-soldiers and declares "there is a positive determination on the part of strongly organized groups with an expert knowledge of how to use propaganda and how to pull political wires to do away with our armed forces if possible, and if that cannot be done to reduce them to a condition of impotency."

It flatly states that the pacifists are in the saddle. That may surprise you. Perhaps you didn't realize how much power you were exercising. We admit we were far from feeling like the powers that be, but perhaps

Source: Belle Rankin, "Carry On," report to AUAM members, AUAM Bulletin no. 37, Oct. 15, 1921, American Union Against Militarism Papers, Swarthmore College Peace Collection.

we were mistaken. The evidence of our power appears to be the fact that we have forced the reduction of the army to a pre-war basis.

The facts about the army reduction are well-known but the status of the naval building program is not. The general impression is that we are continuing our 1916 program as before. That is true, but it is going very slowly. . . . [T]he date of completion of the six battle-cruisers under construction is given as "indefinite" and the furthest advanced of these vessels is only 27.4 per cent completed. Thus you can see what results can be obtained by insisting that appropriations be kept down.

· · · · ·

But the big army and navy advocates are not vanquished. There is a powerful, well-organized propaganda to discount the conference. We are constantly being told of new guns, new gases, perfected plans for a huge army organization, continuance of fortifications in the Pacific, etcetera. There are strong indications that it is going to center on the lat[t]er point. Every effort will be made to frighten the people into demanding a strengthening rather than a lessening of our fortifications in the Pacific and the preparations which must follow such a program would be sufficient to satisfy the most ardent militarist.

· · · · ·

DOCUMENT 58

Secretary of State Charles Evans Hughes Shocks Delegates
at the Washington Disarmament Conference (1921)

Editor's Note: As secretary of state from 1921 to 1925, Charles Evans Hughes, 1862–1948 (former New York governor and Republican presidential candidate in 1916), sought with great political acumen to lead the United States into an independent internationalism and a nonmilitary-oriented foreign policy acceptable to prevailing American opinion in the 1920s. Viewing arms competition within a larger context of conflicting national interests, Hughes saw that continued Japanese expansion endangered the U.S. position in the Far East, especially the "Open Door" in China. The continuing friction between the expanding interests of the United States and Japan in East Asia also raised the ultimate possibility of war between the two countries. This was emphasized by navalists on both sides who sought to expand their fleets and fortify additional island bases.

Given prevailing American sentiment for arms reduction and an unwillingness to threaten military action, let alone go to war with Japan, Hughes sought to modify Japanese expansion through diplomacy. His plan was to weaken Tokyo's position by ending the Anglo-Japanese Defensive Alliance and replacing it with a multilateral agreement on the status quo in the Pacific and the Far East and a restriction on the naval arms race.

The Washington conference was arguably Hughes's finest hour, for he seized the opportunity as presiding chairperson to open the session on November 12, 1921, with an uncharacteristically bold and effective speech, reprinted below. Instead of generalities, Hughes offered specifics; he listed by name the ships the United States, Britain, and Japan should scrap. It was a masterful coup in which Hughes became the dominant figure of the conference and effectively disarmed his critics from the outset. Although Hughes's program underwent considerable revision before its final acceptance, he had made a stunning debut and had established a favorable climate of opinion that would help moderate some of the less popular results of the meeting.

Opening Address to the Conference on the Limitation of Armament

. . . . .

. . . The world looks to this conference to relieve humanity of the crushing burden created by competition in armament, and it is the view of the American government that we should meet that expectation without any unnecessary delay. (*Applause.*) It is therefore proposed that the Conference should proceed at once to consider the question of the limitation of armament.

. . . . .

But if we are warned by the inadequacy of earlier endeavors for limitation of armament, we cannot fail to recognize the extraordinary

Source: Charles Evans Hughes, Address of November 12, 1921. In U.S. Department of State, *Conference on the Limitation of Armament, Washington, November 12, 1921–February 6, 1922* (Washington, D.C.: GPO, 1922), 50–62.

opportunity now presented. We not only have the lessons of the past to guide us, not only do we have the reaction from the disillusioning experiences of war, but we must meet the challenge of imperative economic demands. What was convenient or highly desirable before is now a matter of vital necessity. If there is to be economic rehabilitation, if the longings for reasonable progress are not to be denied, if we are to be spared the uprisings of peoples made desperate in the desire to shake off burdens no longer endurable, competition in armament must stop. (*Great Applause.*) The present opportunity not only derives its advantage from a general appreciation of this fact, but the power to deal with the exigency now rests with a small group of nations, represented here, who have every reason to desire peace and to promote amity. . . . We can no longer content ourselves with investigations, with statistics, with reports, with the circumlocution of inquiry. The essential facts are sufficiently known. The time has come, and this Conference has been called, not for general resolutions or mutual advice, but for action. (*Applause.*)

. . . . .

The question, in relation to armament, which may be regarded as of primary importance at this time, and with which we can deal most promptly and effectively, is the limitation of naval armament. . . .

The first is that the core of the difficulty is to be found in the competition in naval programs, and that, in order appropriately to limit naval armament, competition in its production must be abandoned. Competition will not be remedied by resolves with respect to the method of its continuance. One program inevitably leads to another, and if competition continues, its regulation is impracticable. There is only one adequate way out and that is to end it now. (*Applause*).

. . . . .

It would also seem to be a vital part of a plan for the limitation of naval armament that there should be a naval holiday. It is proposed that for a period of not less than ten years there should be no further construction of capital ships. (*Applause.*)

I am happy to say that I am at liberty to go beyond these general propositions and, on behalf of the American delegation acting under the instructions of the President of the United States, to submit to you a concrete proposition for an agreement for the limitation of naval armament. (*Applause.*)

. . . . .

The principal features of the proposed agreement are as follows:

. . . . .

The United States is now completing its program of 1916 calling for 10 new battleships and 6 battle cruisers. . . . On these 15 capital ships now being built over $330,000,000 have been spent. Still, the United States is willing in the interest of an immediate limitation of naval armament to scrap all these ships. [Hughes listed the ships to be scrapped or not built.]

. . . . .

Thus the number of capital ships [old and new] to be scrapped by the United States, if this plan is accepted, is 30, with an aggregate tonnage (including that of ships in construction, if completed) of 845,740 tons.

The plan contemplates that Great Britain and Japan shall take action which is fairly commensurate with this action on the part of the United States.

It is proposed that Great Britain—[Hughes listed the British ships to be scrapped or not built.]

The total tonnage of ships thus to be scrapped by Great Britain (including the tonnage of the 4 *Hoods,* if completed) would be 583,375 tons.

It is proposed that Japan—[Hughes listed the Japanese ships to be scrapped or not built.]

The total reduction of tonnage on vessels existing, laid down, or for which material has been assembled (taking the tonnage of the new ships when completed), would be 448,928 tons.

. . . . .

Thus, under this plan there would be immediately destroyed, of the navies of the three Powers, 66 capital fighting ships, built and building, with a total tonnage of 1,878,043.

. . . . .

With respect to replacement, the United States proposes—

That it be agreed that the first replacement tonnage shall not be laid down until 10 years from the date of the agreement. . . .

. . . . .

With the acceptance of this plan the burden of meeting the demands of competition in naval armament will be lifted. Enormous sums will be released to aid the progress of civilization. At the same time the proper demands of national defense will be adequately met and the nations will have ample opportunity during the naval holiday of 10 years to consider their future course. Preparation for offensive naval war will stop now. (*Great Applause.*)

DOCUMENT 59

The Five-Power Naval Arms Limitation Treaty at the
Washington Disarmament Conference (1922)

Editor's Note: The Washington conference produced nine treaties, most of which dealt with territorial rivalries of the great powers in the western Pacific and in East Asia. The treaties concerning nonnaval rivalries, provided for mutual respect for each power's rights and territories in the area, and replaced the Anglo-Japanese Defensive Alliance with a four-power treaty in which the United States, Britain, France, and Japan simply agreed to consult in the event of any "aggressive action" in the Pacific.

The main naval armament treaty—the Five-Power Naval Arms Limitation Treaty of 1922, signed by the United States, Britain, Japan, France, and Italy—provided that no additional capital ships (battleships, battle cruisers, or aircraft carriers) would be built during the next ten years. It also consigned specific ships to be scrapped (these amounted to 845,000 tons for the United States, 583,000 tons for Britain, and 480,000 tons for Japan). Finally, it established a ratio of total tonnage of capital ships in surviving fleets of 5-5-3 for the United States, Britain, and Japan respectively and 1.7 and 1.7 for France and Italy.

To compensate the Japanese for their inferior ratio, the treaty prohibited additional fortification of the great powers' naval bases in the Pacific. Although, in essence, the signatories recognized the existing supremacy of the Japanese Navy in the Northwestern Pacific, the Washington treaties also obtained abolition of the Anglo-Japanese Defense Alliance, secured temporary protection of the vulnerable Philippines, still a U.S. territory, and checked a costly naval arms race.

The Five-Power Naval Arms Limitation Treaty, reprinted below, was signed on February 6, 1922. Senator Henry Cabot Lodge, who had been one of the delegates to the conference, easily obtained Senate ratification by a vote of 74 to 1 on March 29, 1922.

The Washington Disarmament Conference was widely hailed as averting a costly naval arms race, indefinitely postponing any war between the United States and Japan, shifting Britain to the American side in any such war, and providing the framework for a workable balance of power arrangement in the Far East. Later criticism in the 1930s that saw it as too favorable to Japan was not entirely valid. Hughes and Harding recognized at the time that success of the conference would ultimately rest on the "will to peace" of the signatory nations. In the 1930s, for various reasons, the mutual trust and confidence underlying and fostered by the Washington agreements were undermined by other events.

Treaty Between the United States of America, the British Empire, France, Italy, and Japan Limiting Naval Armament.

Signed at Washington February 6, 1922; Ratification Advised by Senate March 29, 1922.

The United States of America, the British Empire, France, Italy and Japan;

Desiring to contribute to the maintenance of the general peace, and to reduce the burdens of competition in armament:

Have resolved with a view to accomplishing these purposes, to conclude a treaty to limit their respective naval armament.... [They] have agreed as follows:

CHAPTER I. *General Provisions Relating to the Limitation of Naval Armament.*

ARTICLE I.

The Contracting Powers agree to limit their respective naval armament as provided in the present Treaty.

Source: U.S. Congress, Senate, *Treaties, Conventions, International Acts, Protocols, and Agreements,* 1910–1923. 67th Cong., 4th sess., 1923, S. Doc. 348, 3: 3100–107.

ARTICLE II.

The Contracting Powers may retain respectively the capital ships which are specified in Chapter II, Part 1. On the coming into force of the present Treaty, but subject to the following provisions of this Article, all other capital ships, built or building, of the United States, the British Empire and Japan shall be disposed of as prescribed in Chapter II, Part 2.

. . . . .

ARTICLE IV.

The total capital ship replacement tonnage of each of the Contracting Powers shall not exceed in standard displacement, for the United States 525,000 tons; for the British Empire 525,000 tons; for France 175,000 tons; for Italy 175,000 tons; for Japan 315,000 tons.

. . . . .

ARTICLE XIX.

The United States, the British Empire and Japan agree that the status quo at the time of the signing of the present Treaty, with regard to fortifications and naval bases, shall be maintained in their respective territories and possessions specified hereunder:

(1) The insular possessions which the United States now holds or may hereafter acquire in the Pacific Ocean [i.e., particularly the Philippines], except . . . the Hawaiian Islands.

(2) Hongkong and the insular possessions which the British Empire now holds or may hereafter acquire in the Pacific Ocean . . . except (a) those adjacent to the coast of Canada, (b) the Commonwealth of Australia and its Territories, and (c), New Zealand;

(3) The following insular territories and possessions of Japan in the Pacific Ocean, to wit: the Kurile Islands, the Bonin Islands, Amami-Oshima, the Loochoo Islands [the Ryukyu archipelago, which includes Okinawa], Formosa and the Pescadores, and any insular territories or possessions in the Pacific Ocean which Japan may hereafter acquire [such as the former German colonies in the Mariana and Caroline Islands which the Japanese had occupied in 1914 and formally obtained as League mandates in 1922].

The maintenance of the status quo under the foregoing provisions implies that no new fortifications or naval bases shall be established in the territories and possessions specified that no measures shall be taken to increase the existing naval facilities . . . and the coast defenses of the territories and possessions above specified.

CHAPTER II

. . . . .

PART 2. RULES FOR SCRAPPING VESSELS OF WAR.

The following rules shall be observed for the scrapping of vessels of war which are to be disposed of in accordance with Articles II and III.

I. A vessel to be scrapped must be placed in such condition that it cannot be put to combatant use.

II. This result must be finally effected in any one of the following ways:

(a) Permanent sinking of the vessels;

(b) Breaking the vessel up. This shall always involve the destruction or removal of all machinery, boilers and armour, and all deck, side and bottom plating;

(c) Converting the vessel to target use exclusively.

. . . . .

PART 3. REPLACEMENT

Section II.—*Replacement and scrapping of capital ships*

UNITED STATES.

Ships scrapped (age [in years] in parentheses).

Maine (20), Missouri (20), Virginia (17), Nebraska (17), Georgia (17), New Jersey (17), Rhode Island (17), Connecticut (170), Louisiana (17), Vermont (16), Kansas (16), Minnesota (17), New Hampshire (15), South Carolina (13), Michigan (13), Washington (0), South Dakota (0), Indiana (0), Montana (0), North Carolina (0), Iowa (0), Massachusetts (0), Lexington (0), Constitution (0), Constellation (0), Saratoga (0), Ranger (0), United States (0). . . .

BRITISH EMPIRE.

Ships scrapped (age [in years] in parentheses).

Commonwealth (15), Agamemnon (13), Dreadnought (15), Bellerophon (12), St. Vincent (11), Inflexible (13), Superb (12), Neptune

(10), Hercules (10), Indomitable (13), Temeraire (12), New Zealand (8), Lion (9), Princess Royal (9), Conquerer (9), Monarch (9), Orion (9), Australia (8), Agincourt (7), Erin (7), 4 building or projected. . . .

. . . . .

JAPAN.
Ships scrapped (age [in years] in parentheses).

Hizen (20), Mikasa (20), Kashima (16), Katori (16), Satsuma (12), Aki (11), Settsu (10), Ikoma (14), Ibuki (12), Kurama (11), Amagi (0), Akagi (0), Kaga (0), Tosa (0), Takao (0), Atago (0). Projected program 8 ships not laid down. . . .

. . . . .

[France and Italy, with small navies and no new capital ships under construction were not required to begin scrapping ships until 1930 and 1931 respectively.]

ARTICLE XXIII.

The present Treaty shall remain in force until December 31st, 1936, and in case none of the Contracting Powers shall have given notice two years before that date of its intention to terminate the Treaty, it shall continue in force until the expiration of two years from the date on which notice of termination shall be given by one of the Contracting Powers, whereupon the Treaty shall terminate as regards all the Contracting Powers.

Done at the City of Washington the sixth day of February, One Thousand Nine Hundred and Twenty-Two.

[Signed] Charles Evans Hughes, Henry Cabot Lodge, Oscar W. Underwood, Elihu Root; Arthur James Balfour . . . ; Jusserand; Carlo Schanzer . . . Luigi Albertini; T. Kato, K. Shidehara, M. Hanihara

Chronology
Selected Bibliography
Permission Acknowledgments
Index

Chronology

1898   Anglo-German naval race begins with the legislation and appropriations that authorized a major German fleet.

U.S. war with Spain.

1899   First Hague Peace Conference.

1901   William McKinley assassinated. Vice President Theodore Roosevelt succeeds him.

1904–1905   Russo-Japanese War.

1906   Roosevelt receives Nobel Peace Prize for his successful mediation of the Russo-Japanese War.

1907   Second Hague Peace Conference.

1908   William Howard Taft elected president.

1910   Mexican Revolution begins.

1911   Taft's arbitration treaties with Great Britain and France.

1912   Woodrow Wilson elected president.

1913	Secretary of State William Jennings Bryan's "Cooling Off" treaties.
1914	
August	Outbreak of World War I (1914–1918). Wilson declares U.S. neutrality. Britain declares naval surface blockade of Germany.
1915	
January	Formation of the Woman's Peace party.
February	Germany begins submarine warfare on British and French shipping. Wilson holds Germany to "strict accountability" for loss of American lives or ships.
April–May	International Congress of Women meets at The Hague.
May	Sinking of the British liner *Lusitania*. Beginning of the "preparedness" movement.
June	Formation of Association for a League to Enforce Peace.
November	Wilson recommends "reasonable" expansion and modernization of the army and navy. Formation of the American Union Against Militarism.
December	Henry Ford's "peace ship" sails to Scandinavia.
1916	
February–March	Gore-McLemore resolution defeated.
March	Border raid into New Mexico by Francisco ("Pancho") Villa's irregulars, resulting in seventeen deaths. Wilson calls out the National Guard and sends a regular army Punitive Expedition into Mexico in pursuit.

May	Wilson addresses Association for League to Enforce Peace, his first public endorsement of a postwar international organization.
June	National Defense Act, expanding size of army and National Guard, creating ROTC.
	Clash between U.S. and Mexican army troops at Carrizal, Mexico; thirty-nine killed. War scare.
	American Neutral Conference Committee formed.
August	Congress adopts major U.S. naval expansion.
November	Wilson reelected president.
December	Germany makes peace overtures. Wilson's sends peace note.

1917

January	Allies reject German overtures and Wilson's note.
	Wilson makes "Peace Without Victory" speech.
	Berlin announces unrestricted submarine warfare.
February	United States breaks off diplomatic relations with Germany.
	Formation of Emergency Peace Federation.
March	Zimmermann telegram proposing Mexican alliance with Germany released to American press.
	Russian Revolution; tsar abdicates, replaced by a provisional government headed first by Prince Lvov, later by Alexander Kerensky as premier. Wilson arms American merchant ships.
	Germans sink three American merchant ships.
	Wilson decides for war.
April	Wilson's war message to Congress, April 2.
	Congress declares war, April 6.
June	First units of American Expeditionary Force under General John J. Pershing arrive in France

August   Peace Proposal of Pope Benedict XV.

November   Bolshevik seizure of power, led by Lenin;
                subsequent publication of secret treaties
                and war aims of the European Allies. Lenin
                concludes armistice with the Central Powers.

1918

January   Wilson makes "Fourteen Points" speech.

March   USSR and Germany sign peace treaty of
                Brest-Litovsk. USSR leaves war.

                Reinforced German army begins offensive
                in West.

May   Beginning of arrival of major U.S.
                reinforcements on the Western Front.

July   Defeat of German offensive; beginning of
                major Allied counteroffensive in the West.

August   U.S. detachments join British, French,
                Japanese forces in USSR; withdrawn in
                1919 and 1920.

September   German army commanders seek an armistice.

October   Formation of League of Free Nations
                Association.

November   Revolution in Germany. Kaiser abdicates.

                New German Republic signs armistice,
                November 11.

                U.S. elections give GOP control of Congress.

1919

January   Paris Peace Conference begins.

March   Senator Henry Cabot Lodge's "Round Robin"
                showing more than one-third of Senate
                opposed to Treaty of Versailles and League
                of Nations unless amended.

May	Treaty of Versailles presented to Germans.
	Congress of the Women's International League for Peace and Freedom meets in Zurich.
June	Germans sign Treaty of Versailles.
July	U.S. Senate begins consideration of treaty.
September	Wilson collapses on speaking tour for the treaty.
October	Wilson suffers paralytic stroke, October 2.
November	Senate defeats Treaty of Versailles.

1920

January	Largest of the mass arrests of radicals by Attorney General A. Mitchell Palmer in "Palmer Raids" of the "Red Scare" of 1919–1920.
March	Senate again defeats Treaty of Versailles.
May	National Defense Act, providing for a relatively small army and no universal military training.
August	Nineteenth Amendment (woman suffrage) ratified.
November	Warren G. Harding elected president.
December	Senator William E. Borah's resolution for an international naval disarmament conference.

1921

January	American Civil Liberties Union formed in wake of the extensive "Red Scare."
March	Warren G. Harding inaugurated.
August	Harding invites naval powers to a conference on naval arms reduction and stability in East Asia and the western Pacific.
September	Formation of the National Council on Limitation of Armament.
November	Washington Conference on Limitation of Naval Armament (the Washington Disarmament Conference) opens.

1922

February   Washington conference ends with the signing of nine treaties involving naval arms reduction and stabilization in the Far East.

March   All nine treaties ratified by U.S. Senate.

Selected Bibliography

Addams, Jane. "Feed the World and Save the League." *New Republic* 24 (Nov. 24, 1920): 325–27.

———. *The Long Road of Women's Memory.* New York: Macmillan, 1916.

———. "Patriotism and Pacifists in War Time." [*Chicago*] *City Club Bulletin* 10, no. 9 (June 16, 1917).

———. *Peace and Bread in Time of War.* New York: Macmillan, 1922.

Addresses Given at the Organization Conference of the Woman's Peace Party, Washington, D.C., January 10, 1915. Chicago: Woman's Peace Party Headquarters, [1915]. Pamphlet located in the Woman's Peace Party Papers, Swarthmore College Peace Collection.

Alonso, Harriet Hyman. "Janette Rankin and the Women's Peace Union." *Montana: The Magazine of Western History* 39 (Spring 1989): 34–49.

———. "Suffragist for Peace During the Interwar Years, 1919–1941." *Peace and Change: A Journal of Peace Research* 14 (July 1989): 243–62.

———. *The Women's Peace Union and the Outlawry of War, 1921–1942.* Knoxville: Univ. of Tennessee Press, 1990.

Ambrosius, Lloyd E. *Woodrow Wilson and the American Diplomatic Tradition: The Treaty Fight in Perspective.* Cambridge: Cambridge Univ. Press, 1987.

"American Cavalry Ambushed by Carranza Troops." *New York Times,* June 22, 1916, 1.

Baker, Paula. "The Domestication of American Politics." *American Historical Review* 89 (June 1984): 620–49.

Bartlett, Ruhl. *The League to Enforce Peace.* Chapel Hill: Univ. of North Carolina Press, 1944.

Beale, Howard K. *Theodore Roosevelt and the Rise of America to World Power.* Baltimore: Johns Hopkins Univ. Press, 1956.

Becker, Jean Jacques. *The Great War and the French People.* New York: St. Martin's, 1986.

Beisner, Robert. *Twelve Against Empire: The Anti-Imperialists, 1898–1902.* New York: McGraw Hill, 1968.

Birnbaum, Karl. *Peace Moves and U-Boat Warfare*. Hamden, Conn.: Archon Books, 1970.

Blackbourn, David. "The Politics of Demagogy in Imperial Germany." *Past and Present*, no. 113 (Nov. 1985): 152–84.

Bolt, Ernest. *Ballots Before Bullets: The War Referendum Approach to Peace in America, 1914–1941*. Charlottesville: Univ. of Virginia Press, 1977.

Boulding, Kenneth E. "A Proposal for a Research Program in the History of Peace." *Peace and Change: A Journal of Peace Research* 14, no. 4 (Oct. 1989): 461–69.

Bourne, Randolph S. *War and the Intellectuals: Collected Essays, 1915–1919*. Edited by Carl Resek. New York: Harper and Row, 1964.

Brock, Peter. *Pacifism in the United States: From the Colonial Era to the First World War*. Princeton: Princeton Univ. Press, 1968.

Brock-Utne, Birget. *Educating for Peace: The Feminist Perspective*. Oxford: Pergamon, 1985.

Buckley, Thomas H. *The United States and the Washington Conference, 1921–1922*. Knoxville: Univ. of Tennessee Press, 1970.

Buenker, John D., and Edward R. Kantowicz, eds. *Historical Dictionary of the Progressive Era, 1890–1920*. New York: Greenwood, 1988.

Calhoun, Frederick S. *Power and Principle: Armed Intervention in Wilsonian Foreign Policy*. Kent, Ohio: Kent State Univ. Press, 1986.

Campbell, John P. "Taft, Roosevelt, and the Arbitration Treaties of 1911." *Journal of American History* 53 (1966): 279–98.

Cantor, Milton. "The Radical Confrontation with Foreign Policy: War and Revolution, 1914–1920." In *Dissent: Explorations in the History of American Radicalism*, edited by Alfred F. Young, 215–49. DeKalb: Northern Illinois Univ. Press, 1968.

Carnegie, Andrew. *A League of Peace: A Rectoral Address Delivered to the Students in the University of St. Andrew, October 17, 1905*. New York: New York Peace Society, 1911.

Carroll, Bernice A. "Feminism and Pacifism: Historical and Theoretical Connections." In *Women and Peace: Theoretical, Historical and Practical Perspectives*, edited by Ruth Roach Pierson, 2–28. London: Croom Helm, 1987.

Carsten, Francis Ludwig. *War Against War: British and German Radical Movements in the First World War*. London: Batesford Academic and Educational Publications, 1982.

Cashdan, Laurie. "Anti-War Feminism: New Directions, New Dualities—A Marxist-Humanist Perspective." *Women's Studies International Forum* 12, no. 1 (1989): 81–86.

Ceadel, M. *Pacifism in Britain, 1914–1945*. Oxford: Oxford Univ. Press, 1980.

Challener, Richard D. *Admirals, Generals, and American Foreign Policy, 1898–1914*. Princeton: Princeton Univ. Press, 1973.

Chambers, John Whiteclay II. *To Raise an Army: The Draft Comes to Modern America*. New York: Free Press, 1987.

———. *The Tyranny of Change: America in the Progressive Era, 1890–1920,* 2d edition. New York: St. Martin's, 1992.

———, ed. *The Eagle and the Dove: The American Peace Movement and U.S. Foreign Policy, 1900–1922.* 1st ed. New York: Garland, 1976.

———, ed. *Three Generals Against War.* New York: Garland, 1973.

Chatfield, Charles. *The American Peace Movement: Ideals and Activism.* New York: Twayne, 1992.

———. *For Peace and Justice: Pacifism in America, 1914–1941.* Knoxville: Univ. of Tennessee Press, 1971.

———. "World War I and the Liberal Pacifist in the United States." *American Historical Review* 75 (Dec. 1970): 1920–37.

———, ed. *Peace Movements in America.* New York: Schocken Books, 1973.

———, and Peter van den Dungen, eds. *Peace Movements and Political Cultures.* Knoxville: Univ. of Tennessee Press, 1988.

Chenery, William L. "Conscription in Peace Times." *Survey* 43 (Feb. 14, 1920): 575–76.

Chickering, Roger. *Imperial Germany and a World Without War: The Peace Movement and German Society, 1892–1914.* Princeton: Princteon Univ. Press, 1975.

———. "War, Peace, and Social Mobilization in Imperial Germany: Patriotic Societies, the Peace Movement, and Socialist Labor." In *Peace Movements and Political Cultures,* edited by Charles Chatfield and Peter van der Dungen, 3–22. Knoxville: Univ. of Tennessee Press, 1988.

———. *We Men Who Feel Most German: A Cultural Study of the Pan-German League, 1886–1914.* London: Allen & Unwin, 1984.

Clements, Kendrick A. *William Jennings Bryan, Missionary Isolationist.* Knoxville: Univ. of Tennessee Press, 1982.

———. *Woodrow Wilson: World Statesman.* Boston: Twayne, 1987.

Clifford, J. Garry. *The Citizen Soldiers: The Plattsburg Training Camp Movement, 1913–1920.* Lexington: Univ. Press of Kentucky, 1972.

Cohn, Carol. "Sex and Death in the Rational World of Defense Intellectuals." *Signs* 12, no. 4 (Summer 1987): 687–718.

Coletta, Paolo E. *William Jennings Bryan: Progressive Politician and Moral Statesman, 1909–1915.* Lincoln: Univ. of Nebraska Press, 1969.

Cook, Blanche Wiesen. "The Woman's Peace Party: Collaboration and Non-Cooperation." *Peace and Change: A Journal of Peace Research* 1 (Mar. 1972): 36–42.

———. "Woodrow Wilson and the Anti-Militarists, 1914–1917." Diss., Johns Hopkins Univ., 1970.

———, ed. *Crystal Eastman on Women and Revolution.* New York: Oxford Univ. Press, 1978.

———, Sandi E. Cooper, and Charles Chatfield, eds. *The Garland Library of War and Peace.* 360 vols. New York: Garland, 1970–1980.

Cooper, John Milton, Jr. *Pivotal Decades: The United States, 1900–1920.* New York: Norton, 1990.

————. *The Warrior and the Priest: Woodrow Wilson and Theodore Roosevelt.* Cambridge, Mass.: Harvard Univ. Press, 1983.

Cortright, David. "Assessing Peace Movement Effectiveness in the 1980s. *Peace and Change: A Journal of Peace Research* 16, no. 2 (Apr. 1991): 131–61.

Cott, Nancy F. *The Grounding of Modern Feminism.* New Haven: Yale Univ. Press, 1987.

Curti, Merle E. *Peace and War: The American Struggle, 1636–1936.* New York: Norton, 1936.

Davis, Calvin D. *The United States and the First Hague Peace Conference of 1899.* Ithaca: Cornell Univ. Press, 1962.

————. *The United States and the Second Hague Peace Conference: American Diplomacy and International Organization, 1899–1914.* Durham, N.C.: Duke Univ. Press, 1976.

DeBenedetti, Charles (Charles Chatfield, assisting author). *An American Ordeal: The Antiwar Movement of the Vietnam Era.* Syracuse: Syracuse Univ. Press, 1990.

————. *Origins of the Modern American Peace Movement, 1915–1929.* Millwood, N.Y. : KTO Press, 1978.

————. "Peace History in the American Manner." *History Teacher* 18, no. 1 (Nov. 1984): 75–110.

————. *The Peace Reform in American History.* Bloomington: Indiana Univ. Press, 1980.

————, ed. *Peace Heroes in Twentieth-Century America.* Bloomington: Indiana Univ. Press, 1986.

Degen, Marie L. *The History of the Women's Peace Party.* Baltimore: Johns Hopkins Univ. Press, 1939.

Devlin, Patrick. *Too Proud to Fight: Woodrow Wilson's Neutrality.* New York: Oxford Univ. Press, 1974.

Dingman, Roger. *Power in the Pacific: The Origins of Naval Arms Limitation, 1914–1922.* Chicago: Univ. of Chicago Press, 1976.

"Disarmament Conference and Its Possibilities, The." *Nation* 113 (July 28, 1921): 86.

Early, Frances H. "Feminism, Peace, and Civil Liberties: Women's Role in the Origins of the World War I Civil Liberties Movement." *Women's Studies* 18 (1990): 95–115.

Ekirch, Arthur A., Jr. *The Civilian and the Military.* New York: Oxford Univ. Press, 1956.

Elshtain, Jean Bethke. "On Beautiful Souls, Just Warriors, and Feminist Consciousness.' In *Women and Men's Wars,* edited by Judith Stiehm, 317–28. Oxford: Pergamon, 1983.

————. *Women and War.* New York: Basic Books, 1987.

Enloe, Cynthia. *Does Khaki Become You? The Militarization of Women's Lives.* Boston. South End Press, 1983.

————. "Feminist Thinking About War, Militarism and Peace." In *Analyzing Gender: A Handbook of Social Science Research,* edited by Beth B. Hess and Myra Marx Ferree, 526–47. Newbury Park, Calif.: Sage Publications, 1987.

Everts, Philip P. "Where the Peace Movement Goes When It Disappears." *Bulletin of the Atomic Scientists* (Nov. 1989): 26–30.

———, and G. Walraven. *Vredesbeweging.* Utrecht, 1984.

Falk, Candace. *Love, Anarchy, and Emma Goldman.* New York: Holt, 1984.

Farrell, John C. *Beloved Lady: A History of Jane Addams' Ideas on Reform and Peace.* Baltimore: Johns Hopkins Univ. Press, 1967.

Ferrell, Robert H. *Woodrow Wilson and World War I, 1917–1921.* New York: Harper and Row, 1985.

"Forgiving War-Offenders." *Literary Digest* 67 (Oct. 2, 1920): 18–19.

Gardner, Lloyd C. *A Covenant with Power: America and World Order from Wilson to Reagan.* New York: Oxford Univ. Press, 1985.

———. *Safe for Democracy: The Anglo-American Response to Revolution, 1913–1923.* New York: Oxford Univ. Press, 1984.

———. *Wilson and Revolutions: 1913–1921.* Philadelphia: Temple Univ. Press, 1976.

Garrison, Dee. *Mary Heaton Vorse: The Life of an American Insurgent.* Philadelphia: Temple Univ. Press, 1989.

Gelfand, Lawrence E. "Through the Prism of Seven Decades: The World War, 1914–1918." *Diplomatic History* 14, no. 1 (Winter 1990): 115–21.

Gilderhus, Mark T. *Diplomacy and Revolution: U.S. –Mexican Relations under Wilson and Carranza.* Tucson: Univ. of Arizona Press, 1977.

Gillis, John R., ed. *The Militarization of the Western World.* New Brunswick, N.J. : Rutgers Univ. Press, 1989.

Griffith, William, ed. *Theodore Roosevelt: His Life, Meaning, and Messages.* 3 vols. New York: Current Literature, 1919.

Hallinan, Charles T. "The Mexican Crisis: Some Inside Information." AUAM Bulletin no. 53, July 15, 1916. American Union Against Militarism Papers, Swarthmore College Peace Collection.

Harris, Adrienne, and Ynestra King, eds. *Rocking the Ship of State: Toward a Feminist Peace Politics.* Boulder: Westview, 1989.

Herman, Sondra R. *Eleven Against War: Studies in American Internationalist Thought, 1898–1921.* Stanford: Hoover Institution, 1969.

Holmes, John Haynes. "War and the Social Movement." *Survey* 32 (Sept. 26, 1914): 629–30.

Holsti, Ole R. "Models of International Relations and Foreign Policy." *Diplomatic History* 13, no. 1 (Winter 1989): 15–43.

Holt, Hamilton. "A League of Peace." *Independent* 70 (May 11, 1911): 995–99.

———. "The Way to Disarm: A Practical Proposal." *Independent* 79 (Sept. 28, 1914): 427–29.

Howlett, Charles F. *The American Peace Movement: References and Resources.* Boston: G. K. Hall, 1991.

———, and Glen Zeitzer. *The American Peace Movement: History and Historiography.* AHA Pamphlet no. 261. Washington, D.C.: American Historical Association, 1985.

Hughes, Charles Evans. Address of November 12, 1921. In U. S., Department of State, *Conference on the Limitation of Armament, Washington, November 12, 1921–February 6, 1922*. Washington, D.C. : GPO, 1922.

Individual and the State, The Problem as Presented by the Sentencing of Roger N. Baldwin, The. Pamphlet. New York: National Civil Liberties Bureau, 1918.

Iriye, Akira. "Culture and Power: International Relations as Intercultural Relations." *Diplomatic History* 3 (1979): 115–28.

———. "The Internationalization of History." *American Historical Review* 94, no. 1 (Feb. 1989): 1–10.

———. Jarausch, Konrad. "Armageddon Revisited: Peace Research Perspectives on World War One." *Peace and Change: A Journal of Peace Research* 7, nos. 1–2 (Winter 1981): 109–18.

Jacobs, Aletta H., to Jane Addams, Sept. 15, 1915. Jane Addams Papers, Swarthmore College Peace Collection.

James, William. *The Moral Equivalent of War.* New York: American Association for International Conciliation, 1910. Leaflet no. 27.

Johnson, Donald. *Challenge to American Freedoms: World War I and the Rise of the American Civil Liberties Union.* Lexington: Univ. of Kentucky Press, 1963.

"Joint Debate on the Covenant of Paris." In World Peace Foundation, *League of Nations.* 2 vols. Boston: World Peace Foundaton, 1919.

Joll, James. *1914: The Unspoken Assumptions.* London: Weidenfeld and Nicolson, 1968.

Josephson, Harold. *James T. Shotwell and the Rise of Internationalism in America.* Rutherford, N.J.: Fairleigh Dickinson Univ. Press, 1975.

———, ed. *Biographical Dictionary of Modern Peace Leaders.* Westport, Conn.: Greenwood, 1985.

Katz, Frederich. *The Secret War in Mexico: Europe, the United States, and the Mexican Revolution.* Chicago: Univ. of Chicago Press, 1981.

Kaufman, Burton I. *Efficiency and Expansion: Foreign Trade Organization in the Wilson Administration, 1913–1921.* Westport, Conn.: Greenwood, 1974.

Kennedy, David M. *Over Here: The First World War and American Society.* New York: Oxford Univ. Press, 1980.

Knock, Thomas J. *To End All Wars: Woodrow Wilson and the Creation of the League of Nations.* New York: Oxford Univ. Press, 1992.

Kocka, Jurgen. *Facing Total War: German Society, 1914–18.* Cambridge, Mass.: Harvard Univ. Press, 1985.

Kohn, Stephen M. *Jailed for Peace: The History of Draft Law Violators, 1658–1985.* New York: Praeger, 1986.

Kraft, Barbara S. *The Peace Ship: Henry Ford's Pacifist Adventure in the First World War.* New York: Macmillan, 1978.

Kuehl, Warren F. *Hamilton Holt: Journalist, Internationalist, Educator.* Gainesville: Univ. of Florida Press, 1960.

———. *Seeking World Order: The United States and International Organization to 1920.* Nashville: Vanderbilt Univ. Press, 1969.

————, ed. *Biographical Dicitionary of Internationalists*. Westport, Conn.: Greenwood, 1983.

Landy, Joanne. "Can Summits Replace the Peace Movement?" *Tikkun* 3, no. 6 (Nov./Dec. 1988): 45–49, 105–9.

Lane, Ann J. *To Herland and Beyond: The Life and Work of Charlotte Perkins Gilman*. New York: Pantheon, 1990.

Lawrence, Emmeline Pethick. "Motherhood and War." *Harper's Weekly* 59 (Dec. 5, 1914): 542.

Leffler, Melvyn P. *The Elusive Quest: America's Pursuit of European Stability and French Security, 1919–1933*. Chapel Hill: Univ. of North Carolina Press, 1979.

Leonardo, Micaela di. "Morals, Mothers, Militarism: Antimilitarism and Feminist Theory." *Feminist Studies* 11, no. 3 (Fall 1985): 599–618.

Leuchtenburg, William E. "Progressivism and Imperialism: The Progressive Movement and American Foreign Policy, 1898–1916." *Mississippi Valley Historical Review (now Journal of American History)* 34 (Dec. 1952): 483–504.

Levin, N. Gordon, Jr. *Woodrow Wilson and World Politics: America's Response to War and Revolution*. New York: Oxford Univ. Press, 1968.

Link, Arthur S. *Wilson*. 5 vols. Princeton: Princeton Univ. Press, 1947–1965.

————. *Woodrow Wilson: Revolution, War, and Peace*. Arlington Heights, Ill.: AMH, 1979.

————. *Woodrow Wilson and the Progressive Era, 1910–1917*. New York: Harper, 1963.

————, and Richard L. McCormick. *Progressivism*. Arlington Heights, Ill.: Harlan Davidson, 1983.

————, ed. *Woodrow Wilson and a Revolutionary World, 1913–1921*. Chapel Hill: Univ. of North Carolina Press, 1982.

———— et al., eds. *The Papers of Woodrow Wilson* 65 vols. to date. Princeton: Princeton Univ. Press, 1966– .

Lopez, George A., ed. "Peace Studies: Past and Future," special issue of *The Annals of the American Academy of Political and Social Science* 504 (July 1989).

Lutzker, Michael A. "Can the Peace Movement Prevent War?: The U.S.–Mexican Crisis of April 1914." In *Doves and Diplomats: Foreign Offices and Peace Movements in Europe and America in the Twentieth Century*, edited by Solomon Wank, 127–53. Westport, Conn.: Greenwood, 1978.

————. "Expanding Our Vision: New Perspectives on Peace Research." *Peace and Change: A Journal of Peace Research* 14, no. 4 (Oct. 1989): 444–60.

————. "How We Withdrew from Vietnam in 1965: The Search for an Alternative Past." Paper presented at the conference of the Society of Historians of American Foreign Relations, Williamsburg, Va., June 1989.

————. "The Pacifist as Militarist: A Critique of the American Peace Movement 1898–1912." *Societas* 5 (Spring 1975): 87–104.

————. "The Precarious Peace: China, the United States, and the Quemoy-Matsu Crisis, 1954–55, 1958." In *Arms at Rest: Peacemaking and Peacekeeping in American History*, edited by Robert L. Beisner and Joan R. Challinor, 161–85. Westport, Conn.: Greenwood, 1987.

Mahan, Captain A. T., U.S. Navy. "The Peace Conference and the Moral Aspect of War." *North American Review* 169 (Oct. 1899): 433–47.

Maier, Charles S. "Marking Time: The Historiography of International Relations." In *The Past Before Us: Contemporary Historical Writing in the United States,* edited by Michael Kammen, 355–87. Ithaca: Cornell Univ. Press, 1980.

———. *Recasting Bourgeois Europe: Stabilization in France, Germany, and Italy in the Decade after World War I.* Princeton: Princeton Univ. Press, 1975.

Malloy, William M., comp. *Treaties, Conventions, International Acts, Protocols and Agreements Between the United States of America and Other Powers, 1777–1909.* 2 vols. Washington, D.C.: GPO, 1910.

Marchand, C. Roland. *The American Peace Movement and Social Reform, 1898–1918.* Princeton: Princeton Univ. Press, 1972.

Markowitz, Gerald. "Progressivism and Imperialism: A Return to First Principles." *The Historian* 37 (Feb. 1975): 274.

Marks, Frederick W. *Velvet on Iron: The Diplomacy of Theodore Roosevelt.* Lincoln: Univ. of Nebraska Press, 1979.

Martin, Jane Roland. "Martial Virtues or Capital Vices? William James' Moral Equivalent of War Revisited." *Journal of Thought* 22, no. 3 (Fall 1987).

Martin, Laurence W. *Peace Without Victory: Woodrow Wilson and the British Liberals.* Port Washington, N.Y.: Kennikat, 1973.

May, Ernest R. *The World War and American Isolation, 1914–1917.* Cambridge, Mass.: Harvard Univ. Press, 1959.

Mayer, Arno J. *Political Origins of the New Diplomacy, 1917–1918.* New Haven: Yale Univ. Press, 1959.

———. *The Politics and Diplomacy of Peacemaking: Containment and Counterrevolution at Versailles, 1918–1919.* New York: Knopf, 1967.

Mead, Lucia Ames. "International Police." *Outlook* 74 (July 18, 1903): 705–6.

Meyer, David S. "Peace Movements and National Security Policy: A Research Agenda." *Peace and Change: A Journal of Peace Research* 16, no. 2 (Apr. 1991): 131–61.

Morison, Elting E., and John M. Blum, eds. *The Letters of Theodore Roosevelt.* 8 vols. Cambridge, Mass.: Harvard Univ. Press, 1951–1954.

Moses, John A. *The Politics of Illusion: The Fischer Controversy in German Historiography.* New York: Barnes & Noble, 1975.

Moskos, Charles C., and John Whiteclay Chambers II, eds. *The New Conscientious Secularization of Objection to Military Service.* Forthcoming, 1992.

Murphy, Paul L. *World War I and the Origins of the Civil Liberties Union in the United States.* New York: Norton, 1979.

Mussey, Henry R. Report to the membership, AUAM Bulletin no. 31, Jan. 11, 1921. American Union Against Militarism Papers, Swarthmore College Peace Collection.

National Council on the Limitation of Armament. *An Efficient Disarmament Campaign.* Undated leaflet. Swarthmore College Peace Collection.

Nearing, Scott. *The League of Nations as Seen by an Economist.* Undated leaflet. Swarthmore College Peace Collection.

"New Civil Liberties Union, A." *Survey* 43 (Jan. 31, 1920): 480.

O'Neill, William L. *Everyone Was Brave: A History of Feminism in America.* Chicago: Quadrangle, 1971.

————. *The Last Romantic: A Life of Max Eastman.* New York: Oxford Univ. Press, 1978.

"Pacifist in Charge of Our Foreign Relations, A." *Literary Digest* 46 (May 31, 1913): 1207–9.

Parrini, Carl P. *Heir to Empire: United States Economic Diplomacy, 1916–1923.* Pittsburgh: Univ. of Pittsburgh Press, 1969.

Patterson, David S. *Toward a Warless World: The Travail of the American Peace Movement, 1887–1914.* Bloomington: Indiana Univ. Press, 1976.

————. "The United States and the Origins of the World Court," *Political Science Quarterly* 91 (Summer 1976): 279–95.

————. "Woodrow Wilson and the Mediation Movement, 1914–1917," *The Historian* 33 (Aug. 1971): 535–56.

Peterson, Horace C. and Gilbert C. Fite. *Opponents of War, 1917–1918.* Madison: Univ. of Wisconsin Press, 1957.

Pierson, Ruth Roach, ed. *Women and Peace: Theoretical, Historical and Practical Perspectives.* London: Croom Helm, 1987.

Randall, Mercedes M. *Improper Bostonian: Emily Greene Balch.* New York: Twayne, 1964.

Rankin, Belle. "Carry On." Report to AUAM members, AUAM Bulletin no. 37, Oct. 15, 1921. American Union Against Militarism Papers, Swarthmore College Peace Collection.

————. "Disarmament to Date." Report to AUAM members, AUAM Bulletin no. 35, July 14, 1921. American Union Against Militarism Papers, Swarthmore College Peace Collection.

Reardon, Betty A. *Sexism and the War System.* New York: Teachers College Press, 1985.

Report on the Seventeenth Annual Lake Mohonk Conference on International Arbitration, May 24–26, 1911. Lake Mohonk Conference, 1911.

Resolutions of the First American Conference for Democracy and Terms of Peace, Organized by the People's Council of America for Democracy and Peace, New York City, May 30–31, 1917. Undated [ca. June 1917] pamphlet in the Swarthmore College Peace Collection.

Rodgers, Daniel T. "In Search of Progressivism." *Reviews in American History* 10, no. 4 (Dec. 1982): 113–32.

Roosevelt, Theodore. Statement to the press, Jan. 28, 1917, *New York Times,* Jan. 29, 1917.

"Round Table, A: Explaining the History of American Foreign Relations." *Journal of American History* 77, no. 1 (June 1990): 93–180.

Ruddick, Sara. "Mothers and Men's Wars." In *Rocking the Ship of State: Toward a Feminist Peace Politics,* ed. Adrienne Harris and Ynestra King (Boulder: Westview Press, 1989), 75–92.

———. "Preservative Love and Military Destruction: Some Reflections on Mothering and Peace." In *Mothering: Essays on Feminist Theory,* edited by Joyce Trebilcot, 231–62. Totowa, N.J.: Roman and Allanheld, 1984.

Safford, Jeffrey J. *Wilsonian Maritime Diplomacy, 1913–1921.* New Brunswick, N.J.: Rutgers Univ. Press, 1978.

Salvatore, Nick. *Eugene V. Debs: Citizen and Socialist.* Urbana: Univ. of Illinois Press, 1982.

Schlissel, Lillian, ed. *Conscience in America: A Documentary History of Cosncientious Objectors in America, 1775–1967.* Ithaca: Cornell Univ. Press, 1978.

Scholes, Walter V., and Marie V. Scholes. *The Foreign Policies of the Taft Administration.* Columbia: Univ. of Missouri Press, 1970.

Schott, Linda Kay. "The Woman's Peace Party and the Moral Basis for Women's Pacifism." *Frontiers: A Journal of Women's Studies* 8, no. 2 (1985): 18–24.

Schwabe, Klaus. *Woodrow Wilson, Revolutionary Germany, and Peacemaking, 1918–1919.* Chapel Hill: Univ. of North Carolina Press, 1985.

Scott, Robert, and James Brown, eds. *Addresses on International Subjects by Elihu Root.* Cambridge, Mass.: Harvard Univ. Press, 1916.

Shall We Have War with Mexico? Leaflet, June 26, 1916. American Union Against Militarism Papers, Swarthmore College Peace Collection.

Shand, James D. "Doves among Eagles: German Pacifists and Their Government During World War I." *Journal of Contemporary History* 10, no. 1 (Jan. 1975): 95–108.

Sicherman, Barbara. *Alice Hamilton: A Life in Letters.* Cambridge, Mass.: Harvard Univ. Press, 1984.

Sklar, Kathryn Kish. *Florence Kelley and Women's Political Culture: Doing the Nation's Work, 1820–1940.* New Haven: Yale Univ. Press, 1992.

———. "Hull House in the 1890s: A Community of Women Reformers." *Signs* 10, no. 4 (1985): 658–77.

———. *The Corporate Reconstruction of American Capitalism, 1890–1916: The Market, the Law, and Politics.* Cambridge: Cambridge Univ. Press, 1988.

Smith-Rosenberg, Carroll. *Disorderly Conduct: Visions of Gender in Victorian America.* New York: Oxford Univ. Press, 1985.

Solo, Pam. "The Reagan Era: The Freeze Campaign and Political Power." *Annual Review of Peace Activism, 1989.* Boston: Winston Foundation for World Peace, 1989.

Solomon, Martha. *Emma Goldman.* Boston: Twayne, 1987.

Spencer, The Reverend Anna Garlin. "Woman and the Peace Treaty." *Advocate of Peace* 81 (Dec. 1919): 359–60.

Steinson, Barbara J. *American Women's Activism in World War I.* New York: Garland, 1982.

Stevenson, David. *The First World War and International Politics.* New York: Oxford Univ. Press, 1988.

Stone, Ralph. *The Irreconcilables: The Fight Against the League of Nations.* New York: Norton, 1970.

Taft, William Howard (reported by William Bayard Hale). "World-Peace and the General Arbitration Treaties. *World's Work* 23 (Dec. 1911): 143–49.

Tate, Merze. *The Disarmament Illusion: The Movement for a Limitation of Armaments to 1907.* New York: Macmillan, 1942.

Thomas, Norman. *The Conscientious Objector in America.* New York: B. W. Heubsch, 1923.

Thompson, John A. *Reformers and War: American Progressive Publicists and the First World War.* Cambridge: Cambridge Univ. Press, 1987.

Tompkins, E. Berkeley. *Anti-Imperialism in the United States.* Philadelphia: Univ. of Pennsylvania Press, 1970.

Touraine, Alain. "An Introduction to the Study of Social Movements." *Social Research* 52 (1985).

Trachtenberg, Alexander, ed. *The American Socialists and the War.* New York: Rand School of Social Science, 1917.

"Truth about Carrizal, The." New York *Herald*, June 24, 1916.

U.S., Congress. Senate. Concurrent Resolution 14. *Congressional Record*, 24th Cong., 1st sess., 1916.

———. Senate *Treaties, Conventions, International Acts, Protocols, and Agreements, 1910–1923.* 3 vols. 67th Cong., 4th sess., 1923. S. Doc. 348.

U.S., *Congressional Record*, 66th Cong., 2 sess., 1920, Vol. 59, pt. 5.

———, 66th Cong., 3d sess., 1920, Vol. 60, pt. 1.

U.S., Department of State. *Foreign Relations of the United States, 1917, Supplement I the World War.* Washington, D.C.: GPO, 1931.

———. *Foreign Relations of the United States, 1918, Supplement I.* Washington, D.C.: GPO, 1933.

Vinson, John C. *The Parchment Peace: The United States Senate and the Washington Conference, 1921–1922.* Athens: Univ. of Georgia Press, 1955.

Walworth, Arthur. *Wilson and His Peacemakers: American Diplomacy at the Paris Peace Conference, 1919.* New York: Norton , 1986.

Weinstein, James. *The Decline of Socialism in America, 1912–1925.* New York: Monthly Review, 1974.

"What Happened to the August *Masses?*" *Masses* 9 (Sept. 1917): 3.

Whitney, Edison L. *The American Peace Society: A Centennial History.* Washington, D.C.: American Peace Society, 1928.

"Why Wilson? A Statement by Social Workers." Advertisement. *Survey* 37 (Oct. 21, 1916), back cover.

Widenor, William C. *Henry Cabot Lodge and the Search for an American Foreign Policy.* Berkeley: Univ. of California Press, 1980.

Williamson, Samuel R., Jr., and Peter Pastor, eds. *Essays on World War I: Origins and Prisoners of War.* New York: Brooklyn College Press, 1983.

Winter, J. M. *The Experience of World War I.* New York: Oxford Univ. Press, 1989.

———, and R. M. Wall, eds. *The Upheaval of War: Family, Work and Welfare in Europe, 1914–1918.* Cambridge: Cambridge Univ. Press, 1988.

Wittner, Lawrence S. "Peace Movements and Foreign Policy: The Challenge to Diplomatic Historians." *Diplomatic History* 11 (Fall 1987): 355–70.

———. *Rebels Against War: The American Peace Movement, 1933–1983.* Philadelphia: Temple Univ. Press, 1984.

———. "The Transitional Movement Against Nuclear Weapons, 1945–1986: A Preliminary Survey." In *Peace Movements and Political Cultures,* edited by Charles Chatfield and Peter van den Dungen, 265–94. Knoxville: Univ. of Tennessee Press, 1988.

"Women of the World." *Survey* 46 (Apr. 16, 1921): 75.

Women's International League for Peace and Freedom. *Towards Peace and Freedom.* Pamphlet. New York: Women's International League for Peace and Freedom, 1919.

Wreszin, Michael. *Oswald Garrison Villard: Pacifist at War.* Bloomington: Indiana Univ. Press, 1965.

Young, Nigel. "The Contemporary European Anti-Nuclear Movement: Experiments in the Mobilization of Public Power." *Peace and Change: A Journal of Peace Research* 9, no. 1 (Spring 1983): 1–16.

———. "Why Peace Movements Fail: An Historical and Sociological Overview." *Social Alternatives* 4, no. 1 (1984): 9–16.

Permission Acknowledgments

Permission to quote from the following sources and to reprint the photographs noted is gratefully acknowledged:

DOCUMENT 40. Excerpts from *The Individual and the State: The Problem as Presented by the Sentencing of Roger N. Baldwin*. Reprinted with permission of the American Civil Liberties Union.

DOCUMENT 15. Alice Hamilton to Mary Rozet Smith, May 5, 1915, printed in Barbara Sicherman, *Alice Hamilton: A Life in Letters* (Cambridge, Mass.: Harvard Univ. Press, 1984), 189–90. By permission of W. Rush G. Hamilton.

DOCUMENT 48. Alice Hamilton to Mary Rozet Smith, May 19, 1919, printed in Barbara Sicherman, Alice Hamilton: A Life in Letters (Cambridge, Mass.: Harvard Univ. Press, 1984), 228–32. By permission of W. Rush G. Hamilton.

DOCUMENT 4. Theodore Roosevelt to Andrew Carnegie, August 6, 1906. Reprinted by permission of the publishers from THE LETTERS OF THEODORE ROOSEVELT: VOLUME V, THE BIG STICK, edited by Elting E. Morison, Cambridge, Mass.: Harvard University Press, Copyright © 1952 by the President and Fellows of Harvard College.

DOCUMENT 10. Elihu Root, Nobel Peace Prize Address, in Robert Scott and James Brown, eds., *Addresses on International Subjects by Elihu Root* (Cambridge, Mass.: Harvard Univ. Press, 1916), 153–74.

DOCUMENT 57. "The Disarmament Conference and Its Possibilities," *The Nation* magazine/The Nation Company, Inc., Copyright © 1921.

DOCUMENT 42. Scott Nearing, *The League of Nations as Seen by an Economist*, undated [ca. March/April 1919] leaflet, located in the Scott Nearing Papers, Swarthmore College Peace Collection. By permission of Helen Nearing.

DOCUMENT 17. Socialist Party of America, Position Against the War (1915); document 32, Socialist Party Position on American Belligerency (1917). By permission of Tamiment Library, New York University.

DOCUMENT 16. Woodrow Wilson, "An Address in Philadelphia to Newly Naturalized Citizens," May 10, 1915, in Arthur S. Link et al., eds., *The Papers of Woodrow Wilson,* 65 vols. to date (Princeton: Princeton Univ. Press, 1966–), 33: 149.

DOCUMENT 18. Woodrow Wilson to Juliet Barrett Rublee, June 2, 1915, in Arthur S. Link et al., eds., *The Papers of Woodrow Wilson,* 65 vols. to date (Princeton: Princeton Univ. Press, 1966–), 33: 314.

DOCUMENT 19. Woodrow Wilson to Senator William J. Stone, February 25, 1916, in Arthur S. Link et al., eds., *The Papers of Woodrow Wilson,* 65 vols. to date (Princeton: Princeton Univ. Press, 1966–), 36: 213–14.

DOCUMENT 20. Transcript of the meeting of May 8, 1916, made by Wilson's personal stenographer, Charles L. Swem, printed in Arthur S. Link et al., eds., *The Papers of Woodrow Wilson,* 65 vols. to date (Princeton: Princeton Univ. Press, 1966–), 35: 634–46.

DOCUMENT 21. "An Address in Washington to the League to Enforce Peace," May 27, 1916, reprinted in Arthur S. Link et al., eds., *The Papers of Woodrow Wilson,* 65 vols. to date (Princeton: Princeton Univ. Press, 1966–), 37: 113–16.

DOCUMENT 22. Wilson to Colonel House, June 22, 1916; Jane Addams telegram to Wilson, June 27, 1916; Woodrow Wilson, Remarks to the New York Press Club, June 30, 1916, reprinted in Arthur S. Link et al., eds., *The Papers of Woodrow Wilson,* 65 vols. to date (Princeton: Princeton Univ. Press, 1966–), 37: 281, 308, 333–34.

DOCUMENT 23. "A Colloquy with Members of the American Neutral Conference Committee," August 10, 1916, transcript by Wilson's stenographer, Charles L. Swem, printed in Arthur S. Link et al., eds., *The Papers of Woodrow Wilson,* 65 vols. to date (Princeton: Princeton Univ. Press, 1966–), 38: 108–17.

DOCUMENT 29. "A Visit to the President," *The Friends; Intelligencer,* 74 (March 10, 1917): 147–48, reprinted in Arthur S. Link et al., eds., *The Papers of Woodrow Wilson,* 65 vols. to date (Princeton: Princeton Univ. Press, 1966–), 41: 302–4.

DOCUMENT 36. Woodrow Wilson to Max Eastman, September 18, 1917, reprinted in Arthur S. Link et al., eds., *The Papers of Woodrow Wilson,* 65 vols. to date (Princeton: Princeton Univ. Press, 1966–), 44: 210–11.

DOCUMENT 41. The Diary of "Colonel" House, entry for August 15, 1918, Edward M. House Papers, Manuscripts and Archives, Yale Univ. Library, reprinted in Arthur S. Link et al., eds., *The Papers of Woodrow Wilson*, 65 vols. to date (Princeton: Princeton Univ. Press, 1966–), 49: 256–68.

DOCUMENT 47. Jane Addams to Woodrow Wilson, ca. May 13, 1919; Wilson to Addams, May 16, 1919, reprinted in Arthur S. Link et al., eds., *The Papers of Woodrow Wilson*, 65 vols. to date (Princeton: Princeton Univ. Press, 1966–), 59: 117, 189.

DOCUMENT 49. "A Conversation with Members of the Senate Foreign Relations Committee; Conference at the White Hosue, Tuesday, August 19, 1919," reprinted in Arthur S. Link et al., eds., *The Papers of Woodrow Wilson*, 65 vols. to date (Princeton: Princeton Univ. Press, 1966–), 62: 304–44.

DOCUMENT 57. An Efficient Disarmament Campaign, leaflet. Swarthmore College Peace Collection.

Photograph of the U.S. Delegation at the International Congress of Women at The Hague, May 1915, The Women's International League for Peace and Freedom—U.S. Section Papers, Swarthmore College Peace Collection.

Photograph of Jane Addams and Mary McDowell, The Jane Addams Papers, Swarthmore College Peace Collection.

DOCUMENTS 14 and 38. *Addresses Given at the Organization Conference of the Woman's Peace Party, Washington, D.C., January 10, 1915,* and *Our War Record: A Plea for Tolerance.* Woman's Peace Party Papers, Swarthmore College Peace Collection.

DOCUMENT 18. Aletta Jacobs to Jane Addams, September 15, 1915. Jane Addams Papers, Swarthmore College Peace Collection.

DOCUMENTS 22, 25, and 57. *Shall We Have War with Mexico?* "Bulletin No. 53"; Crystal Eastman *A Review;* and Bulletins 31, 35, and 37. American Union Against Militarism Papers, Swarthmore College Peace Collection.

DOCUMENT 46. *Towards Peace and Freedom,* Women's International League for Peace and Freedom Papers, Swarthmore College Peace Collection.

DOCUMENTS 27 and 30. "Jane Addams Recalls Wilson and Peace Efforts, 1915 to 1917"; "Jane Addams' Recollection of the February 1917 Meeting with Wilson," *Peace and Bread in Time of War,* 1922. Women's International League for Peace and Freedom.

DOCUMENT 50. The Reverend Anna Garlin Spencer, "Woman and the Peace Treaty," *The Advocate of Peace* 81 (December 1919): 359–60. World Affairs.

DOCUMENT 44. Excerpts from "Joint Debate [between Henry Cabot Lodge and A. Lawrence Lowell] on the Covenant of Paris," reprinted in *League of Nations,* vol. 2 (Boston: World Peace Foundation, 1919).

DOCUMENT 41. In the Edward M. House Papers, Diary entry for August 15, 1918. Edward M. House Papers, Manuscripts and Archives, Yale University Library.

Index

Abbott, Grace, 58
ACLU. *See* American Civil Liberties
  Union
Addams, Jane, xlvii, xlviii, liii, 168,
  176–77; and Carrizal incident,
  82; and first international
  women's congress, 57, 58, 66,
  101–2; and formation of
  Woman's Peace party, 50, 54–56;
  on League of Nations, 177–78;
  on naval disarmament, 183; and
  Nobel Peace Prize, xvi, xxxix,
  177, on patriotism in wartime,
  54, 119–22; and peace delegation
  to Wilson, 105, 106, 107–8; on
  positive peace, xvii, xxxvii–
  xxxviii; and second international
  women's congress, 152, 153, 156,
  158–59, 160; on Wilson's peace
  efforts, 100–102; and Wilson's
  reelection, 91
African Americans, and peace, 157.
  See also Terrell, Mary Church
Algeciras Conference (1905), lxxxii
American Civil Liberties Union
  (ACLU), xix, xx, xxii, 39, 133,
  166–168; and postwar amnesty
  campaign, lxxii, 167. *See also*
  National Civil Liberties Bureau
American Defense Society, lxxiii

American Expeditionary Force, lxiii
American Federation of Labor, lxxii,
  lxxiii, 176
American Friends Service
  Committee, xxii, 14, 159
American Legion, lxxiii
American Neutral Conference
  Committee, xv, lii, 66, 88–90
American Peace Society, xxxiv, xxxv,
  li, lxviii, 165; during World War
  I, xlv, lv, lvii
American School Peace League, lviii
American Society for the Judicial
  Settlement of International
  Disputes, xxxvi, xlv
American Society of International
  Law, xxxvi, xxxviii, xlv
American Union Against Militarism
  (AUAM), xv, xix, lix–lx, 119,
  188; and Carrizal incident, xx,
  xlix–l, 76–77, 79–81, 83–87, 95;
  founding of, xxii, xlviii–xlix,
  lxxx, 39, 70; postwar activities
  of, lxxi, lxxiv, 168, 181–82,
  184–86; wartime role of, lii, lv,
  70–74, 92–96, 101. *See also*
  American Civil Liberties Union;
  National Civil Liberties Bureau
Amnesty campaign, lxxi–lxxiii,
  175–76

223

THE EAGLE AND THE DOVE
was composed in 10 on 12 Sabon on a Linotronic 300
by Partners Composition;
printed by sheet-fed offset on 50-pound, acid-free Glatfelter,
Smyth-sewn and bound over binder's boards in Holliston Roxite B
and notch bound with paper covers printed in 2 colors
by Edwards Brothers, Inc.;
and published by
Syracuse University Press
Syracuse, New York 13244-5160

Syracuse Studies on Peace and Conflict Resolution
HARRIET HYMAN ALONSO, CHARLES CHATFIELD, AND LOUIS KRIESBERG
Series Editors

A series devoted to readable books on the history of peace movements, the lives of peace advocates, and the search for ways to mitigate conflict, both domestic and international. At a time when profound and exciting political and social developments are happening around the world, this series seeks to stimulate a wider awareness and appreciation of the search for peaceful resolution to strife in all its forms and to promote linkages among theorists, practitioners, social scientists, and humanists engaged in this work throughout the world.

Other titles in the series are: